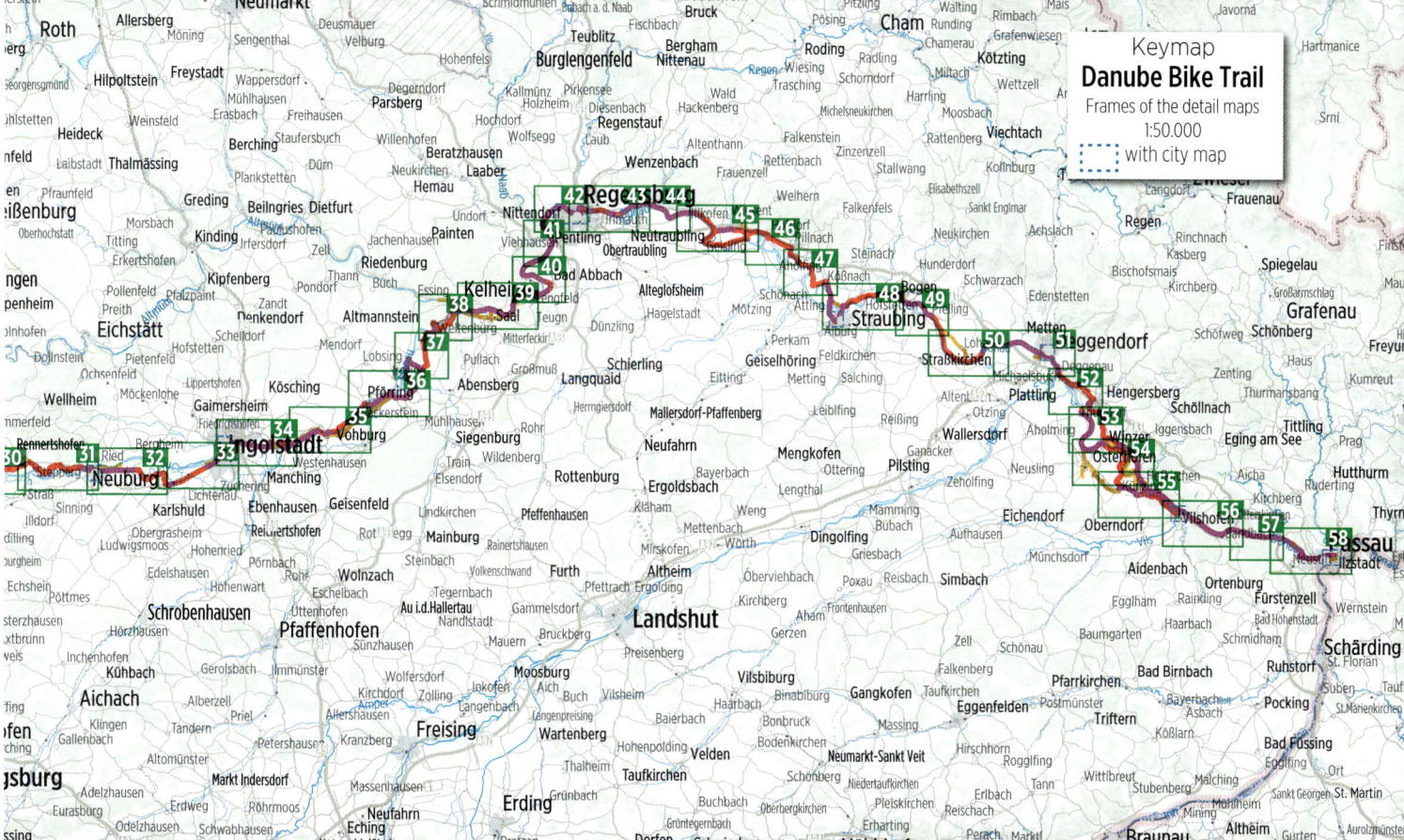

Keymap
Danube Bike Trail
Frames of the detail maps
1:50.000
with city map

bikeline®-Cycling guide
Danube Bike Trail 1
© 2008-2019, **Verlag Esterbauer GmbH**
A-3751 Rodingersdorf, Hauptstr. 31
Tel.: +43/2983/28982-0, Fax: -500
E-Mail: bikeline@esterbauer.com
www.esterbauer.com
4th Edition 2019
ISBN: 978-3-85000-786-3

Please quote edition and ISBN number in all correspondence!

We are especially grateful to Ms. Kathy Kist of Cincinnati, whose generous support made the translation of this book possible.
We wish to thank all the people who contributed to the production of this book, see p. 161

The *bikeline*-Team: Birgit Albrecht-Walzer, Katharina Amon-Schneider, Sabine Bacher-Baumgartner, Beatrix Bauer, Michael Binder, Veronika Bock, Petra Bruckmüller, Roland Esterbauer, Dagmar Güldenpfennig, Martina Kreindl, Nora Ludolph, Gregor Münch, Karin Neichsner, Carmen Paradeiser, Sabrina Pusch, Claudia Retzer, Petra Schartner, Sonja Schleifer, Isabella Tillich, Christian Thoren, Martin Trippmacher, Carina Winkelhofer, Martin Wischin, Wolfgang Zangerl

Cover photos:Umschlagbilder: Münster: © pure-life-pictures - Fotolia; Danube: Arbeitsgemeinschaft Deutsche Donau; Regensburg: Arbeitsgemeinschaft Deutsche Donau

Photo credits: Arbeitsgemeinschaft Deutsche Donau: 29, 36, 74, 96, 134; Arbeitsgemeinschaft Deutsche Donau/ flymovies.de: 106; Archiv: 138; Bürgermeisteramt Inzigkofen: 32; Fouad Vollmer Werbeagentur: 78; Ingolstadt Tourismus und Kongress GmbH – Tanja Lehner: 100; © karamba2106 - Fotolia: 68; © katcya_design - Fotolia: 128; © kranidi - Fotolia: 122; Landkreis Regensburg: 121; © mojolo - Fotolia: 52; © m.schuckart - Fotolia: 112; pixabay: 11, 108; Regensburg Tourismus GmbH: 116; © Schlesier - Fotolia: 24, 30; Schloss Leitheim: Markus Schnitzler: 88; Stadt Blaustein/Jens Burkert: 56; Stadt Donaueschingen: 16; Stadt Kelheim: 102; Stadt Mühlheim/ Uwe Steinbächer: 26; Stadt Schelklingen: 51; Stadt Tuttlingen/Jens Burkert: 20; Stadtverwaltung Riedlingen: 40; © Stiefi - Fotolia: 86; © Thomas - Fotolia: 114; Tourismus-Marketing GmbH Baden-Württemberg/TMBW: 64

Cartography produced with *axpand* (www.axes-systems.com)

bikeline

What is bikeline?

We are a team of writers, cartographers, geographers and other staff united by our enthusiasm for bicycling and touring. Our project first „got rolling" in 1987, when a group of Vienna cyclists came together to begin producing bicycling maps. Today we are a highly successful publisher that offers a wide range of bikeline® books in five languages covering many European countries.

We need your help to keep our books up-to-date. Please write to us if you find errors or changes. We would also be grateful for experiences and impressions from your own cycling tours.

We look forward to your letters and e-mails (redaktion@esterbauer.com),

Your bikeline team

Preface

From its headwaters in the Black Forest of southwestern Germany, the Danube flows through some of the most beautiful landscapes in Europe. Pristine flood-plains, picturesque villages and small towns, and a wealth of cultural landmarks line the river as it begins its long march to the distant Black Sea.

These tranquil valleys are also ideal for cycling. In recent years, many of the paths and lanes along the river have been paved specifically for bicycle tourists. As a result, almost the entire route follows smooth quiet roads that make it ideal for families with children.

Precise maps, reliable route descriptions, information about historic and cultural attractions plus a comprehensive list of overnight accommodation – this book provides everything you need for a cycling tour along the German Danube. The one thing it cannot provide is great cycling weather, but we hope you encounter nothing but sunshine and gentle tailwinds.

Map legend

Cycling routes (Radrouten)

Main cycle route, low motor traffic
(Hauptroute, wenig KFZ-Verkehr)
— Paved surface (asphaltiert)
– – – Unpaved surface (nicht asphaltiert)
▪▪▪▪ Bad surface (schlecht befahrbar)

Main cycle route, without motor traffic / cycle path
(Hauptroute, autofrei / Radweg)
— Paved surface (asphaltiert)
– – – Unpaved surface (nicht asphaltiert)
▪▪▪▪ Bad surface (schlecht befahrbar)

Excursion or alternative cycle route, low motor traffic
(Ausflug od. Variante, wenig KFZ-Verkehr)
— Paved surface (asphaltiert)
– – – Unpaved surface (nicht asphaltiert)
▪▪▪▪ Bad surface (schlecht befahrbar)

Excursion or alternative route, without motor traffic / cycle path (Ausflug od. Variante, autofrei / Radweg)
— Paved surface (asphaltiert)
– – – Unpaved surface (nicht asphaltiert)
▪▪▪▪ Bad surface (schlecht befahrbar)

Other cycle routes (Sonstiges)
— Other cycle route (sonstige Radroute)

●●●●● Cycle route with significant motor traffic (verkehrsreiche Radroute)
Cobbled street (Kopfsteinpflaster)
Cne-way connection (Einbahnführung)
Ferry connection (Fährverbindung)
Road surface unknown (unbekannter Belag)
Tunnel (Tunnel)
Dismounting recommended (Schiebestrecke)
Train connection (Zugverbindung)
ooooooo Planned cycle path (Radweg in Planung)
xxxxxxx Closed cycle path (Radweg gesperrt)
Cycle lane (Radfahrstreifen)
Cycle path along road (straßenbegleitender Radweg)
xxxxx Road closed to cyclists (Straße für Radfahrer gesperrt)
⟹ Described direction (Beschriebene Fahrtrichtung)
⑤ Waypoint (Wegpunkt)

Gradient / Distance (Steigungen / Entfernungen)

➤ Steep gradient, uphill (starke Steigung)
➤ Light gradient, uphill (leichte bis mittlere Steigung)
2,4 Distance in km, rounded (Entfernung in Kilometern, gerundet)

Important cycling information (Radinformationen)

🔧 Bike workshop* (Fahrradwerkstatt*)
🚲 Bike rental* (Fahrradvermietung*)
🚲 Covered bike stands* (überdachter Abstellplatz*)
🚲 Lockable bike stands* (abschließbarer Abstellplatz*)
🔌 E-bike charging station (E-Bike Ladestation)
🚲 Information board* (Infotafel*)
⚠ Dangerous section (Gefahrenstelle)
⚠ Read text carefully (Text beachten)
▬ Stairs (Treppe)
🚲 Bicycle must be carried! (Tragestrecke)
✕ Constriction, bottleneck* (Engstelle*)
○17 ○42 Nodal point (Knotenpunktnummer der Wegweisung*)

⬜ Town or city map (Stadt- /Ortsplan)

Symbols only in the city maps (Nur in Ortsplänen)

🅿 Garage* (Parkhaus*)
🎭 Theatre* (theater*)
✉ Post office* (Post*)
💊 Pharmacy* (Apotheke*)
🅷 Hospital* (Krankenhaus*)
🅵 Fire brigade* (Feuerwehr*)
🛡 Police* (Polizei*)

* Selection (* Auswahl)

Scale 1 : 50.000

1 cm ≙ 500 m   1 km ≙ 2 cm

0   1   2   3   4   5   6   7   8   9   10 km

Sights of interest / Facilities (Sehenswertes / Einrichtungen)

- Church; Chapel (Kirche; Kapelle)
- Monastery/Convent (Kloster)
- Synagogue; Mosque (Synagoge; Moschee)
- Palace, Castle; Ruin (Schloss, Burg; Ruine)
- Tower; Lighthouse (Turm; Leuchtturm)
- Watermill; Windmill (Wassermühle; Windmühle)
- Power station (Kraftwerk)
- Mine; Cave (Bergwerk; Höhle)
- Airport, Monument (Flughafen , Denkmal)
- Other sight of interest (sonstige Sehenswürdigkeit)
- Museum (Museum)
- Excavations; Roman site (Ausgrabungen; röm. Objekte)
- Zoo; Nature info (Tierpark; Naturpark-Information)
- Nature reserve/Monument (Naturpark, -denkmal)
- Natural sight of interest (sonstige Natursehenswürdigkeit)
- Panoramic view* (Aussichtspunkt*)
- Tourist information; Restaurant (Tourist-Info; Gasthaus)
- Hotel, Guesthouse; Youth hostel (Hotel, Pension; Jugendherberge)
- Campground; Simple tent site* (Camping-; Lagerplatz*)
- Shopping facility*; Kiosk* (Einkaufsmöglichkeit*; Kiosk*)
- Picnic tables*; Covered stand* (Rastplatz*; Unterstand*)
- Outdoor pool; Indoor pool (Freibad; Hallenbad)
- Natural pool; Thermal baths/Waterpark (Naturbad; Thermal-/Erlebnisbad*)
- Drinking fountain*; Parking lot* (Brunnen*; Parkplatz*)
- <u>Schönern</u> Picturesque town (sehenswertes Ortsbild)
- Facilities available (Einrichtung im Ort vorhanden)

Topographic information (Topographische Informationen)

- Church; Chapel (Kirche; Kapelle)
- Monastery/Convent (Kloster)
- Synagogue; Mosque (Synagoge; Moschee)
- Palace, Castle; Ruin (Schloss, Burg; Ruine)
- Tower; Lighthouse (Turm; Leuchtturm)
- Watermill; Windmill (Wassermühle; Windmühle)
- Power station, Solar power station (Kraftwerk)
- Mine; Cave (Bergwerk; Höhle)
- Monument; Burial mound (Denkmal; Hügelgrab)
- Airport; Airfield (Flughafen; Flugplatz)
- Windturbine (Windkraftanlage)
- TV/Radio tower (Funk- und Fernsehanlage)
- Transformer station (Umspannwerk, Trafostation)
- Wayside cross; Boundary stone (Wegkreuz; Grenzstein)
- Playing field, Stadium (Sportplatz, Stadion)
- Golf course; Tennis courts (Golfplatz; Tennisplatz)
- Boat landing; Sluice/lock (Schiffsanleger; Schleuse)
- Natural spring; Wastewater treatment plant (Quelle; Kläranlage)
- International border crossing (Staatsgrenze; Übergang)
- State border (Landesgrenze)
- District border (Kreis-, Bezirksgrenze)
- Nature reserve, National park (Naturschutzgebiet, Naturpark, Nationalpark)
- Prohibited zone (Truppenübungsplatz, Sperrgebiet)
- Contour line 100m/50m (Höhenlinie 100m/50m)
- UTM-grid (2 km-grid) (UTM-Gitter)

- Motorway/Freeway; Expressway (Autobahn; Schnellstr.)
- Highway (Fernverkehrsstraße)
- Main road (Hauptstraße)
- Secondary main road (untergeordnete Hauptstraße)
- Secondary road; Access road (Nebenstraße; Fahrweg)
- Track; Ferry (Weg; Fähre)
- Road planned/under construction (geplant/in Bau)
- Railway/station; S-train station (Eisenbahn/Bahnhof; S-Bahnhof)
- Railway disused; planned (Eisenbahn stillgelegt; geplant)
- Narrow gauge railway (Schmalspurbahn)
- Mountain railway; Cable car (Bergbahn; Seilbahn)
- Forest; Park (Wald; Parkanlage)
- Marsh/Bog; Heath (Sumpf; Heide)
- Vineyards; Allotment gardens* (Weinbau; Gärten*)
- Quarry; Open cast mine* (Steinbruch, Tagebau*)
- Cemetery; Dunes/Beach (Friedhof; Düne, Strand)
- Tidal flats; Glacier (Watt; Gletscher)
- Rock; Cliff; Scree (Felsen; Geröll)
- Greenhouse; Plantation (Gewächshäuser, Plantage)
- Commercial/Industrial area (Gewerbe-, Industriegebiet)
- Urban area; Public building (Siedlung; öffentl. Gebäude)
- Defensive wall/Wall (Stadtmauer, Mauer)
- Embankment, Dike (Damm, Deich)
- Canal (Kanal)
- River/Dam/Lake (Fluss/Staumauer/See)

Content

Citymaps

The German Danube

The Danube is not merely one of Europe's great rivers. At 2,888 kilometers from the source of the Breg and 2,845 kilometers from the confluence of the Breg, Brigach and Danube Spring in Donaueschingen, it is the second longest river in Europe; only the Volga (3,534 kilometers) is longer. It is one thousand kilometers longer than the Rhine, and collects water from a catchment basin that is more than four times as large. The Danube flows through or along the borders of ten nations and has long served

Donau-Radwanderweg

Donauradweg

as one of the most important transportation links between Europe and Asia.

Let us follow the Danube from its modest beginnings in southwestern Germany. Deep in the Black Forest, a few kilometers northwest of Furtwangen, the map notes the source of the Danube. If one follows this tiny stream, it reaches the village of Zindelstein, where it acquires a name: the Breg. It keeps this name as far as Donaueschingen, where it meets a second stream, the Brigach, coming from near Triberg to the north. The two streams merge and acquire a new name, the Danube (Donau in German), which it keeps in various forms and languages all the way to the Black Sea.

The Danube is unique in Europe for another reason. As the only river in the continent which measures its kilometers from the mouth towards the source, it "ends" in Donaueschingen.

In the 19th century, the residents of Donaueschingen erected an impressive basin around a karst-spring in the city's Schlosspark and declared it the river's

LIVE-UPDATES

On our web page we offer an online-service, that provides updated information and current changes concerning this cycling guide. This information is brought up-to-date regularly and enables you, in combination with the current edition of this book, to plan your trip in the best possible way. The Live-Update for this book is freely available under:

www.esterbauer.com/db_detail.php?buecher_code=DRW1_E

Have you noticed some changes or mistakes during your journey concerning the itinerary, the overnight accommodation or the tourist information along the route? Then you have the possibility to bring the bikeline-team up-to-date using the Update-section on our web page. We are looking forward to getting your information and say Thank You in the name of all cyclists.

The latest bikeline GPS-Track for this book is freely available under:

www.tracks.world/?dir=de/trk09tx780

source. This basin is decorated with a marble sculpture that shows the Danube as a small girl next to a woman who represents the Baar, the rolling hill country that surrounds the city. The Baar points the girl eastward towards the sea. The site does little to suggest a great river, however, as the waters from this purported "source" immediately disappear between metal bars into underwater pipes leading to the nearby Brigach.

Downstream from Donaueschingen, the Danube has barely begun its meandering march eastward when it reaches the foothills of the Swabian Alb near the town of Immendingen. This plateau is formed of porous limestone and provides the conditions for a remarkable and curious phenomenon called the Danube Sink. With a spooky gurgling and hissing, the river's waters disappear into the ground and flow beneath the surface until they reemerge 12 kilometers further East.

The banks of the Danube offer a rich diversity of natural and cultural sights. In Mühlheim, for instance, the medieval Enzberger castle and curious St. Gallus church look down on the river. Rocky promontories rise above the valley floor and provide habitat for many unusual birds and plants.

Ancient strongholds and castles keep guard over the river from strategic points along the valley. There is the massive Beuron Archabbey, for instance, built by the Austrian architect Franz Beer, or nearby Wildenstein Castle where the hard-drinking Count Gottfried von Zimmer sought refuge from the Black Plague in 1528 and thus also avoided the peasant uprisings that followed. Werenwag Castle is where the minstrel Hugo von Werenwag wrote his verse around 1260. Nearby Kreenheinstetten was the birthplace in 1644 of Johann Ulrich Megerle, who later became famous in Vienna as the eloquent preacher Abraham a Sancta Clara. Each of these castles offers interesting views of the valley that the Danube has carved into the jurassic rock.

The valley widens near Inzigkofen before the river

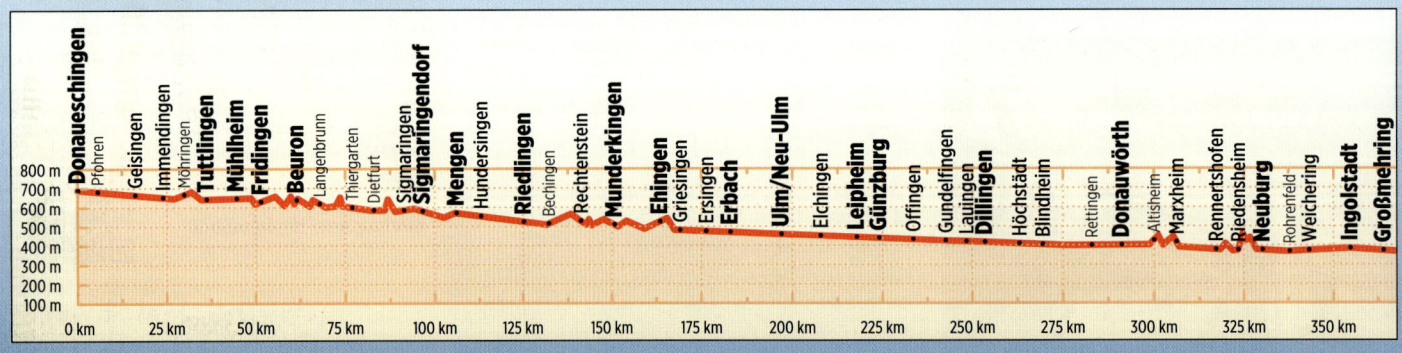

reaches Sigmaringen, where a proud castle, the one-time residence of the Hohenzollerns, rises above a confusion of ancient roofs. From Sigmaringen the river continues in leisurely loops before emerging from the Swabian Alb at Ulm.

On its way to the Ingolstadt basin your cycling tour passes through a number of particularly scenic areas, including the Leibi nature preserve near Günzburg, many pristine flood plain areas, past Donauried and Donaumoos.

This stretch of the ride also visits the charming towns of Dillingen, Gundelfingen, the renaissance city of Neuburg, and Vohburg with its city walls and gates, before entering the Danube Gorge between Weltenburg and Kelheim.

From Regensburg, the Danube is navigable by ships and meets the Rhein-Main-Danube canal, which emerges from the Altmühl valley. With its 18 locks, the canal passes through the Upper Palatinate and Franconia to enable river traffic to travel from the North Sea to the Black Sea. The character of the Danube's valley also changes at Regensburg, which is the northern-most city along the river. North of the river, the Bavarian Forest rises away toward the Czech border and the central German highlands. To the South, the fertile soils of Bavaria's breadbasket extend towards the foothills of the Alps.

The Danube leaves Germany at Passau, the three-

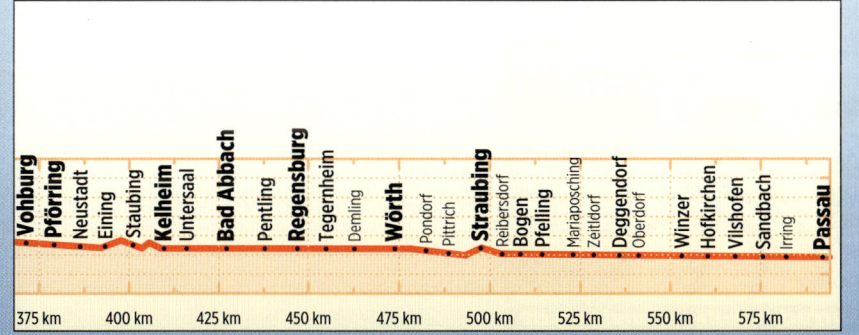

rivers city situated at the confluence of the Danube, Inn and Ilz rivers. They join to make the Danube qualify as a great river worthy of legend and fame.

The route

Length
The Danube cycle path between Donaueschingen and Passau is about 600 kilometres long. In this book you will also find approx. 260 kilometres of variants and excursions.

Classification by ADFC
The „ADFC Quality Cycle Route" award is given to cycle routes that have been completely travelled by bicycle by ADFC route inspectors. The quality of the rideability, safety, signposting and other criteria such as accommodation, gastronomy and accessibility by train are evaluated. All the data put together then result in a classification between one and five stars for the respective route. The rating is valid for three years, after which, if desired, it must be reviewed again.
The Danube Cycle Route was awarded 4 stars in 2017, so it is a great pleasure for cyclists.

Surface quality and traffic
Most of the route follows quiet country lanes or dedicated cycling paths. Sections with heavier traffic are rare and usually short. With only a few exceptions, the roads and paths have a hard surface. Gravel sections are usually in good condition. Because the route follows the course of the river, it is almost completely flat. It is mostly on the excursions into the surrounding countryside that must expect some steep sections. It is possible that during flooding part of the route is unusable or closed and you need to use alternative routes.

Signage
Signposting along the Danube bicycle route is gener-

ally reliable and signs are located at every change in direction at forks and intersections.
The signs show the green-yellow-blue logo of the Deutsche Donau and are also marked with the logo of the D-Route 6 and the Eurovelo-6 sign.

Planing your tour

Central information sources
Arbeitsgemeinschaft Deutsche Donau, 89073 Ulm, Neue Str. 45, ✆ 0731/1612814, www.deutsche-donau.de

Arrival & departure by air
Visitors from countries beyond Europe can reach Germany easily with commercial airlines.
Once you have arrived in Europe, trains and buses offer excellent alternatives to air travel.

Arrival & departure by rail
The starting point of the Danube Bike Trail, Donaueschingen, can be easily reached by rail; from Munich about 4 hrs, from Stuttgart about 2 hrs and from Frankfurt 3 to 4 hrs.
For the return trip from Passau you have good rail connections; to München about 2 hrs, to Stuttgart 4 to 5 hrs.
Advance reservations are recommended, and are required at least one day in advance on most long-

Regensburg

distance trains that accept bicycles in Germany. Due to the constantly changing prices and conditions for transport of a bicycle by rail we suggest that you inform yourself about your personal rail travel at the following addresses.

German Rail (DB):
General Service Number: ✆ 0180/6996633
Timetable Information: ✆ 0800/1507090
(€ 0.20/call from landline, mobile max. € 0.60/call)
www.bahn.de, www.bahn.de/bahnundbike
Automatic DB timetable information:
✆ 0800/1507090 (toll-free from the fixed network)

ADFC, Allgemeiner Deutscher Fahrrad-Club e. V.: further information and broken down individual connections at www.adfc.de/bahn

Bike & train
With a few exceptions, the villages in the Danube valley are connected by a railway line. So you can always change to the alternative train if necessary. www.bahn.de/fahrrad-bayern
Bike rental stations
You can rent a bicycle along the Dan-

ube cydle path at the following stations: **Donaueschingen, Rad Center Rothweiler**, Max-Egonstr. 11 (500 m north of the railway station), 78166 Donaueschingen, ✆ 0771/13148. Bikes can be returned anywhere up to Passau, www. rotrad.de. **Regensburg**, **RENT A BIKE und Bikeambulanz**, Bahnhofstr. 18, ✆ 0941/5999194 od. ✆ 0177/4608460, **www.fahrradverleih-regensburg.de**
Passau, **RENT A BIKE**, Bahnhofstr. 29, ✆ 0851/9662570, www.fahrradverleih-bahnhof-passau.de
You should always check prices and opening hours at the rental station in advance. To rent a

bicycle you need a valid photo ID and about € 30,- for the deposit. The rental fees are sometimes very different, they amount to about € 13 per day. For further information, please contact **Deutsche Bahn AG cyclist hotline**: ✆ 01806/996633 (0,20-0,60 € per call) Within Baden-Württemberg and Bavaria, regional trains can be used inexpensively with the state ticket..

Bike & ship

Excursion steamers on the Danube offer another interesting alternative to riding the entire stretch by bicycle. Ships stop in Kelheim, Regensburg and Passau. Addresses and schedules are reviewed in the town descriptions that follow in this guide.

There is also scheduled passenger service by ship between Deggendorf and Passau. Ship operators and addresses can be found in the town descriptions. Danube passenger ships do carry bicycles. For current departure and arrival times inquire at the ship landings or call the ship operators (for instance Wurm+Noé, D-94032 Passau, Höllg. 26, ✆ 0851/929292 or 93047 Regensburg, Osteng. 3, ✆ 0941/50277880, info@donauschiffahrt.de, www.donauschiffahrt.de). The 5-kilometer section of the Danube bicycle route between Weltenburg and Kelheim is not

to be recommended. It follows busy roads and has a long climb. The ships and boats that shuttle between Weltenburg and Kelheim offer an attractive alternative, and also enable you to enjoy the spectacular narrow gorge from the river. The ships run frequently during the summer season (daily every half-hour between 10 am and 6 pm, information ✆ 09441/5858, Kelheim office).

Overnight accommodation

A comprehensive list of overnight accommodation is provided at the end of this book. We have endeavoured to put together the largest possible choice of providers for you. The following internet addresses of accommodation providers, who also provide alternative types of accommodation, are recommended for those who are looking for alternatives or even more choice:

ADFC-Dachgeber works on the principle of reciprocal benefit: Here you find offers of private accommodation for cycling enthusiasts by cycling enthusiasts. More under www.dachgeber.de.

The **Deutsche Jugendherbergswerk** introduces itself and its 14 national associations under www.djh.de. Also the **Naturfreunde** offer an alternative form of accommodation with their Naturfreunde Houses. More under www.naturfreunde.de.

You will find just the **camping ground** you are looking for under www.campingplatz.de.

Additionally, you will find further information about the ADFC listed **Bett+Bike** providers all over Germany under www.bettundbike.de.

Bicycle tours with children

Generally children over the age of 10 will be able to ride most of the routes detailed in the guide. Do not overestimate a child's stamina, however, and keep open options like taking a train or ship for some section of the trip. Depending on their physical condition, most children can easily manage distances of 30 to 50 kilometers in a day. But remember that most children will not ride safely and with full concentration for hours on end. Finally, no child will enjoy the ride if his or her bicycle is poorly adjusted, heavy or poorly equipped for long distances. If riding with children in a trailer you will find the route near the start between Fridingen and Sigmaringen or between Rennertshofen and Neuburg somewhat difficult.

Bicycle tour operators

EUROBIKE, A-5162 Obertrum am See, Mühlstr. 20, ✆ 0043/6219/7444 or ✆ 0800/5889718, www.eurobike.at, eurobike@eurobike.at

Austria Radreisen GmbH, A-4780 Schärding, Joseph-Haydn-Str. 8, ☎ 0043/7712/55110, www.austria-radreisen.at, office@austria-radreisen.at
PEDALO Touristik GmbH, A-4710 Grieskirchen, Kickendorf 1a, ☎ 0800/2400999 (free of charge from DE, AT & CH), www.pedalo.com, info@pedalo.com
Augustus Tours, D-01097 Dresden, Turnerweg 6, ☎ 0049/351/563480, www.augustustours.de, info@augustustours.de
Rückenwind Reisen GmbH, D-26125 Oldenburg, Am Patentbusch 14, ☎ 0049/441/485970, www.rueckenwind.de, info@rueckenwind.de
Velociped Fahrradreisen, D-35039 Marburg, Alte Kasseler Str. 43, ☎ 0049/6421/886890, www.velociped.de, info@velociped.de

About this Book

This cycling guide contains all the information you need for your cycling vacation along the Danube from Donaueschingen to Passau: Precise maps, a detailed description of the route, a comprehensive list of overnight accommodation, numerous detail maps of cities and towns, and information about the most significant sights.

And all that information comes with our **bikeline guarantee**: The route described in this book has been tested and evaluated in person by one of our editors! To assure that the book is as up-to-date as possible, we welcome corrections submitted by readers and local officials or businesses. We cannot, however, always check and confirm such changes before deadline.

The maps

The detail maps are produced in a scale of 1:50,000 (1 centimetre = 500 meters). In addition to exactly describing the route, these maps also provide information about roadway quality (paved or unpaved), climbs (gentle or steep), distances, as well as available cultural and culinary highlights.

Even with the most precise map, consulting the written description of the route may be necessary at times. Locations where the route is difficult to follow are shown by the ⚠ symbol on the maps, the same symbol can then be found in the written description where the route is explained in detail.

Note that the recommended main route is always shown in red or purple; alternative and excursion routes in orange. The individual symbols used in the maps are described in the legend on pages 4 and 5.

Height and distance profile

The detailed route altitude profiles at the beginning of each section provide a graphic depiction of elevations along the route, the total length as well as waypoints and the location of towns and cities along the way. The waypoints enable a direct reference to the maps and route description. The altitude profile does not show every individual small hill and dip, but only the major changes in elevation. On the detail maps smaller gradients are shown by arrows that point uphill.

The text

The maps are supplemented by a written text that describes the route starting in Passau and proceeding down the Danube to Vienna. Key phrases about the route description are indicated with the ～ symbol.

Many distinctive or important positions along the route are marked as waypoints with consecutive numbers **1**, **2**, **3**, ... and, to help with navigation, are to be found with the same symbol in the maps. The description of the main route is also interrupted by passages describing alternative and excursion routes. These are printed in orange colour.

TIP Text printed in purple indicates that you must make a decision about how your tour shall continue. For instance, there may be an alternative route that is not included in the tour description, or a turn-off to another location.

EXCURSION These also indicate excursion suggestions, interesting sights or recreational facilities that are not directly on the main route.

Furthermore, the names of important **villages**, towns and cities are printed in bold type. If a location or community has important points of interest, addresses, telephone numbers and opening times are listed under the headline with the name of the place. *Descriptions of the larger towns and cities, as well as historic, cultural and natural landmarks help round out the travel experience. These paragraphs are printed in italics to distinguish them from the route description.*

Opening hours - Categories

🕑 Opening hours
24 freely accessible
7 daily
🖰 frequently (5-6 days/week)
🖰 average (3-4 days/week)
🖰 rare (up to 2 days/week)
🕑 after tel. request

This information is valid during the cycling season and serves as a guide. The daily opening hours can be found via the web link.

Weblink

In the location data block at the respective tourist entry there is a six-digit number and a letter combination after the @ symbol (e.g. @ abc123). Entering this weblink ID on our website www.esterbauer.com will take you directly to the corresponding website and thus replace the tedious entry of long web addresses.

Accommodation and service directory

On the last pages of this cycle tour book you will find a list of overnight accommodations in almost every place along the route, from simple campsites to 5-star hotels. You will also find extensive information about bike workshops and bike rental stations.

Donaueschingen to Ulm

m/km: ↗ 5.6 (1104m) ↘ 6.7 (1322m) | cycle path: 62 % | unpaved: 17 % | busy road: 3 %

The first section of this ride passes through especially scenic landscapes. The Danube, which is little more than a stream at this point, curves in leisurely loops across the countryside. Near Geisingen the valley narrows, and the river's meandering course becomes ever more impressive. Tall limestone cliffs with romantic pinnacles line the valley. An unusual spectacle is the Danube Sink between in the Upper Danube Nature preserve between Immendingen and Möhringen. The river then winds along the southern edge of the Swabian Alb, passing numerous castles, abbeys and palaces. Especially impressive: the castle Wildenstein, Beuron Archabbey and the Hohenzollern castle at Sigmaringen.

The route follows mostly flat terrain and is generally well-paved. The only climbs and gravel stretches come in the narrow Danube valley. Downstream from Sigmaringen, the river becomes wider as it passes through a broad valley. In Ehingen you can turn your back on the Danube and follow an alternative route through the Blau valley. Ulm with its old city and huge cathedral offers a fitting end to this stage.

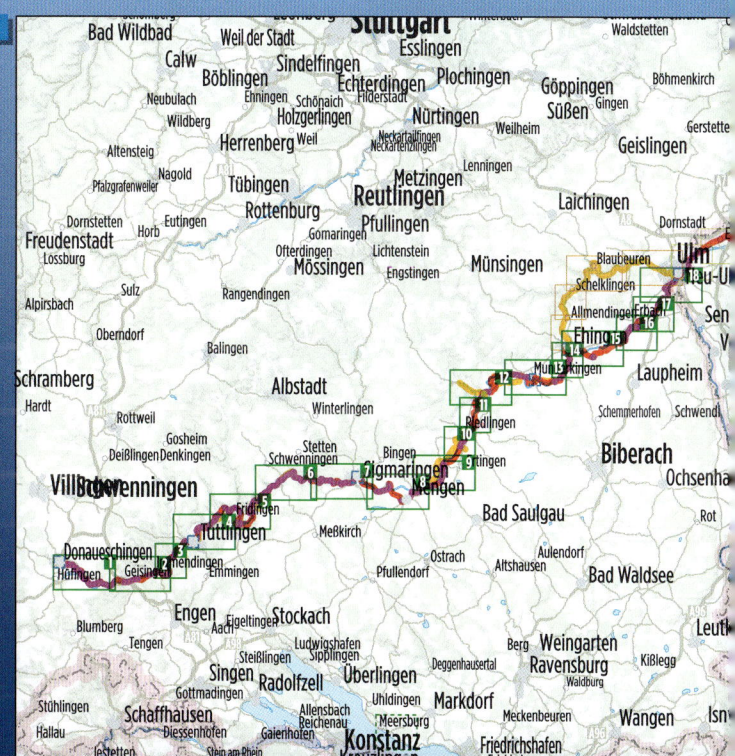

The Danube Source

"Brigach and Breg set the Danube on its way" goes an old classroom rhyme to help geography students with their lessons. But it does not completely explain the source of Europe's second-longest river. The Breg carries more water and is longer than the Brigach, and it was at the Breg's source near Furtwangen that locals placed a small monument marking the spot as the Danube's source. When residents of Furtwangen applied to have "their" Danube source officially recognized in 1965, city leaders in Donaueschingen were not amused. After all, the Roman emperor Tiberius had long ago recognized a spring in the city's Fürstenberg Park as the Danube's source. The dispute was settled in that the official Danube spring was allowed to remain in Donaueschingen, while the Breg spring was marked on maps as the Danube's headwaters.

Donaueschingen

prefix: 0771

- **Tourist-Information**, Karlstr. 58, ✆ 857221, @ axq611
- **Fürstlich Fürstenbergische Sammlungen (Princely Fürstenberg collections)**, Am Karlspl. 7, ✆ 229677563 The exhibition deals with the eventful history of the House of Fürstenberg and shows natural history exhibits as well as an art collection. @ fkj365
- **Fürstlich Fürstenbergische Brauerei (princely Fürstenberg brewery)**, Postpl. 1, ✆ 86206 Guided tour through traditional buildings, brewery museum and production. @ har786

Briach an Breg confluence

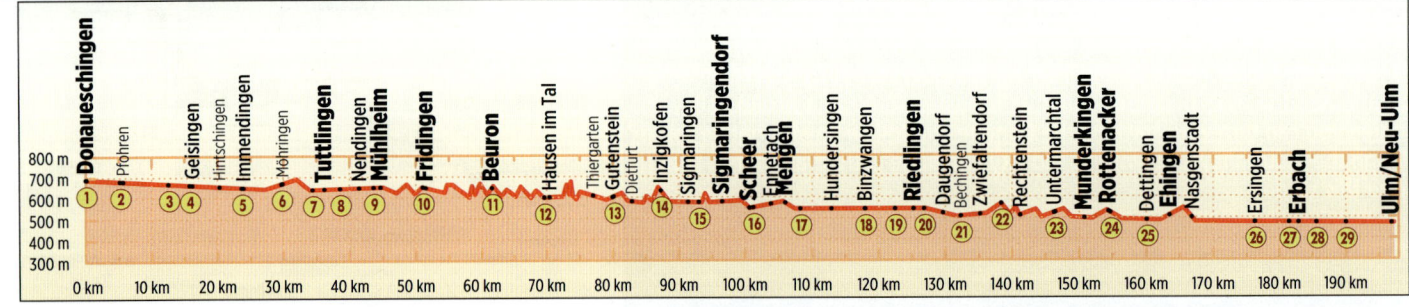

🏛 **Kinder- und Jugendmuseum (museum for children and youth)**, Haldenstr. 5, ☎ 92947426 ⊜ Explore nature, technical objects or man himself! @ mgm661

🏛 **Museum Art.Plus**, Museumsweg 1, ☎ 8966890 ⊜ Contemporary art is presented in changing exhibitions. @ gdu118

🏛 **Zunftmuseum (carnival and guilds museum)**, Sennhofstr. 8a ☾ Immerse yourself in the colourful hustle and bustle of carnival and take a look at historical and contemporary carnival figures and traditional costumes from the region. @ kxr751

🚹 **Stadtkirche St. Johann (town church)**, An der Stadtkirche, ☎ 897820. The landmark of the town was built from 1724-47 in the style of the Bohemian Baroque. @ gum686

🚹🏰 **Fürstlich Fürstenbergisches Schloss (Princely Fürstenberg palace)**, An der Stadtkirche, ☎ 229677563 ☾ The palace is one of the most important buildings of the Belle Epoque in Germany. The park impresses with historical monuments, watercourses and old trees. @ tvx238

✳ **Donauquelle (source of Danube)**, Fürstenbergstr., ☎ 857221 the Danube is located between the town church St. Johann and the palace. @ lei488

✳ **Donauzusammenfluss (Danube confluence)**, Brigachweg ㉔

▭ **Parkschwimmbad (park pool)**, Brigachweg, ☎ 857221, @ dqj683

The name Fürstenberg has long been associated with the city of Donaueschingen. The German baronial family has left numerous marks on the city, which has been the family's residence since 1723. There is the Fürstenberg Brewery and the Fürstlich Fürstenberg Palace near St. Johann, a Bohemian baroque church. The palace park is also the location of the Danube spring, an artfully constructed basin decorated with figures representing the Mother Baar who points the young maiden Danube toward the east. The spring can also be reached from Josefstraße and Straße An der Stadtkirche.

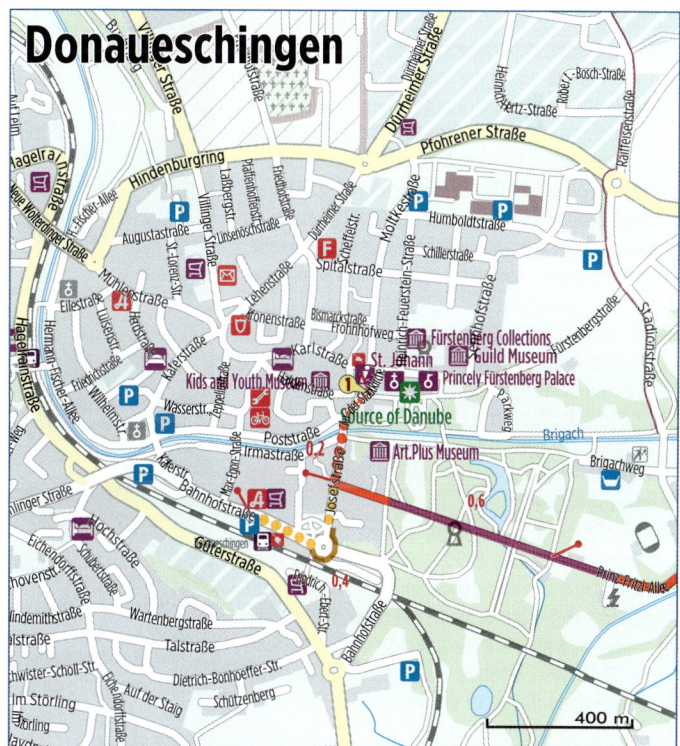

CENTRE If you want to get to the source of the Danube and also to the starting point of the Danube cycle path, turn right at the station into **Bahnhofstraße**, at the roundabout follow the sign Donauquelle and take the second exit (**Josefstraße**). Cross the Brigach and follow the road to the church St. Johann. Here you can park your bikes and walk a few meters to the source of the Danube. **1** Starting point for the tour is the diagonally opposite **Lammplatz** ⌇ on the street An der Stadtkirche back to Brigachbrücke ⌇ at the second possibility turn left into **Prinz-Fritzi-Allee** ⌇ ride through the palace park ⌇ keep right after the transformer station ⌇ along the Breg.

TIP To reach the confluence of the Brigach and Breg, follow the path along the creek which begins just after the bridge.

Turn right over the bridge across the Breg ⌇ continue under the **B 27** ⌇ immediately turn right before the wastewater treatment plant ⌇ follow the paved path between fields to Pfohren ⌇ **2** at the intersection turn left onto the **K 5749**, which takes you across the Danube and into the village of Pfohren.

At the source of the Danube

Pfohren (Donaueschingen)

prefix: 0771

✉ **Riedsee-Camping**, Am Riedsee 11, ☎ 5511, @ uwo337

🏰 **Jagdschloss Entenburg (hunting lodge)**, Entenburgweg. The old moated castle was built in 1471 by Count Heinrich von Fürstenberg.

In the village turn right on **Entenburgweg** ⌇ ride past the **Entenburg** hunting lodge ⌇ turn right on **Wiesenstraße** ⌇ at the edge of the village turn right into the paved field road ⌇ this takes you under the main road ⌇ follow the paved field road, at first beside the main road ⌇ turn right between meadows and fields ⌇ along the main road, then right.

TIP Tip: At the 5-way-intersection by the river you can make an excursion to the nearby Neudingen. Simply turn right over the bridge. On the main route ride straight on.

Neudingen (Donaueschingen)

🏰 **Fürstliche Gruftkirche (Princely crypt church)**, Gutmadinger Str. 15. Distinctive domed building from 1850, in the middle of a park, former location of the monastery Maria-Hof.

Keep left by the building and continue to the main road ⌇ follow the route along the **B31** and through the underpass towards Geisingen. **3**

Wartenberg

On the left you can see the 821 meter Wartenberg. It is one of the extinct Hegau volcanos and offers fine views into the surrounding landscape. The lords of Wartenberg and of Fürstenberg, whose castles stood on opposite sides of the Danube, fought each other

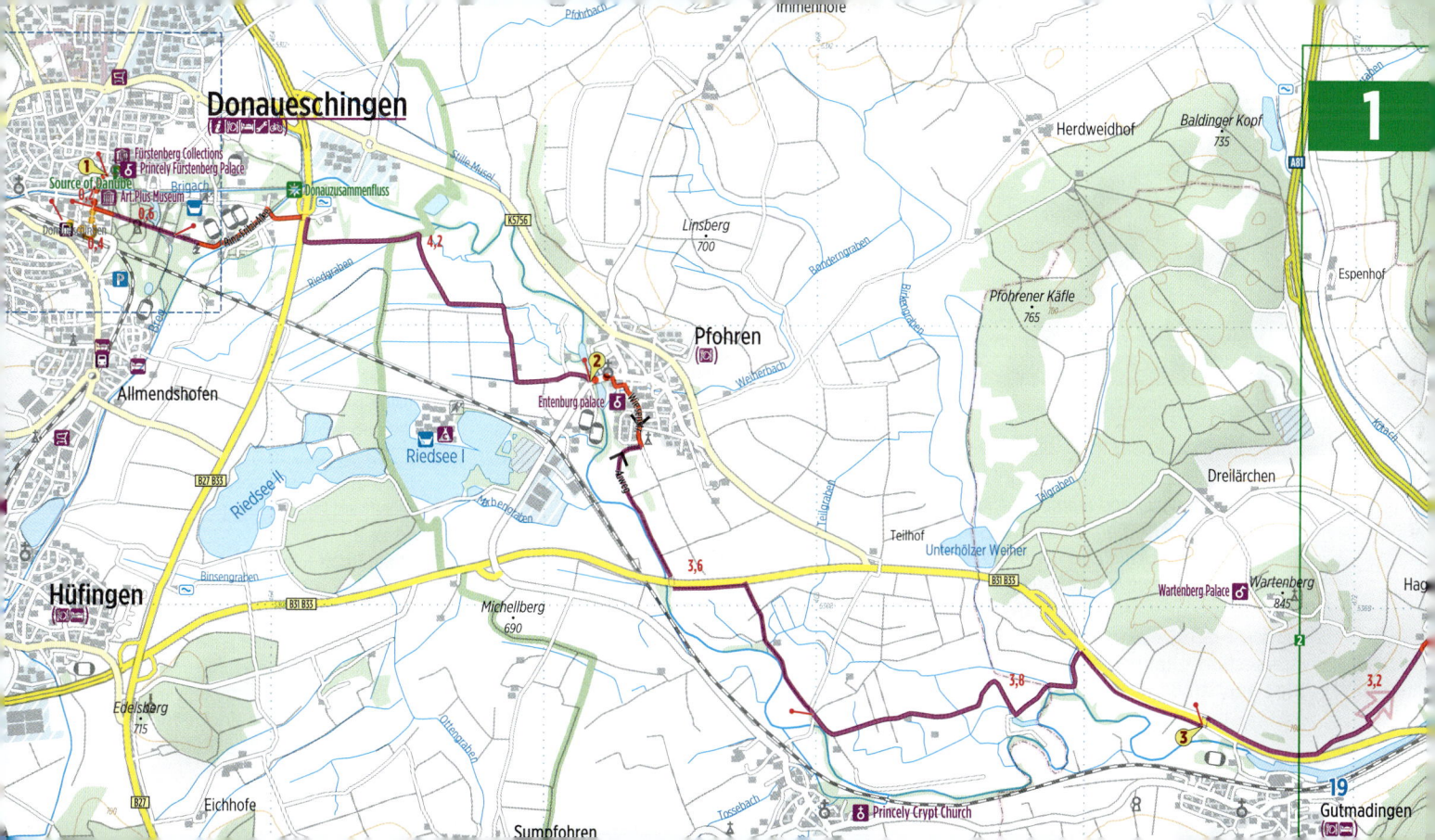

Donaueschingen

Fürstenberg Collections
Princely Fürstenberg Palace
Art.Plus Museum

Source of Danube

Brigach

Donauzusammenfluss

1

Immenhöfe

Herdweidhof

Baldinger Kopf
735

Espenhof

Pfohren

Linsberg
700

Pfohrener Käfle
765

4,2

2

Entenburg palace

Allmendshofen

Riedsee I

Riedsee II

Hüfingen

Michellberg
690

3,6

Teilhof

Unterhölzer Weiher

Dreilärchen

Wartenberg Palace

Wartenberg
845

3,8

2

3,2

3

Edelsberg
715

Eichhöfe

Sumpfohren

Princely Crypt Church

19

Gutmadingen

Nature education at the Danube Seepage

for centuries until Count Heinrich II of Fürstenberg got tired of the feud and married the last female member of the Wartenberg line around 1300. It was a shrewd move, which ended the rivalry and enabled the Fürstenbergs to take over all Wartenberg possessions.

As you reach Geisingen turn right at the T-intersection ⌁ immediately right again onto the Hauptstraße. **4**

ALTERNATIVE The busy main road of Geisingen can be bypassed on the Donaustraße.

Geisingen
prefix: 07704

- ℹ️ **Rathaus (Town hall)**, Hauptstr. 36, ✆ 8070, @ qbg367
- 🔯 **Wallfahrtsstätte Heilig-Kreuz-Kapelle (pilgrimage site Heilig-Kreuz-chapel)**, Hauptstr. 58. The church is a station on the pilgrim's way to Santiago Donau-Randen. The architectural style reflects the transition from Renaissance to Baroque.
- ♟ **Schloss Ruine Wartenberg (castle ruin)**, Wartenberg. Ruin on mountain of the same name. The castle was once the seat of the Lords of Geisingen.
- ✳️ **arena geisingen**, Am Espen 16, ✆ 9233980 ⛸ Germany's first roofed inline skating arena, beautifully situated leisure and sports area in the immediate vicinity of the Danube. @ cku626

Geisingen is one of the oldest towns in the Baar plateau, being first mentioned in deeds from the monastery of St. Gallen in 724. According to documents, the town of Geisingen was founded beside the village of the same name around 1300 by the Counts von Wartenberg. The first mention of the town dates to 1329, as the Wartenberger property went to the Counts von Fürstenberg after the Wartenberger line died out in 1321.

Geisingen to Tuttlingen   19.4 km

Turn right at the roundabout ⌁ cross the railway tracks ⌁ immediately left onto the bicycle path ⌁ follow the path beside the tracks ⌁ you pass underneath the freeway and the **B 31** ⌁ under a railway bridge ⌁ by the house turn right across the Danube ⌁ left onto the bicycle path at the T-intersection ⌁ turn right into Hintschingen.

Immendingen
prefix: 07462

- ℹ️ **Tourist-Information**, Schlosspl. 2, ✆ 24228, @ plx546
- 🏛 **Heimatmuseum (museum of local history)**, Hindenburgstr. 2, ✆ 24228 ⏰ Unique fossil finds, including the sabre-toothed tiger and mammoth, customs, exhibits on the development of industry and landscape document the history of the region. @ ilo623
- ♟ **Oberes Schloss (upper palace)**, Schlosspl. 2. The castle (12th century) was originally a moated castle, but its moats were buried. The Tourist Information is located in the castle. @ hkh243
- ✳️ **Donauversinkung (Danube seepage)** 🕐 The river without water - the Danube disappears. @ rxc383

Take the pedestrian and bicycle bridge across the tracks ⌁ after the bridge turn right on the bike path that leads into **Blumenweg** **5** turn

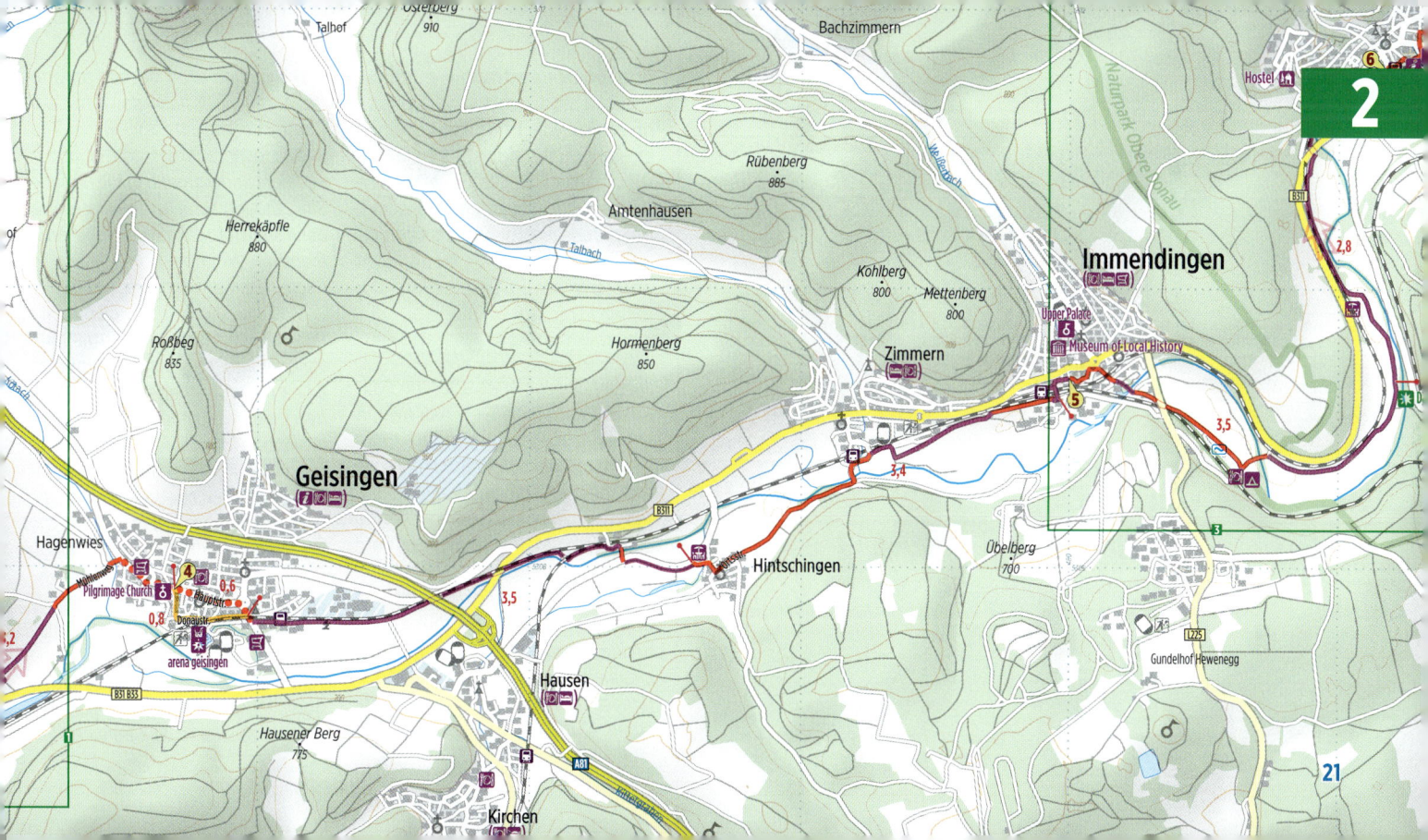

Talhof

Osterberg
910

Bachzimmern

Naturpark Obere Donau

Hostel

6

2,8

Herrekäpfle
880

Amtenhausen

Rübenberg
885

Immendingen

Roßberg
835

Talbach

Hormenberg
850

Kohlberg
800

Mettenberg
800

Zimmern

Upper Palace

Museum of Local History

5

3,5

D

Geisingen

B311

3,4

Übelberg
700

3

Hagenwies

Pilgrimage Church

4   0,6

Hauptstr.

0,8   Donaustr.

3,5

Hintschingen

Hütsch.

225

3,2

arena geisingen

B31 B33

Gundelhof Hewenegg

Hausen

Hausener Berg
775

A81

Kirchen

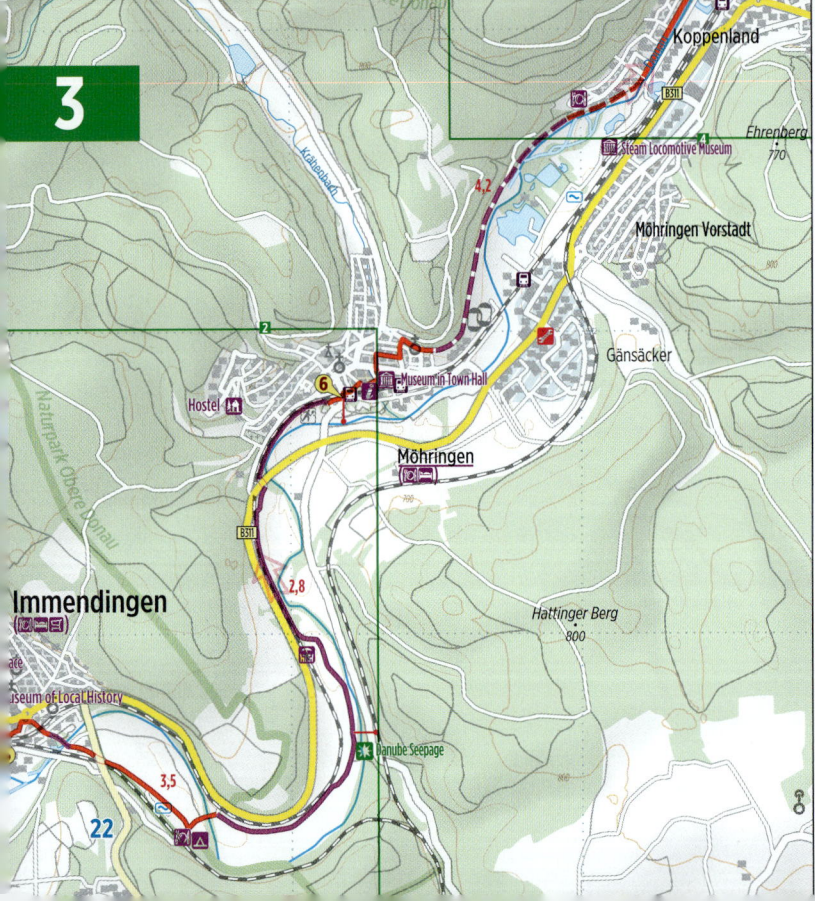

right on **Donaustraße** ∼ continue straight and cross the Danube on the bicycle bridge ∼ continue straight on the side street ∼ along the railroad tracks ∼ after the wastewater treatment plant turn left across another bicycle bridge over the Danube ∼ keep right onto the paved lane before the railway tracks.

The Danube Seepage

Just a few kilometers after the Danube starts to look like a real river, it seems to magically disappear into the ground with a mysterious gurgling and splashing. When the river is low, the riverbed above ground dries up completely as the river seeps into the porous limestone layers beneath the soil. For about 12 kilometers the Danube's waters wind through an underground labyrinth of caves and channels. It resurfaces at Germany's largest spring, the Aachtopf, where some 10,000 litres bubble up out of the ground every second to form the Aach, which flows down to Lake Constance and into the Rhine. The water spends an average of about 60 hours underground in the Danube Sink, though some of the water has been shown to take weeks and even months to resurface.

People used salt and dyes as early as 1877 to investigate the underground river. The first places where the river vanishes into the ground are visible as an earthen funnel on the south bank near the Immendingen railroad bridge. Whirlpools form there when the water is high. During the summer months, if the water is low, one can find fantastic stone formations on a walk along the dry river bed to Möhringen. Although the caves form one of Europe's largest underground river systems, divers and researchers have explored only a small part of the network.

To assure that some of the Danube's water reaches downstream communities, a canal was built between Im-

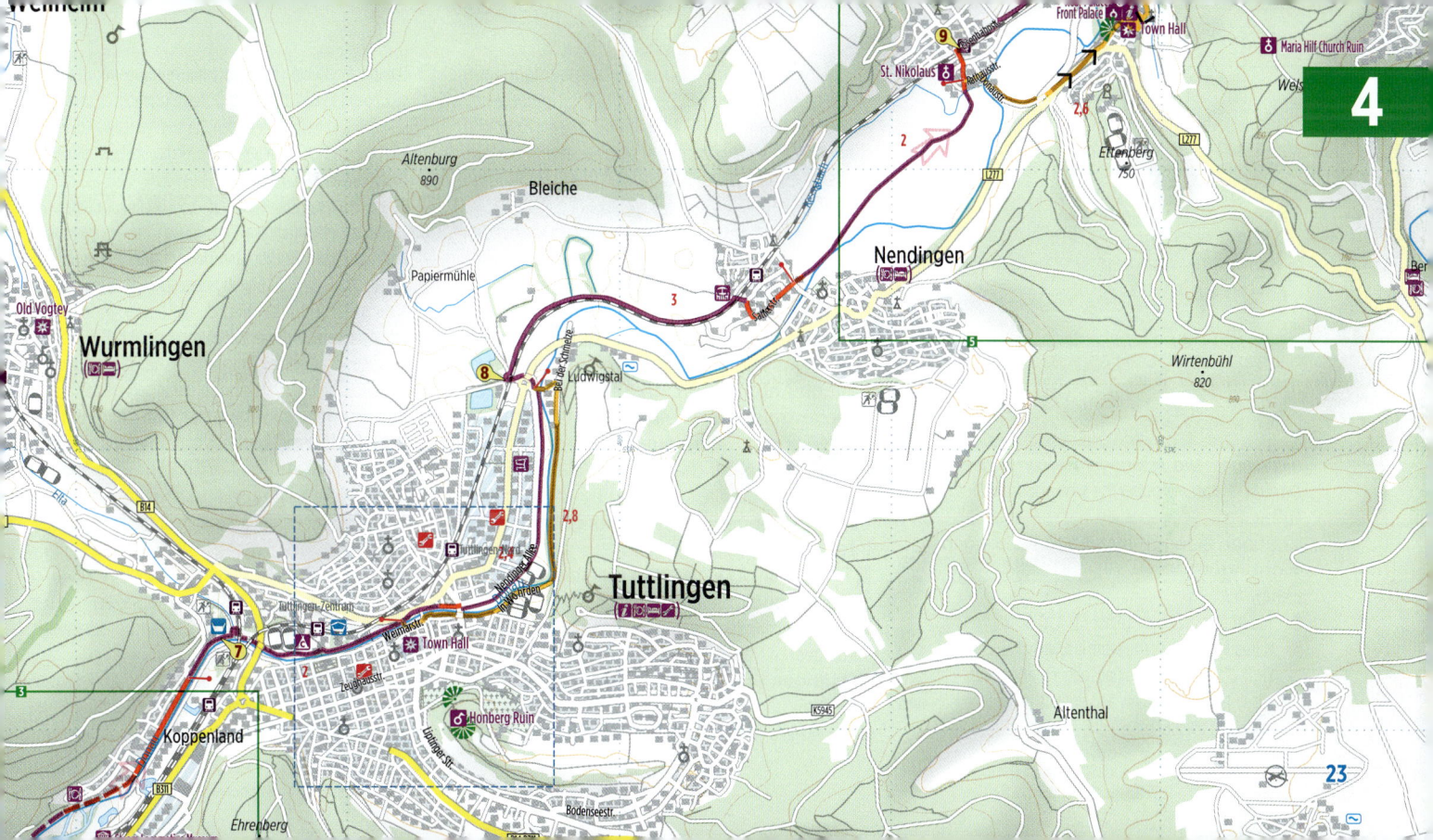

Danubevalley close to Tuttlingen

mendingen and Möhringen to carry some of the Danube's water around the sink and into the Danube valley.

Continue along the tracks to Möhringen.

Möhringen (Tuttlingen)
prefix: 07462

- ℹ **Tourist-Info**, Hermann-Leiber-Str. 4, ☎ 94820, @ fan532
- 🏛 **Museum im Rathaus (museum in town hall)**, Hermann-Leiber-Str. 4, ☎ 94820 ⊜ Exhibitions about the history of Möhringen, old stringed instruments and exhibits around the Möhringer Fasnet. @ uwd867

The earliest documented reference to Möhringen dates from the year 882, and in 1308 it gained city and market status. In 1470, Austrian Emperor Friedrich II awarded the city its coat of arms showing a Moor. Its name comes from "Moringas," or city of Moring, a local ruler.

6 At the first intersection in Möhringen turn left across the tracks ~ then immediately right on **Hermann Leiber Straße** ~ pass the tourist information and the museum ~ turn right into **Marktgasse** ~ at the last possibility turn left ~ straight ahead over the main road ~ turn right on **Anton Braun Straße** and then left on **Bleichestraße** ~ at the T-intersection right on **Am Mühlberg** ~ continue into the gravel road along the edge of the woods ~ **7** on a paved cycle path you pass directly by the outdoor pool in Tuttlingen ~ further along the Danube into the Donaupark.

CENTRE To reach the city's interesting pedestrian area, cross the Danube on the wooden bridge **Rathaussteg** and after approx. 20 m you reach the market place of Tuttlingen.

Tuttlingen
prefix: 07461

- ℹ **Tourist-Info**, Rathausstr. 1, ☎ 99340, @ yai822
- 🚂 **Dampflokmuseum (steam locomotive museum)**, Beim Lokschuppen 1, ☎ 07462/9116827 ⊙ Steam locomotives, passenger, sleeping and freight wagons in the original railway depot, as well as buildings and numerous exhibits of railway history are presented on 4 ha. @ blt687
- 🏛 **Galerie (gallery)**, Rathausstr. 7, ☎ 15551 ⊜ Regular temporary exhibitions of contemporary art. @ ikq371
- 🏛 **Heimatmuseum Fruchtkasten (local history museum)**, Donaustr. 50, ☎ 15135 ⊙ The museum shows informative facts about settlement, urban and industrial history. @ tnr462
- 🏛 **Tuttlinger Haus (Tuttlinger house)**, Donaustr. 19, ☎ 15135 ⊜ From the cellar to the granary, experience the history of the town on the basis of the former inhabitants of the Tuttlinger Haus! @ fiu118
- ⛪ **Evangelische Stadtkirche (protestant town church)**, Bahnhofstr. 13, ☎ 162228. The church was consecrated around 15 years after the Tuttlingen town fire on 31 October 1817. @ tqe372
- 🏰 **Ruine Honberg (ruin)** 🕐 Every year in July, the Honberg Open Air Festival takes place in the ruins of the former fortress. @ hrv575
- ✳ **Rathaus (town hall)**, Rathausstr. 1, ☎ 990. After the town fire of 1803, Carl Leonard von Uber not only planned the town plan but also the town hall with late baroque and classical elements. @ okb773
- 🏊 **Freibad Tuttlingen (public pool)**, Badstr. 4, ☎ 72405, @ hdv336
- 🛁 **TuWass, Freizeit- und Thermalbad (thermal bath)**, Mühlenweg 1-5, ☎ 9665566, @ uky161

After a catastrophic fire in 1803, Tuttlingen was rebuilt and emerged as an important district city with about 35,000 residents. The city's main attraction is the Lutheran church, which is one of the most beautiful art nouveau churches in Germany. Rising above the city is the Honberg, which is crowned by the ruins of an old castle and offers fine views onto the surrounding city.

Tuttlingen to Beuron   25.5 km

The main route runs along the busy Nendinger Allee. You can avoid this section on a signposted route along the Südufer. After crossing the river, turn left on **Weimarstraße**, then continue on the street **In Wöhrden**. Near the river bank to Ludwigstal, where you cross the Danube again.

To take the main route, pass the wooden bridge and continue beside the river ~ you depart Tuttlingen on the bike path along the **Nendinger Allee** ~ at the roundabout proceed straight and

under the main road ~ **8** turn right immediately after crossing the railway line ~ follow the paved lane beside the tracks to Nendingen.

Follow the lane to the right across the railway line ~ turn right on **Industriestraße** ~ at the next T-intersection turn left onto **Sattlerstraße** ~ continue straight into the **Austraße**, a paved lane takes you towards Stetten.

Stetten (Mühlheim an der Donau)

8 Pfarrkirche St. Nikolaus, Zellstr. 7. The church was built from 1864-67 according to the plans of the Viennese cathedral architect Friedrich von Schmid. @ bpc721

In Stetten you can either continue along the signposted main route or take a short excursion through the pretty medieval centre of Mühlheim.

Via Mühlheimer Oberstadt   2.6km

After crossing the Kesselbach turn right into **Rathausstraße** ~ right

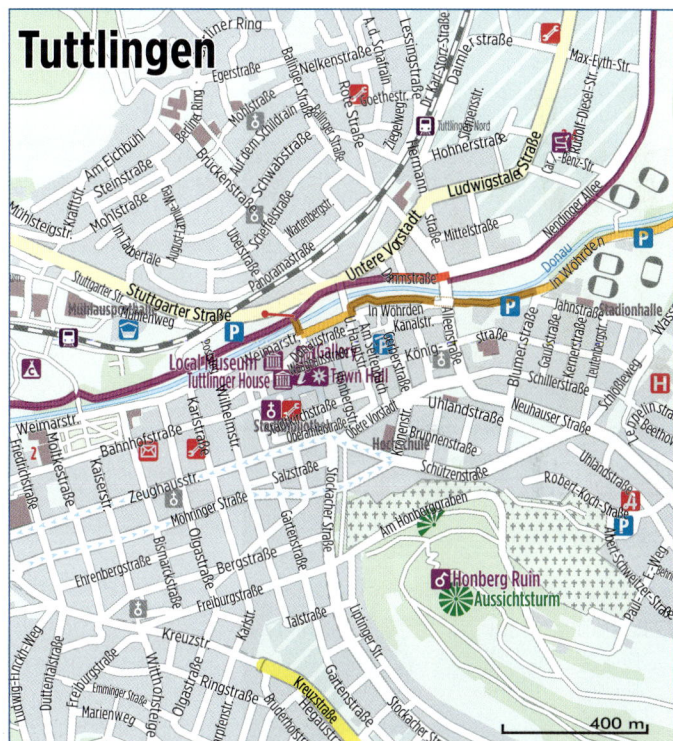

Town Hall of Mühlheim

on **Donaustraße** ~ cross the Danube ~ along the bicycle path under the **L 443** ~ keep left onto **Tuttlinger Straße** ~ continue into **Haldenstraße** ~ follow the right-hand bend..

Mühlheim-Oberstadt

prefix: 07463

Verkehrsamt, Schloßstr. 1, ✆ 8903, ✆ 0174/3264445, @ krc852

Vorderes Schloss mit Museum (front palace with museum), Schlossstr. 1 ☺ ☾ City history, history of the lords of Mühlheim, the church and the Welschenberg mountain. Probably the origin of the second palace in Mühlheim can be explained by the dual rule of Friedrich and Engelhard von Enzberg. The palace was used as a widow's residence and was purchased and repaired by the town of Mühlheim in 1987. @ diq276

Hinteres Schloss (rear palace), Schlossstr. 3, ☾ private possession, not open to the public. The palace was built around 1200, at the time the town was founded, on the so-called Nussbühl. The reconstruction in the years 1751-1753 changed the palace and gave it its present appearance. Mühlheim Castle is still the residence of the von Enzberg family and cannot be visited. @ pnk582

Mühlheimer Rathaus (Townhall), Hauptstr. 16. As one of the oldest buildings in the city, the town hall has been the centre of the city's interesting history for 800 years. A column with a Romanesque capital refers to its founding period around 1200.

The picturesque old city of Mühlheim is visible from afar perched on a ridge above the Danube. If you have a weakness for romantic old cities, you should find the strength to pedal up the steep but short road to the upper city. The narrow streets and half-timbered houses with pointed roofs are built on a rocky ledge and surrounded by the old city wall. During much of the year, colourful flowers line the window sills to complete the quaint atmosphere. The first known mention of Mühlheim can be found in a document dated 799 from the Reichenau abbey. Mühlheim was awarded city status in 1300, and in 1409 the brothers Friedrich and Engelhardt von Enzberg purchased authority over the city from the Weitingen Knights. Descendents of the von Enzbergs still live here today.

Take the **Hauptstraße** through the historic upper town of Mühlheim ~ at the next possibility turn left through the city gate ~ turn left into **Hintere Straße** ~ at the end turn right into **An der Steig** street ~ the street leads down to the Danube ~ at the roundabout turn into **Bahnhofstraße**.

For the main route, continue straight on **Bachstraße** and cross the railway line.

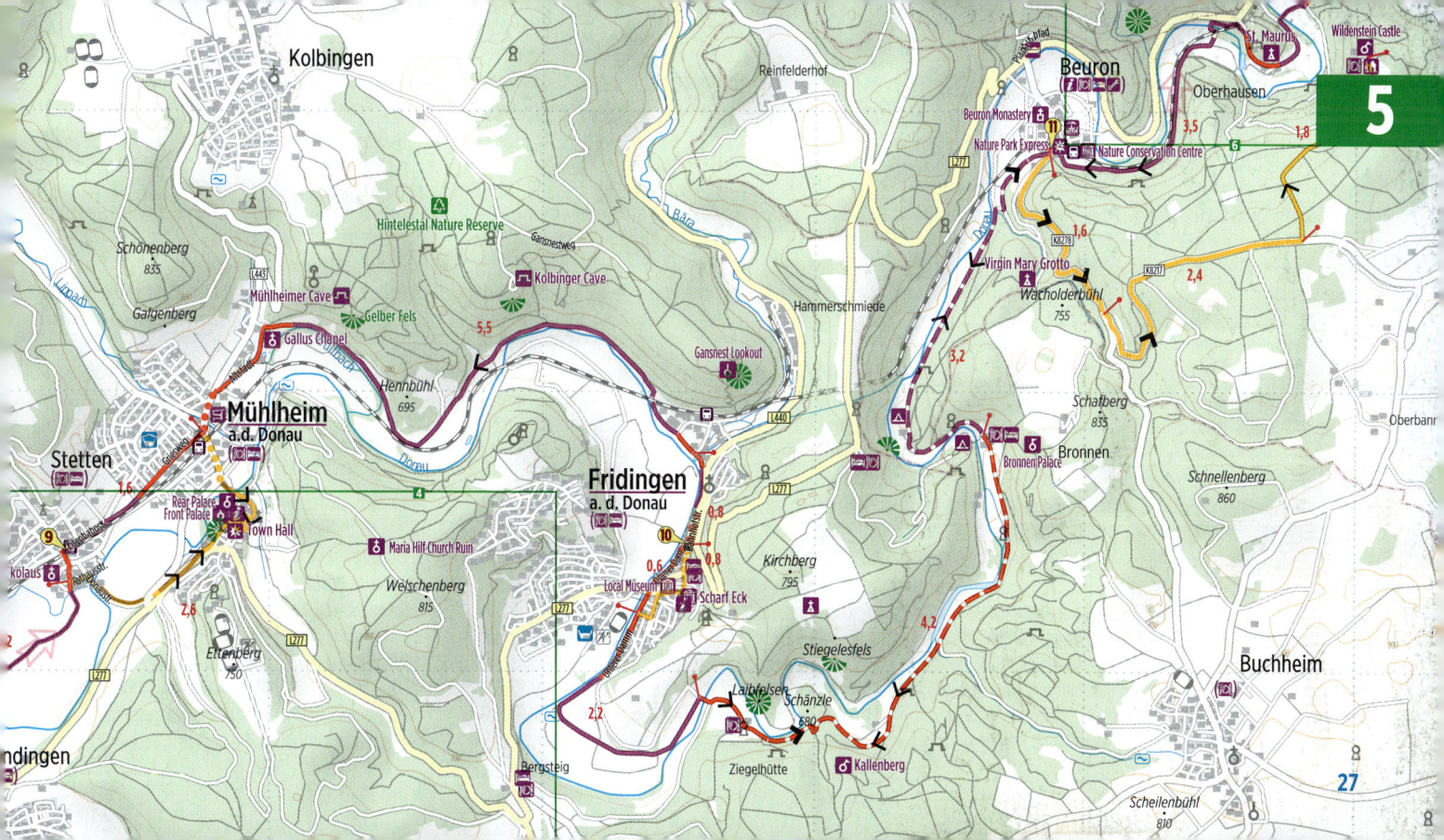

Kolbingen

Schönenberg
835

Galgenberg

Mühlheimer Cave

Gelber Fels

Reinfelderhof

Gansnestweg

Hintelestal Nature Reserve

Kolbinger Cave

5,5

Gallus Chapel

Henbühl
695

Hammerschmiede

Gansnest Lookout

Stetten

Mühlheim
a.d. Donau

Rear Palace
Front Palace

Town Hall

1,6

Maria Hilf Church Ruin

Welschenberg
815

Ettenberg
750

Nikolaus

2,6

Fridingen
a. d. Donau

0,8

10

0,6

Local Museum

0,8

Scharf Eck

Kirchberg
795

2,2

Bergsteig

Stiegelesfels

Laibfelsen

Schänzle
680

Ziegelhütte

Kallenberg

Beuron

Oberhausen

3,5

1,8

6

Beuron Monastery

Nature Park Express

Nature Conservation Centre

Virgin Mary Grotto

1,6

K8278

2,4

K8277

Wacholderbühl
755

3,2

Schafberg
835

Bronnen

Bronnen Palace

Schnellenberg
860

Oberbann

4,2

Buchheim

Scheilenbühl
810

27

St. Maurus

Wildenstein Castle

5

9

Donau

Donau

L443

L440

L277

L277

L277

Stetten (Mühlheim an der Donau)

9 In Stetten turn right onto the cycle path ⮑ the cycle path leaves the **Eisenbahnstraße** ⮑ straight on **Griesweg** ⮑ at the T-intersection, where the excursion rejoins the main route from the right, turn left onto **Kolbinger Straße** (L443).

Mühlheim an der Donau

prefix: 07463

- 🔷 **Galluskirche (Gallus church)**, Altstadt 4. In Mühlheim's oldest church (10th/11th century) you can admire frescos from the 14th and 15th centuries.

- 🔷 **Ruine Maria Hilf (ruin)**, Welschenberg ㉔ The former pilgrimage church was demolished in the 19th c., only a small open chapel remained.

- 🔶 **Veitskapelle (Veits chapel)**, Altstadt 5, close to Gallus church. The chapel with its outer pulpit was formerly used as an ossuary.

- ◻ **Mühlheimer Höhle (cave)**, ✆ 668, ✆ 838977, ✆ 0174/3610067 ☺ ✆ In the stalactite cave impressive ice sculptures form again and again. @ ami567

- ✳ **Mühlheimer Nachtwächter (night watchman)**, ✆ 8903, ✆ 9952952 ☺ The tradition existing from 1496-1936 is continued by Heinz-Dieter Wettki now on Saturdays and in the season also every Tuesday at 21 o'clock, meeting point is at the town hall. @ xru185

- 🔵 **Hallenbad (indoor pool)**, Schillerstr. 18, ✆ 7515, @ ras776

At the edge of town turn right into a paved lane ⮑ follow the lane between scattered houses ⮑ turn right just after the Gallus church and cemetery ⮑ the narrow, paved lane takes you through a beautiful nature reserve ⮑ continue between fields and forest and then along the Danube to Fridingen ⮑ continue beside the river to the main road ⮑ turn right onto a bicycle path along the road ⮑ **10** after 300 m turn right into the street **Oberer Damm**.

ALTERNATIVE If you would like to take the alternative through the historic city centre, then stay on **Bahnhofsstraße**, turn left shortly after Gasthof Sonne, turn right at **Mittlerer Gasse**, turn left into Gartenstraße, turn right at **Friedenstraße**, shortly thereafter you will find the main route at Unteren Damm.

Fridingen an der Donau

prefix: 07463

- ℹ **Verkehrsamt Donau-Heuberg (tourist office)**, Kirchpl. 2, ✆ 8370, @ kcy825

- 🏛 **Künstlerhaus „Scharf Eck" (house of artists „Scharf Eck")**, Am Oberen Tor 3, ✆ 9912055, ✆ 83718 ☺ ✆ The 16th century farmhouse features a rustic inn and a museum dedicated to the Danube valley painter Hans Bucher (1929-2002). @ fqt736

- 🏛🔷 **Museum Oberes Donautal im Ifflinger Schloss (museum upper Danube valley)**, Schloßg. 20, ✆ 8474, ✆ 83728 ☺ ✆ Ifflinger Castle, built around 1300 as a residential tower castle, is named after the last noble owners, the barons of Ifflingen-Granegg. In addition to temporary exhibitions in seven departments, the museum exhibits collections on the cultural history of the Upper Danube Valley: archaeology, castle ruins, Danube valley gallery, historical carnival masks and dresses, Fridinger artists. @ mxt281

- 🔷 **Aussichtsturm Gansnest (observation tower)** ㉔ The former Schieberhaus of the high storage facility of the Danube power plant was built in 1923 and shut down in 1960. Since 1967 it belongs to the Schwäbischen Albverein (Swabian hiking association?) and the tower can be visited at any time.

- ◻ **Kolbinger Höhle – Stephanshöhle (cave)** ☺ The name Stephanshöhle (cave) is ascribable to a thief named Stephan, who hid here in the 19th century. The entrance he is said to have used can be seen in the first room of the cave. The Kolbinger cave is one of the largest and most important caves in the southwestern Swabian Alb. It has a length of approx. 330 metres, of which approx. 90 metres are accessible as a show cave. The cave with its impressive stalactites was made permanently accessible in 1968 by stairs, paths and electric lighting. @ tyw184

- ✳ **Historischer Stadtkern (historic town centre)** ㉔ In addition to the Ifflinger Castle, the Zehntscheuer with the oversized Austrian double eagle and the city wall with its houses in Kirchstraße and Litschenberg are worth seeing. The church square with the town hall built in 1876/77 in classicist style and the parish church Sankt Martin are also worth a visit. @ bci734

✉ **Freibad (open air pool)**, ✆ 7558, @ umo612

The prettiest half-timbered house in the town is called Scharf Eck at the upper gate where the city wall stood. It was recently converted into an artists' house in which exhibition spaces document the life and work of the well-known Fridingen artist Hans Bucher. The Ifflinger Schloss contains an interesting local history museum, the Museum Oberes Donautal. If you have time and interest in theatre, the natural amphitheatre at Steintäle presents high-quality performances from June to September.

The route segment from Fridingen to Beuron goes through some of the most beautiful landscape along the German Danube. Rocky formations crowd the valley so that only the railroad and a simple track have room on the valley floor. Shining white limestone cliffs rise almost vertically and suggest the eons that the Danube needed to wear a course through the 300 meters tall stone formation.

Keep right to continue along the river as you leave Fridingen ～ follow the left curve in the paved lane by the wastewater treatment plant ～ at the T-intersection, turn right across the bridge over the Danube ～ keep left after the bridge and continue to the left ～ keep left as you pass the **Scheuerlehof** ～ after another 3 km you reach the "Jägerhaus" inn. The next 3 km follow an unpaved forest track ～ after a gate the track is paved, ahead you can see the Monastery of Beuron ～ the paved lane takes you up a steep hill to the main road ～ **11** cross the road and then immediately turn right.

EXCURSION Wildenstein Castle, which also contains a youth hostel, can be reached by bicycle from Beuron via the K 8278 and Leibertingen. The first 5 km are quite steep, but thereafter the ride up to the castle is no problem.

Wildenstein (Leibertingen)
prefix: 07466

⌂ **Burg Wildenstein (Wildenstein castle)**, Wildenstein 1, ✆ 411 Ⓒ The imposing castle towers on a rock above the Danube and was built in the 13th century. It belongs to a Wildenstein castle chain consisting of Unterwildenstein, Altwildenstein, Wildenstein, Hexenturm and Hahnenkamm. It received its present appearance between 1520 and 1550. Today the castle houses a youth hostel. An annual medieval festival takes place at the castle area. @ spo221

CENTRE To reach the Benedictine monastery of Beuron simply continue straight across the bridge.

On the cycle path near Beuron

Beuron
prefix: 07466

ℹ **Tourist-Information**, Kirchstr. 18, Hausen im Tal (Beuron), ✆ 07579/92100, @ nwy258

🏛 **Naturschutzzentrum Obere Donau (nature conservation centre)**, Wolterstr. 16, ✆ 92800. Permanent exhibitions on earth history, cultural history and natural spaces in the Upper Danube Nature Park, as well as temporary exhibitions. @ eie287

⌂ **Erzabtei Beuron (archabbey)**, Abteistr. 2, ✆ 170. The Augustinian canons' monastery, secularised in 1802, was revived again in 1862 by a foundation of Princess Katharina von Hohenzollern and reopened one year later as a Benedictine monastery. The archabbey houses the largest German monastery library with around 405,000 volumes. @ nga611

* **Naturparkexpress (nature park express)**, ✆ 928014 ☺ The express stops at 22 stations in the Danube Valley. The transport of bicycles is free of charge. @ ufd876

The archabbey Beuron was mentioned as part of the possessions of the St. Gallen abbey as early as 861. The Benedictine monastery that stands there today was established in the 11th century as an Augustine abbey. The abbey has a long tradition of artistic and scientific study, and today generates its own electricity.

Schloss Werenwag

Beuron to Sigmaringen   **31.7 km**

The route between Beuron and Wildenstein runs along the Petersfelsen cliffs, with the Danube winding its way through the valley below ∼ after the railway underpass cross the Danube ∼ after a short gradient follow the sign to the right ∼ a little later past the St.-Maurus-chapel ∼ after the bridge turn left towards Sigmaringen.

On the way to Sigmaringen you will pass Langenbrunn and the impressive Werenwang Palace.

Langenbrunn (Beuron)

⚐ **Schloss Werenwag (Werenwag palace)**. The palace was built around 1100 and is now owned by the House of Fürstenberg. It is inhabited and therefore not open to the public.

The Danube Valley and its Castles

The upper reaches of the Danube, with its many valleys, hillsides and rocky outcrops, was well suited for medieval fortifications. Nowhere else does the Danube feature as many castles as on the short stretch between Donaueschingen and Sigmaringen. Possibly the most impressive of these bastions is Wildenstein Castle, perched high on a rocky summit.

Known to have existed as early as 1077, the castle enjoyed its heyday in the 15 th and 16 th centuries. Today it ranks as the jewel of the Swabian Danube, having survived the turmoils of Europe's darkest periods thanks to its massive walls and double moat. It was only due to the occupants' carelessness that the Swedish armies were able to temporarily seize the castle in 1642. This stretch of the cycle route passes many famous outcroppings, like the Bishop's rock, the Glasträger rock and the Kornelius rock near Hausen.

Follow the right bank of the Danube until you reach Hausen ∼ **12** turn right just before you reach the bridge over the Danube.

ALTERNATIVE For those wishing to ride through Hausen im Tal simply follow the alternative route given in the map. You will rejoin the main route across the bridge down from the railway crossing by Neidingen.

Hausen im Tal (Beuron)
prefix: 07579

ℹ **Tourist-Information**, Kirchstr. 18, ✆ 92100, @ nwy258

Neidingen (Beuron)

The poet Anton Schlude wrote the following about Neidingen in 1858:

„After the traveler has patiently poked around in the ruins of the old palace at Hausen and made his way back down the mountain, the tree-lined road

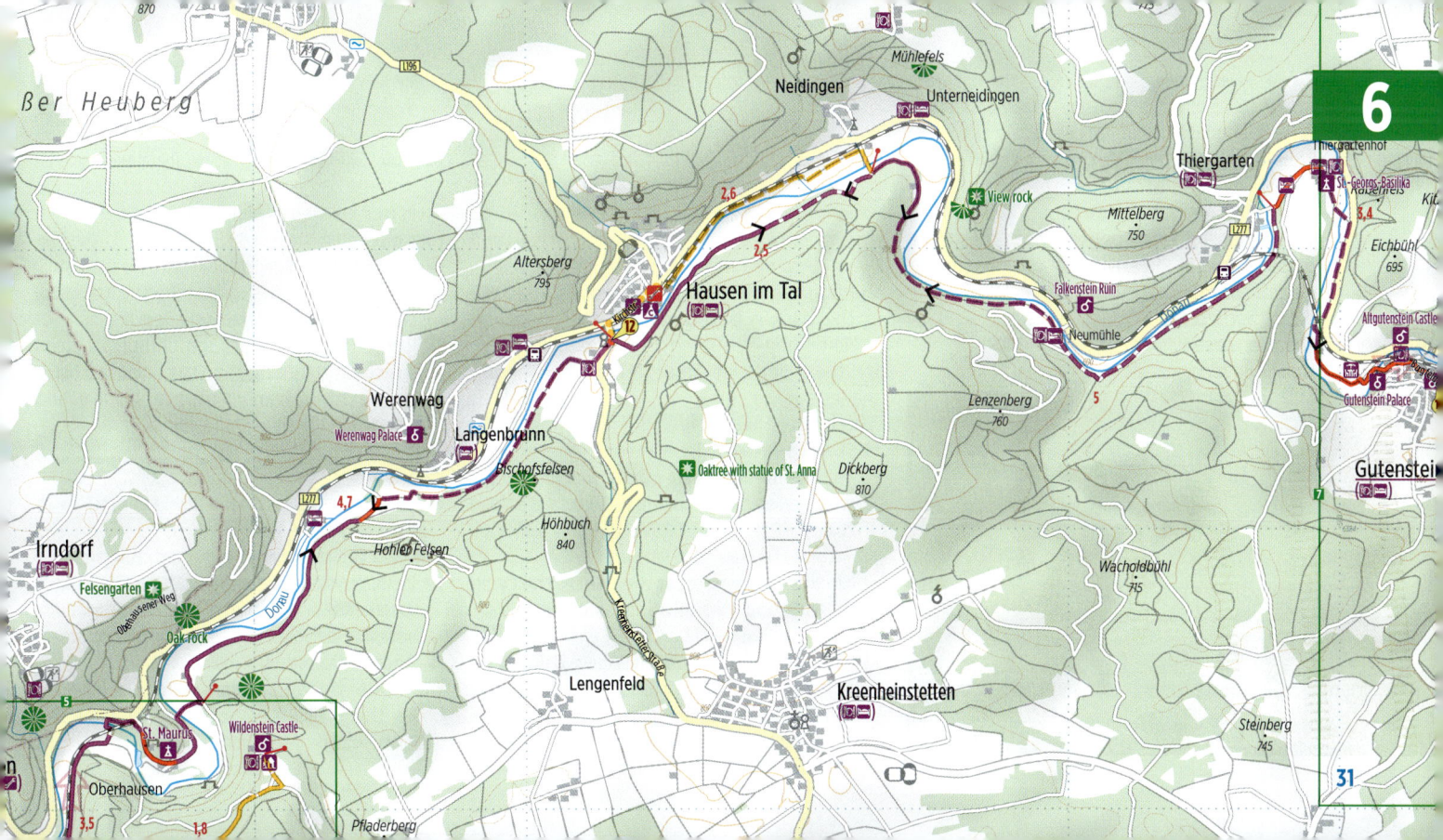

ßer Heuberg

870

L196

Mühlefels

Neidingen

Unterneidingen

Thiergarten

Thiergartenhof

6

St.-Georgs-Basilika

Kützenfels

3,4

Mittelberg
750

Eichbühl
695

View rock

2,6

2,5

Altersberg
795

Hausen im Tal

Falkenstein Ruin

Altgutenstein Castle

Neumühle

Werenwag

Lenzenberg
760

Gutenstein Palace

Gutenstei

Werenwag Palace

Langenbrunn

Oaktree with statue of St. Anna

Dickberg
810

Bischofsfelsen

L277

4,7

Höhbuch
840

5

Wacholdbühl
715

Irndorf

Hohler Felsen

Donau

Felsengarten

Oberhausener Weg

Oak rock

Lengenfeld

Kreenheinstetten

Steinberg
745

5

St. Maurus

Wildenstein Castle

31

n

Oberhausen

3,5

1,8

Pfladerberg

along the left bank of the Danube leads him into the little hamlet of Neidingen not half-an-hour away. Neidingen consists of three parts. Upper and Lower Neidingen and the five hillside houses across from the mountain on the road to Stetten. The 130 inhabitants, like those in Hausen, live exclusively from farming. Further downstream from Neidingen there once stood Schaufels palace. The crag at this location still bears that name. But the most remarkable thing about Neidingen is that a city of the same name supposedly once occupied the right bank of the Danube, on a moderate hill named Buchtbühl, where ruins of old

walls can still be found in the ground. What makes this legend yet more probable is that a 12 th century map documents this Neidingen as a significant locale. Another piece of evidence is, that when the French first came to us in 1796, their maps also showed this Neidingen. Despite all that, however, we can do no more than voice our conjectures because there is no official document that names the place."

Continue along the right bank of the Danube ~ the track is paved initially, then unpaved ~ Neidingen is situated on the opposite bank. By the village of **Thiergarten** the Danube makes a large curve.

Thiergarten (Beuron)

- St.-Georgs-Basilika 🕖 The estate encloses a restaurant and you will find the smallest three-aisled basilica north of the Alps. It was mentioned for the first time in 1275, but was probably built around the year 1000. If you want to visit the basilica, you will get the key in the nearby restaurant.

Still in this loop you cross the river ~ the cycle path leads you through Gutenstein.

Gutenstein (Sigmaringen)

- Pfarrkirche St. Gallus (parish church), Lindenstr., ✆ 07571/52089. Built in 1542 as a Gothic church with saddle roof. A renewal of the nave in Baroque style took place in the 18th c. The „black organ" of the church was built in 1890 by the organ building

company Wilhelm Schwarz & Sohn from Überlingen. Next to the church there is a memorial in remembrance of the war dead. @ gxx554

- Schloss Gutenstein, Grimmerriedweg. The castle was probably built in the 16th c. and rebuilt in the 18th c.. It captivates with its great location. Unfortunately not accessible, since it is in private property since 1978.
- Burgruine Altgutenstein. Built in the 12th c., the castle was already visibly dilapidated in the 16th c. From the former castle only a few remnants of the keep can be seen.

13 Turn left after the village church ~ cross the tracks and turn right on the unpaved track along the railway line ~ cross the bridge ~ and ride past Dietfurth with its ruins.

Dietfurt (Inzigkofen)
prefix: 07571

- ℹ Gemeindeverwaltung Inzigkofen (municipal office), Ziegelweg 2, Inzigkofen, ✆ 73070, @ hgg253
- Ruine Dietfurt und Burghöhle (ruin and castle cave). From the former castle only the bergfried (keep) is preserved, which dominates the village. Important archaeological finds were made in the castle cave below the ruin. However, the ruins and the cave are not open to the public.

Continue between train and Danube ~ cross the little river Schmeie ~ after the station Inzigkofen turn right ~ turn right

Känzele lookout, Inzigkofen

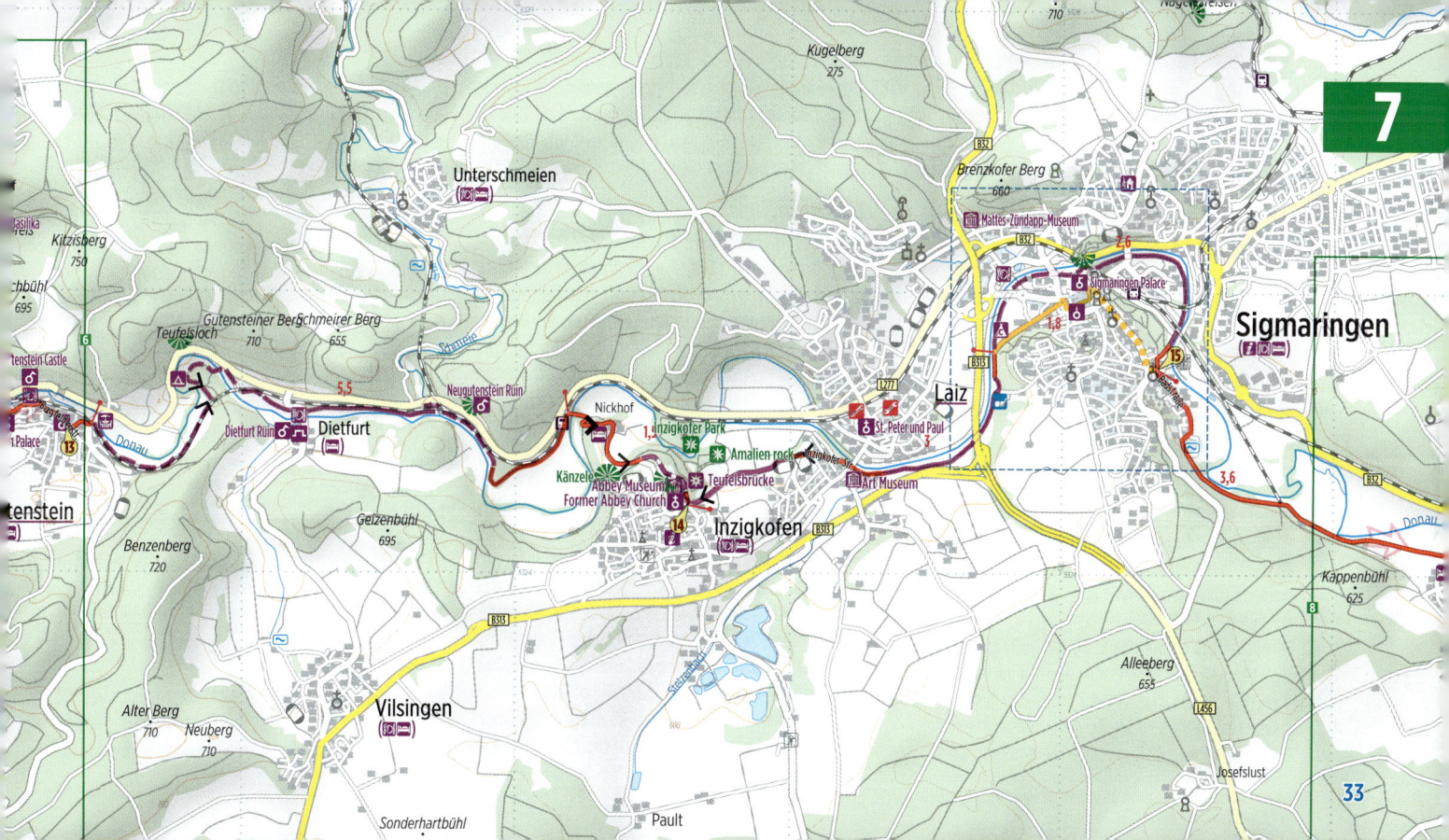

7

Kugelberg
275

Nagelbreisen

Unterschmeien

Kitzisberg
750

chbühl
695

Teufelsloch

Gutensteiner Berg Schmeirer Berg
710   655

Neugutenstein Ruin

Nickhof

Brenzkofer Berg
660

Mattes-Zündapp-Museum

Sigmaringen Palace

2,6

Sigmaringen

tenstein Castle

Donau

Dietfurt Ruin   Dietfurt

5,5

1,Inzigkofer Park

1,1

Amalien rock

Känzele

Abbey Museum
Former Abbey Church   Teufelsbrücke

St. Peter und Paul

Laiz

B313

1,8

15

3,6

Palace

13

Inzigkofen

Art Museum

Geizenbühl
695

B313

1,Palace

tenstein

Benzenberg
720

Kappenbühl
625

Donau

8

Alter Berg
710

Neuberg
710

Vilsingen

Alleeberg
655

L456

Josefslust

Pault

Sonderhartbühl

across the bridge ~ you must ride uphill to Inzigkofen ~ the view from the top of the hill is excellent.

Inzigkofen

prefix: 07571

- ℹ **Gemeindeverwaltung Inzigkofen (municipal office)**, Ziegelweg 2, ✆ 73070, @ hgg253
- 🏛 **Bauernmuseum (farmer museum)**, Parkweg, ✆ 52415 😊 © Topic: How did one live and work on a farm in former times?
- 🏛 **Klostermuseum (monastery museum)**, ✆ 73980 😊 © The history of the monastery, from its foundation in 1354 until its dissolution, is illustrated with numerous exhibits. @ wnw571
- ⛪ **ehem. Klosterkirche (former monastery church)**. The collegiate church of St. John the Baptist with a nun's gallery in late Rococo style, an artistic lattice of twigs and papier-mâché, is used today by the Catholic parish.
- ⛪ **ehem. Kloster Inzigkofen (former monastery)**, Parkweg 3, ✆ 73980. Since the middle of the 20th c., the former Augustinian women's convent has served as an adult education centre. @ uaj268
- ✳ **Fürstlicher Park (princely park)** 🕓 The wildly romantic park stretches out amidst the imposing slopes of the Danube with the rugged Jurassic limestone cliffs, crossed by footpaths and stairs. Special attractions are the Amalienfelsen, the Teufelsbrücke, the Känzele vantage point and the grottos.

- ✳ **Schau-Kräutergarten (show herbs garden)**, im ehem. Klostergelände, at the former monastery grounds, ✆ 5686 🕓 Various medicinal and culinary herbs, some of which are little known, are cultivated here. @ avm815

Inzigkofer Park

Bicycle tourists who have the time should not miss the opportunity to take a walk through the park in Inzighofen. It was built through the generosity of Count Anton von Hohenzollern, who wanted to give every citizen the possibility of exploring this spectacular terrain in a park-like setting. Riders can park their bicycles at the entrance and follow hiking paths towards the Amalien rock at the eastern end of the park.

From the Amalien rock there is a steep path to the Teufelsbrücke (Devil's bridge). The bridge's name is said to have its origin in the following story. In 1843, when the Count Karl instructed his court architect to build a wooden bridge over the gorge, the architect told his master, "The devil can build it, but I won't!" No sooner had he spoken those words when the devil appeared and promised to build the bridge, but only under the condition that he be given the soul of the first to cross the finished structure. The deal was agreed, but when the bridge was completed, a

dog was chased across the span and the devil was cheated of his prize. The concrete bridge that stands at the site today was built in 1895, apparently without satanic support.

Past the bridge, there is a small tunnel that leads to the Inzigkofen-Nickhof road. About 100 meters further a trail goes to the left over a meadow towards a woods and the "Känzele", a picturesque rocky point that offers fine views into the "Degerau" valley. From the Känzele the trail drops down to the "grottos," a mighty cave and rocky formations. Hikers can then proceed to a romantic stone gate up steps that lead to a wooded avenue back to the abbey.

14 In Inzigkofen turn left just past the abbey ~ follow the paved lane into the valley and over to Laiz.

Laiz (Sigmaringen)

prefix: 07571

- 🏛 **Kunstmuseum Laiz (art museum)**, Ablacher Str. 2, ✆ 51923 😊 © The former Siechenhaus (infirmary) accommodates a private museum with works by the sculptor Prof. Josef Henselmann and his wife, the painter Marianne Henselmann. @ ugt324
- ⛪ **St. Peter und Paul**, Römerstr. Although the church was built as early as 1308, the choir paintings and frescoes were only made in the 18th c. by the Baroque painter Andreas Meinrad von Ow.

Continue along the Danube to Sigmaringen, where the mighty Hohenzollern palace looms above the small city's historic centre.

ALTERNATIVE At the camping ground you have a choice of following the official route along the Danube or taking a detour through the city.

To continue along the main route, simply follow the path along the Danube.

Sigmaringen

prefix: 07571

🛈 **Tourist-Information**, Fürst-Wilhelm-Str. 15, ✆ 106224, @ kom881

🏛🔆 **Heimatmuseum „Runder Turm" (Local history museum in the round tower)**, Anton-str. 22, ✆ 62974 📷 In the defensive tower of the old town fortification, exhibits on the town's history are shown. There are also regular special exhibitions on various topics. @ fig864

🏛 **Mattes-Zündapp-Museum**, Leopoldstr. 40, ✆ 0170/7774427 ☺ More than 100 exhibits of the legendary Nürnberg motorcycle brand Zündapp. @ yfa571

🔆 **Schloss Sigmaringen (Sigmaringen castle)**, Karl-Anton-Pl. 8, ✆ 729230 📷 Explore the second largest castle in Germany on a guided tour and learn about the important roles played by the Princes of Hohenzollern in European history. Stroll through the private chambers of the Princesses and take a look at a Princely bathroom. One of the largest private weapon collections in Europe is also housed in the castle. You can explore more than 3,000 exhibits from the 14th to the 20th c. with an audio guide. @ ojl884

✳ **out & back Erlebnis-Welt**, Georg-Zimmerer-Str. 6, ✆ 50411. Camping site, canoeing, adventure camp etc.

✳ **Paddel & Pedale (Paddles & Pedals)**, Leopoldstr. 22, ✆ 2448. Canoe trip through the Danube valley, bicycle transfer, @ pqt764

🌊 **Beheiztes Freibad (heated public pool)**, Roystr. 31, ✆ 106333, @ ofv541

🌊 **90° Sauna & Bad (indoor pool with sauna)**, Maximilian-Haller-Str. 12, ✆ 683150. Various sauna rooms, heated outdoor swimming pool, inhalation bath, @ ihu472

The Sigmaringen royal Hohenzollern palace on a rocky outcrop above the

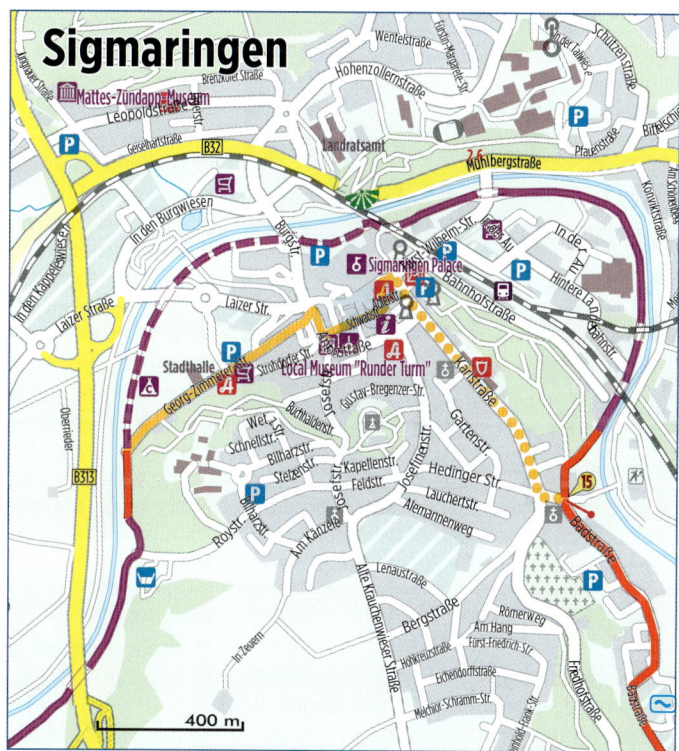

In Mengen

Danube is built on the site of an 11th century castle that belonged to the Counts of Werdenberg. After a devastating fire in 1893, it was rebuilt in its current form by, among others, Emanuel von Seidl for the Hohenzollerns.

Sigmaringen to Mengen   **11.4 km**

15 From the Hedinger Church take **Badstraße** out of Sigmaringen ⌁ pass the city's waste-

water treatment plant ⌁ and ride between the edge of the forest and the Danube towards Sigmaringendorf.

Sigmaringendorf
prefix: 07571

- ℹ **Gemeindeverwaltung (municipal office)**, Hauptstr. 9/Wilhelm-Lehmann-Pl., ✆ 73050, @ mue645
- **Bruckkapelle (Bridge chapel)**, Krauchenwieser Str. ㉔ The chapel is dedicated to St. Mary and, according to legend, was built where a flood had washed up a Madonna figure.

At the Bruckkapelle (bridge chapel) turn right onto the moderately busy Krauchenwieser Straße ⌁ at the next junction turn left ⌁ proceed on the unpaved track along the Danube ⌁ riding between the woods and the river towards Scheer ⌁ at the beginning of the village the road narrows and widens again after the railway underpass ⌁ the Danube cycle path makes a loop through the village.

Scheer
prefix: 07572

- ℹ **Stadtverwaltung (town office)**, Hauptstr. 1, ✆ 76160, @ hvu614
- **St. Nikolaus (St. Nicholas)**, Schloßsteige/Kirchberg. Kirchberg. Built in the 13th c. as a three-nave Gothic basilica, it was consecrated to St. Nicholas of Myra. @ ffs275

- **Grafenschloss (count's palace)**, Schloßsteige. Private property. The triple-gable Renaissance fortress was built in the years 1485-1496. @ gvj176
- **Schloss Bartelstein (Bartelstein palace)**, Sigmaringer Str. Built in the 11th and 12th c. over a limestone cave system. Today privately owned. @ wew333

The small town of Scheer lies at the eastern end of the upper Danube valley. This is where the river leaves the Swabian Alb and enters a wider valley. The city's historic structures include the renaissance palace and the Bartelstein palace, and testify to the 700-year history of Scheer and the Grafschaft Friedberg-Scheer.

16 Keep right across the railway line before reaching the railway station ⌁ follow the street along the right side of the railway line to Ennetach.

Ennetach (Mengen)
prefix: 07572

- ✳ **Gaggli Nudelhaus**, Mühlstr. 8-10, ✆ 759444 ⟲ ⟳ During the guided tour you will vividly experience the production of pasta from cracking eggs to packaging. @ ymv588
- ✳ **Archäologischer Wanderweg (archaeological hiking trail)** ㉔ Follow the traces of the Romans in Ennetach, who were once stationed in a fort here. You can also explore the area on other signposted paths. @ wby162

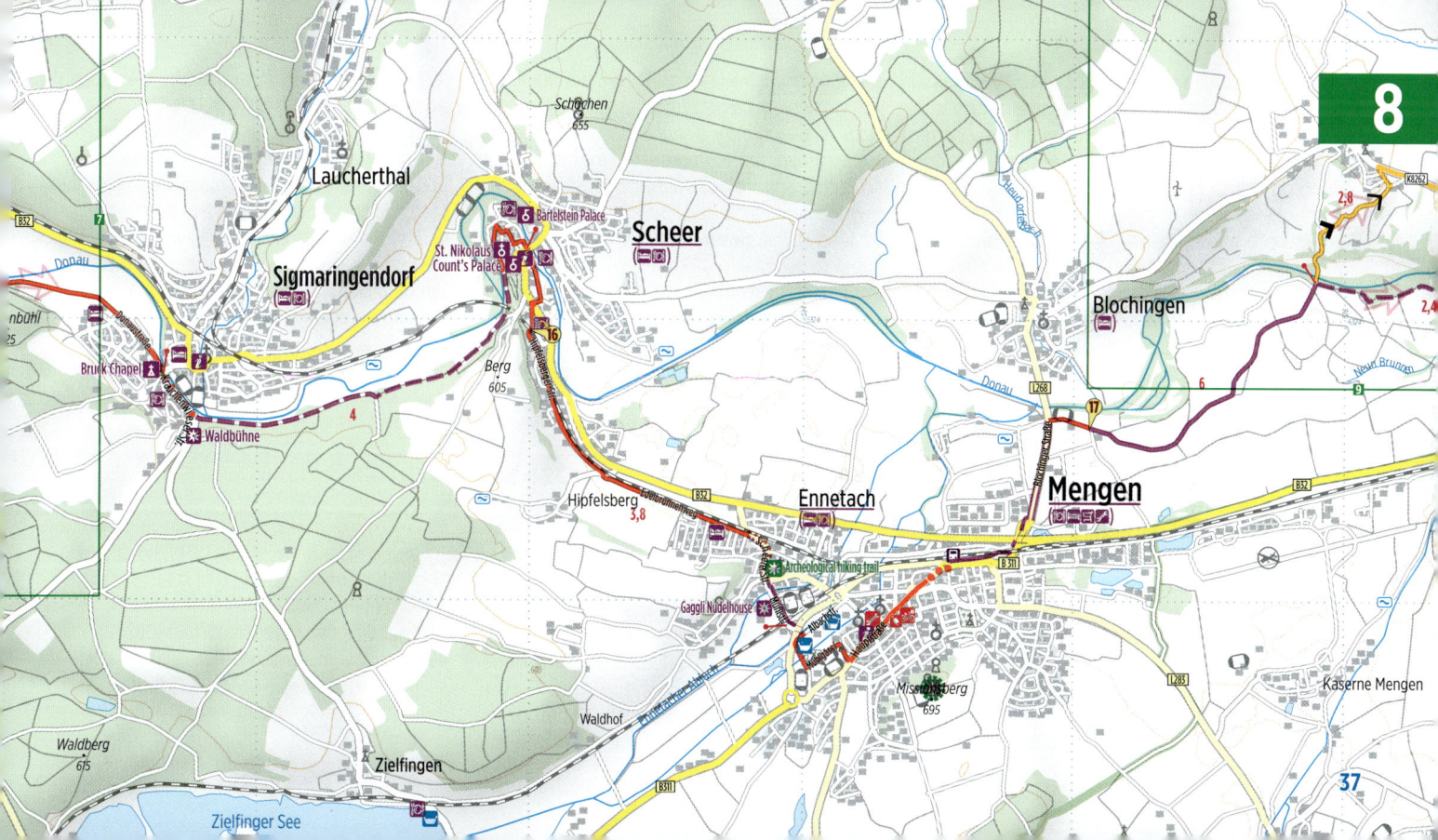

8

Laucherthal

Schochen
655

Bartelstein Palace

Scheer

St. Nikolaus
Count's Palace

Sigmaringendorf

Blochingen

2,8

K8262

2,4

Bruck Chapel

4

Waldbühne

Berg
605

16

6

9

17

Donau

L1268

Hipfelsberg

3,8

Donau

Ennetach

Mengen

B32

Archeological hiking trail

B 311

Gaggli Nudelhouse

Missionsberg
695

Kaserne Mengen

Waldhof

L283

Waldberg
615

Zielfingen

B311

Zielfinger See

At the main road turn right onto the bicycle lane along Scheerer Straße ∿ straight on into **Mühlstraße** ∿ past **Gaggli Nudelhaus** ∿ after crossing the railway tracks, keep left through the underpass into **Ablachstraße** ∿ immediately right ∿ past the outdoor pool ∿ over the bridge left into **Mühlgassle** ∿ follow the right bend, then turn left onto the Hauptstraße in Mengen.

Mengen

prefix: 07572

- 🛈 **Stadtverwaltung Mengen (town office)**, Hauptstr. 90, ✆ 6070, @ fyo116
- 🏛 **Alte Posthalterei – Stadtmuseum Mengen (old post office)**, Hauptstr. 96, ✆ 607100, ✆ 2458 ☺ The half-timbered building was built around 1702 as a post office for the Thurn- und Taxis'sche postal line. Now temporary exhibitions take place here two to three times a year. @ art641
- 🔭 **Aussichtsturm auf dem Missionsberg (observation tower)**. Beautiful view of the Danube valley and the city. @ xkt266
- ✱ **Mittelalterliches Stadtbild (medieval townscape)**
- 🏊 **Freibad (outdoor pool)**, Mühlgässle 32, ✆ 607460, @ ydr544
- 🏊✱ **Zielfinger Seen (lakes)**, Uferweg, about 3 km southwest of Mengen near Zielfingen. In addition to the swimming lake, there are other lakes with rich fish stocks, which are a real pleasure for anglers. @ kik324
- 🏊 **Hallenbad (public pool)**, Ablachstr. 7, ✆ 607450, @ hwk671

The old city centre of Mengen contains numerous well-preserved half-timbered houses. A written guide is available for a short tour or one can join guided groups to learn more about the city's history. Artifacts from region's Hallstatt and Roman past have been found throughout the region and can be seen at the award-winning Mengen-Ennetach Römermuseum which reopened in July 2001. It stands directly on the Danube hiking trail and also features a multi-media presentation that provides insights into life in Roman times. Mengen acquired city status under the Staufers before becoming a possession of the Habsburgs. In 1276 it obtained the same rights and freedoms as the city of Freiburg im Breisgau. Mengen was one of the five so-called Eastern Austrian Danube cities until 1806, when it became part of Württemberg.

Mengen to Riedlingen   20.7 km

At both roundabouts take the second exit ∿ continue on **Riedlinger Straße** ∿ before the next roundabout take the cycle path along the road ∿ at the **B 311** turn left and under the railway tracks ∿ continue on the cycle path next to **Blochinger Straße** ∿ before the Danube turn right ∿ **17** at the fork take the

left option, so go straight on ∿ keep right at the next fork ∿ take a left turn ∿ at the next fork turn right ∿ follow the road to the Beurener bridge.

ALTERNATIVE Here you have the option of continuing straight ahead to enjoy the fabulous views into the Danube valley from the heights along the Beuren-Hundersingen road on the way to Hundersingen. From there you can continue to Binzwangen, passing the Heuneburg Museum and open-air museum Heuneburg on the way. The route is given in orange on map 8.

Via Hundersingen   *8 km*

Hundersingen (Herbertingen)

prefix: 07586

- 🛈 **Gemeinde Herbertingen (municipal office)**, Holzg. 6, Herbertingen, ✆ 92080, @ fef334
- 🏛 **Freilichtmuseum Keltischer Fürstensitz Heuneburg (celtic open-air museum)**, Heuneburg 1-2, ✆ 8959405 ☺ You can see a partially reconstructed early Celtic settlement on the upper Danube (600 BC) as well as original finds. Archaeological hiking trail to the highest burial mound in Central Europe. @ ctv785
- 🏛 **Keltenmuseum Heuneburgmuseum (celtic museum inside the Heuneburg)**, Binzwanger Str. 14, ✆ 1679, ✆ 920838 ☺ ⌚ Excavated pieces testify life, art and trade relations of the Celts. @ orb875

Landauhof

Wolfsbühl
585

Binzwangen

Heselberg
· 590

Brettried

Ertingen

Dollhof

Celtic open-air Museum Heuneburg

Donau

5

Maria Chapel

Ertinger Bach

Kreusbühl
· 600

5

Bettelbühlbach

Beuren

Brauwanger Str.

Leisure centre Schwarzachtalseen

Heuneburg Museum

Hundersingen

Surfing lake

Natural lake

2,8

Beurener Str.

0,8

K8262

Donau

2,4

K 8261

3,0

4,5

10

L278

18

0,7

B311

B311

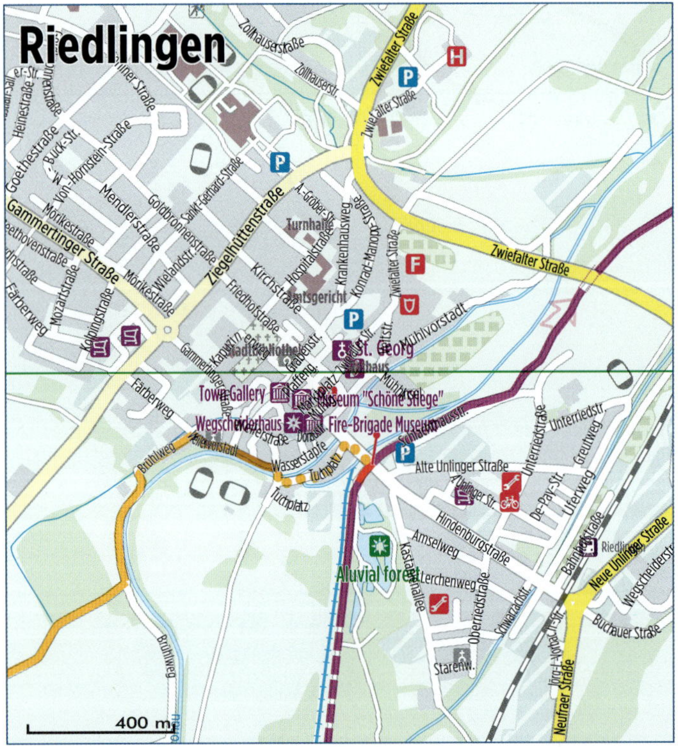

Riedlingen

To stay on the main route, turn right in front of the bridge into the unpaved field road ∿ keep left ∿ then left again onto **Mühlenweg** ∿ turn right when you reach the main road (K 8261) from Hundersingen ∿ turn left after a short distance onto a small paved road ∿ ride straight ahead in the right bend ∿ follow the field road all the way to the **L 278** after the playing fields in Binzwangen **18**.

Binzwangen (Ertingen)

There are attractive and well-marked bicycle routes on both sides of the Danube between Binzwangen and Riedlingen. You can choose from either the direct route on the right bank or the somewhat longer route via Altheim on left bank. The left bank route has the advantage of being paved the entire way. Through Binzwangen industrial estate ∿ after 200 m turn right and then follow the road to Neufra ∿ **19** at the T-junction turn left and proceed to the Danube.

Riedlingen

EXCURSION At this T-intersection you can also turn right and visit the palace at Neufra, which is about 1.5 km distant.

Neufra (Riedlingen)
prefix: 07371

- **Schloss Neufra (Neufra palace)**, Schlossberg 12, ☎ 5700 ⊜ The castle is probably the smallest castle hotel in Germany with only 4 rooms and a total of 9 beds. @ fmp756

- **Historische Hängegärten (historical hanging gardens)**, Schlossberg 12, ☎ 5700 ⊜ The monument was built in 1569 on accessible vaults and walls and unites garden and architecture. @ yss631

The „Hanging Garden" is one special attraction of the Neufra palace. The former Renaissance garden built on 16-meters tall support walls by Count Georg von Helfenstein between 1569 and 1573 has been redesigned and opened to the public. It also offers fine views into the Danube valley.

Before the Danube turn right into the grave cycle path ～ at first beside the Danube, you come to ride beside the Danube ca-nal ～ after 2.5 km you reach Riedlingen.

Riedlingen
prefix: 07371

- ℹ️ **Verkehrsamt im Rathaus (municipal office)**, Marktpl. 1, ☎ 1830, @ kkp815

- 🏛 **Feuerwehrmuseum (fire-brigade museum)**, Mühlg. 13/15, ☎ 7140, ☎ 0172/7009724 ☺ ☺ Historical exhibits about the fire brigade. @ jvf455

- 🏛 **Museum „Schöne Stiege"**, Rössleg. 1, ☎ 909633 ☺ In the half-timbered house from 1556, permanent exhibitions bear witness to the city and church history and the oldest newspaper (1712). @ wjq734

- 🏛 **Städtische Galerie (town gallery)**, Wochenmarkt 3, ☎ 909633. Works by important Riedlinger artists from the 18th-20th centuries and a special exhibition of contemporary art are exhibited in the late Gothic refectory. @ nda844

- **Stadtpfarrkirche St. Georg (city parish church)**, Kirchstr. 1, ☎ 93350. The late Gothic style dates back to the 15th century, with the baptistery and organ built in 1997 by Hartwig Späth being of particular interest.

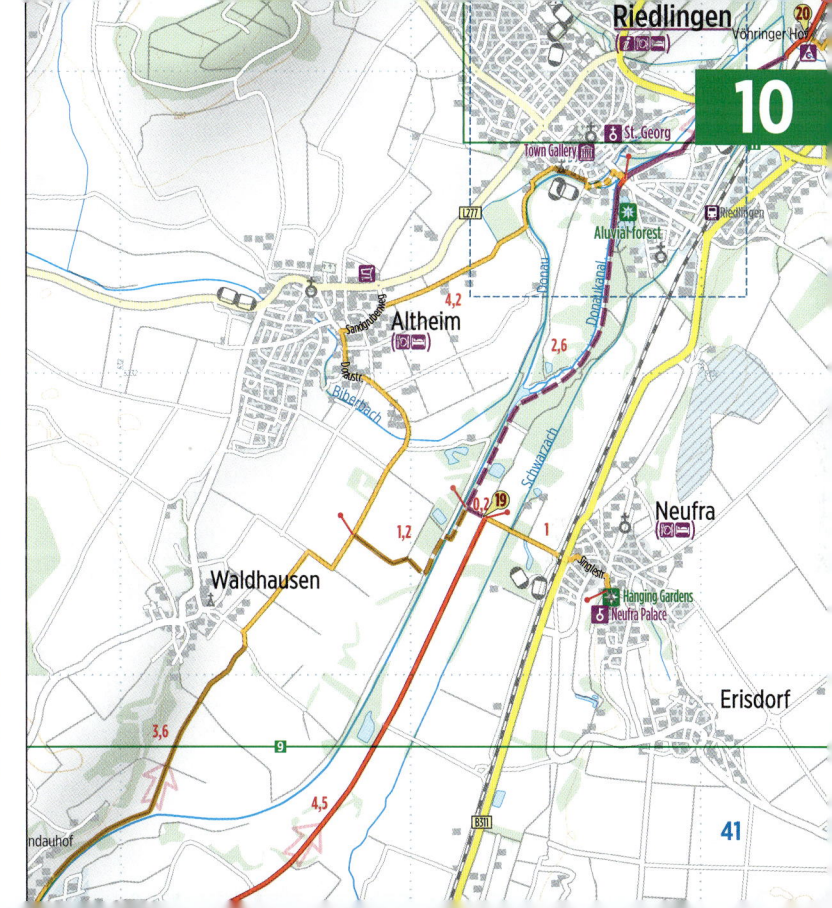

* **Rathaus (town hall)**, Marktpl. 1, ☏ 1830. Riedlingen's most distinctive building in Gothic style with two staggered gables. @ kpj261
* **Wegscheiderhaus**, Weibermarkt. Designed in the 18th c. by the famous Riedlinger painter Josef Ignaz Wegscheider.

The settlement of Riedlingen dates back to lands owned by Louis I (Louis the Pious, or Ludwig der Fromme in German) from the year 835. Between 1247 and 1255 the Counts of Veringen founded a typical new city east of the original settlement with streets laid out at right angles. The main street became the market square.

In the 14th century town residents then enlarged their city by adding the original hamlet and extending the city's area down to the Danube. Its location at the intersection of the river with the main road helped the town to grow. Its prosperity is reflected by the impressive town hall, the city walls and the elaborate half-timbered houses.

Riedlingen is in one of the few communities in the region that managed to mostly avoid the devastation brought by war and plundering armies during Europe's most violent periods.

A tour through the old town starts at the town hall, a distinctive structure with stepped gables built in 1447 as a storehouse for grain and goods. On the roof there is a stork's nest that attracts a family of the great migrating birds every summer. Across the market square one comes to the "Alte Kaserne" on Apothekergasse, a granary from 1686. Next stop is the house with the "Schönen Stiege", which today holds the town museum. Across from it, the "Altes Spital". Through the city gate one comes to the moat along the city wall and the cemetery that belonged to the former Kapuzinerkloster. The church "Spitalkirche" contains works by the famous Riedlingen artists J. J. Christian and Johann de Pay.

Cross Hospitalstraße and Gammertinger Straße to reach the old Weilervorstadt part of town, with the baroque Weiler chapel from 1721, which was built to honor 14 holy "Nothelfer," or helpers in times of need, a group of saints who provide help or solace in times of crisis. Images of the group can be found in many church paintings made after the 14th century. Returning to the town hall one passes the Wegscheider Haus on Lange Straße. It is a baroque city palace from 1742 which today contains the city library. Finally, one should pass through the small park behind the town hall, where the Zwiefalter Gate and the Zellemess tower of the city wall can be found.

Riedlingen to Munderkingen — 26km

After crossing the road, continue along the bicycle path beside the canal out of Riedlingen ∼ you pass under the main road ∼ and reach **Vöhringer Hof** after crossing a small bridge.

> **TIP** Here the Donau-Bodensee (Danube-Lake Constance) bicycle route forks off to the right over the railway tracks.

Keep left of the tracks ∼ **20** past the waste-water treatment plant ∼ and along the lane towards Daugendorf.

Daugendorf

At the intersection in Daugendorf turn left across the bridge ∼ turn right immediately after the bridge ∼ at the intersection in the fields, turn right and proceed to Bechingen ∼ before the houses keep right then left and ride to the main street.

Bechingen

21 In Bechingen turn right onto the bicycle path along the **K 7545** ∼ cross the Danube just before Zell and stay on the K 7545 through Zell.

Zell

Turn left immediately after the bridge over the railway tracks ∼ follow the lane beside the railway tracks to the railway bridge, which you use to cross the river — after another 500 m turn left across the tracks and follow the street into Zwiefaltendorf.

Zwiefaltendorf (Riedlingen)

St. Michael. Mentioned for the first time at the end of the 8th century, the late Gothic building, built in the 15th c., was rebuilt in 1756 in the Baroque style.

Schloss Zwiefaltendorf (castle), Von-Speth-Str. 11, ☎ 07323/170430 A moated castle already existed here in the 11th c. The castle as well as the whole village were burned down by Duke Ulrich of Württemberg. @ wur326

From here you can make a side-trip to Zwiefalten and the interesting Benedictine abbey. The town is several kilometers to the west and can be reached on a bicycle path along the left side of the Zwiefacher Ach creek.

Zwiefalten excursion 10.4 km

Zwiefalten
prefix: 07373

Tourist-Information, Marktpl. 3, ☎ 20520, @ gjw222

Foto-Museum (photo museum), Sägmühlstr. 15, ☎ 921395 A private collection of exhibits related to photography, from its beginnings to the present day. @ lfj725

Peterstormuseum, Hauptstr. 9, ☎ 366 In the former western entrance of the abbey there are exhibits on popular piety in the 19th and 20th cs. @ vdg318

Psychiatriemuseum (pychiatric museum), Armsündergässle, ☎ 103223 In the First Württemberg Psychiatric Museum you can expect exciting insights into the development of psychiatry. @ qmq622

Ehem. Benediktinerkloster und Münster Zwiefalten (former Benedictine monastery and cathedral), Beda-Sommerberger-Str. 5, ☎ 2252. In the former Benedictine monastery and Zwiefalten cathedral, the lush art of the late Baroque and Rococo periods once unfolded. Today the monastery houses the „Centre for Psychiatry". @ rdn363

Höhenfreibad (public pool), Brunnensteige, ☎ 2050, @ kat766

Return to Zwiefaltendorf by the same route.

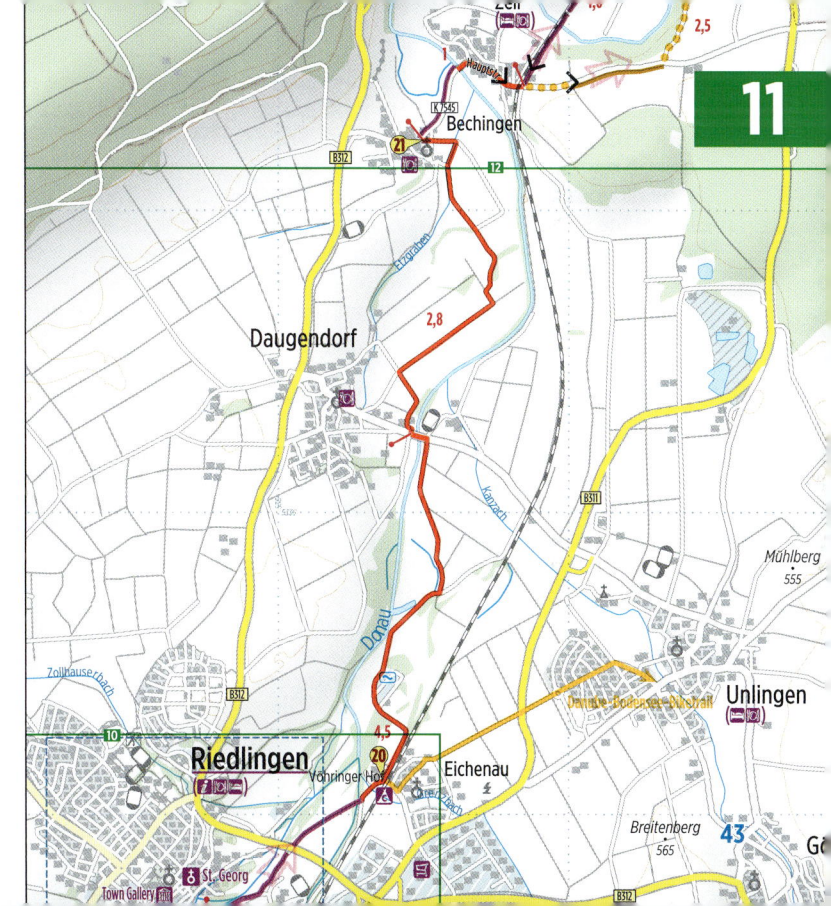

11

43

In Zwiefaltendorf turn right on the **Von-Speth-Straße** ⁓ cross the Danube and turn left on the gravel path before the railway crossing ⁓ ride along the tracks ⁓ after crossing the tracks the road climbs steeply up to Datthausen ⁓ ride out to the **B 311** main road.

After crossing the busy road, turn left onto the paved lane which runs beside the **B 311** ⁓ continue through the underpass and keep left up to the T-intersection **22**.

FORK Here you have two possibilities for continuing: The longer main route to the left takes you through Rechtenstein, with its imposing castle, while the alternative route to the right bypasses Rechtenstein, taking you directly to Obermarchtal and the noteworthy abbey church, which can also be easily reached from the main route.

Via Obermarchtal   5.8 km

Turn right at the T-intersection and follow the paved field road beside the **B 311** to Obermarchtal ⁓ keep left onto the main street ⁓ turn right into the first side street to continue on the **Sebastian-Sailer-Straße** ⁓ ride 200 m to the centre of the town.

FORK Turn left here if you want to visit the Abbey or take the connection to the main route along the river.

Obermarchtal
prefix: 07375

ℹ **Bürgermeisteramt (mayor's office)**, Hauptstr. 21, 📞 205, @ vea816

🏛 **Museum Marchtal**, Hauptstr. 2, 📞 1308 ⊙ ℂ Precious historical and sacral exhibits. @ eke266

⚲ **Klosterkirche Obermarchtal (monastery church)**. The former Premonstratensian canons' monastery with the Baroque church, which was elevated to a cathedral in 2001, is the only monastery in Upper Swabia that is architecturally self-contained and completely preserved. It houses art-historical treasures such as the summer refectory, the Hall of Mirrors and a chapter house from 1708. @ aip211

✳ **Galerie im Petrushof (art gallery)**, Maiertorweg 12, 📞 950671 ⊙ ℂ Presentation of current, contemporary art of all genres, housed in the historic solid stone and half-timbered barn. @ oro763

✳ **MuM-Maschinen unterm Münster (MuM machines under the cathedral)**, Alfredstal 1, 📞 07373/915299, 📞 0172/6374863 ℂ The exhibition on hydropower and energy generation is located in the power plant, which has been producing electricity for over a hundred years. @ fhe437

✳ **Soldatenfriedhof (military cemetery)**. Also known as the „Cemetery of Strangers", as travellers, pilgrims and many soldiers have been buried here since 1790, @ wbv534

The former Premonstratensian monastery in Obermarchtal contains some of the most beautiful examples of German baroque stucco church decorations of the Wessobrunner school. Marie Antoinette, the youngest daughter of Empress Maria, stayed here on her way to Paris. In the early 19th century the monastery was closed and the grounds were turned over to the Counts of Thurn und Taxis. Since 1973 it has been the property of the Rottenburg-Stuttgart diocese.

To continue on the alternative route to Untermarchtal, ride straight ahead ⁓ after a short distance on the **Hauptstraße** turn right into the **Oberwachinger Str.** ⁓ after passing under the main road, turn left ⁓ follow the right bend along the small street ⁓ turn left at the intersection in the fields ⁓ follow the paved road ⁓ at the next intersection continue straight ahead into the field road ⁓ turn left at the T-intersection ⁓ follow the paved lane through a small wooded ravine down to Untermarchtal. **22** To follow the main route via Rechtenstein, turn left at the T-intersection ⁓ shortly after the level crossing turn left onto the **L 249** ⁓ cross the Danube and turn right into Rechtenstein.

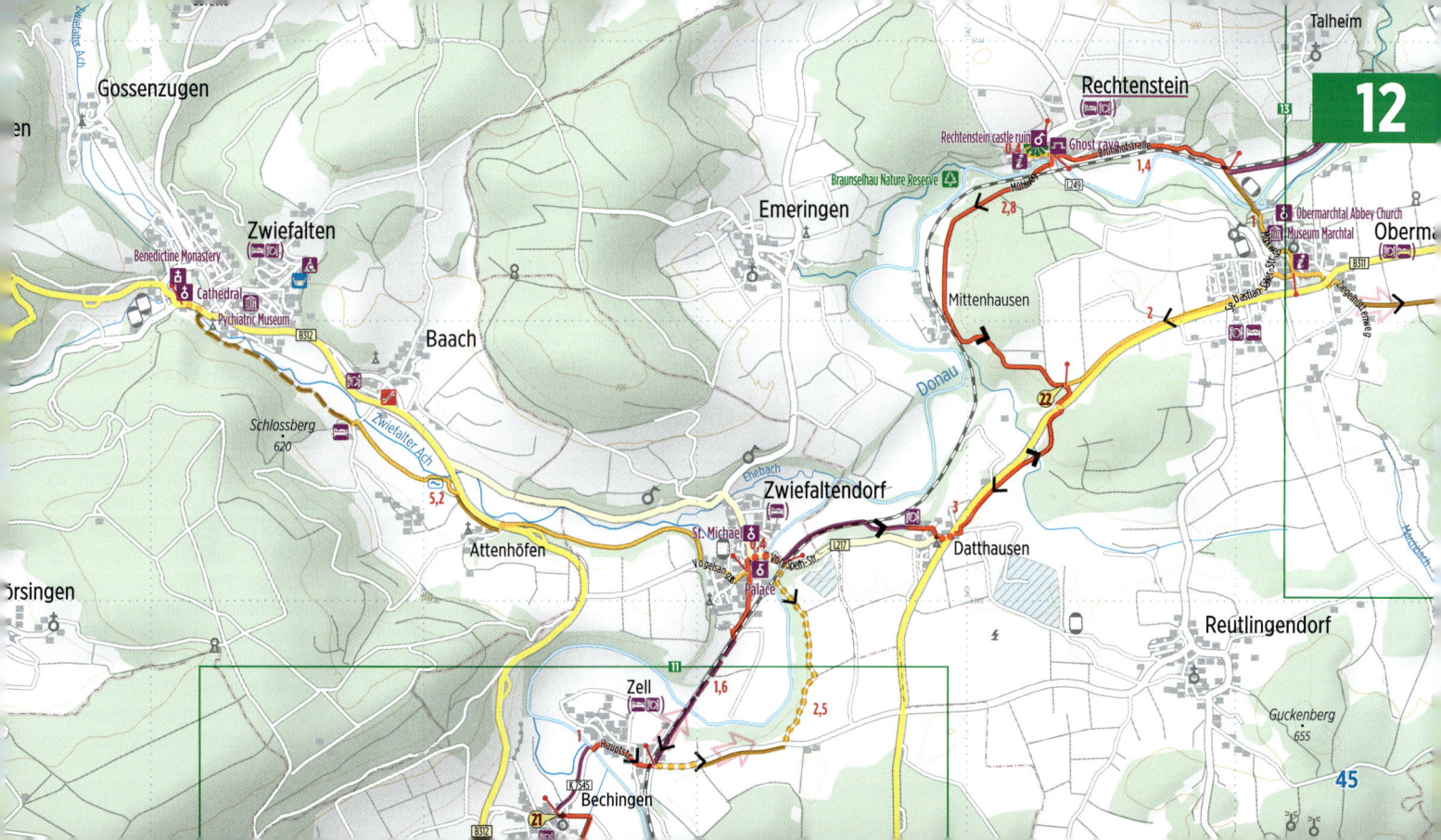

Talheim

Gossenzugen

Rechtenstein
Rechtenstein castle ruin 0,4
Ghost cave
Kahlotstraße
1,4
13

Braunselhau Nature Reserve

Emeringen

Obermarchtal Abbey Church
Museum Marchtal
Oberma
L249
2,8
Mühlweg
1
B311

Zwiefalten
Benedictine Monastery
Cathedral
Pychiatric Museum
B312

Mittenhausen
2
Ziegelhüttenweg
<Dattau-See-Str.>

Baach

Donau

22

Schlossberg
620
Zwiefalter Ach
5,2

Ehebach

Zwiefaltendorf
St. Michael
Vogelsangk.
Von-Speth-Str.
Palace
L217
3
Datthausen

Attenhöfen

Reutlingendorf

örsingen

Zell
11
1,6
2,5

Guckenberg
655

1
Hauptstr.
Bechingen
L245
21
B312

45

Munderkingen

Rechtenstein

prefix: 07375

- ℹ **Bürgermeisteramt (mayor´s office)**, Braunselweg 2, ☎ 244, @ uxi228
- ⚲ **Burgruine Rechtenstein (castle ruin)**, Burgstr., ☎ 244. The remains of the castle are witnesses of wealth and importance of its owners, the Lords of Stain. The key to the tower is available in the courtyard. @ wme244
- ⬛ **Geisterhöhle (ghost cave)**. If you feel like a small cave expedition, you can make a detour into the ghost cave. The cave is open to the public in summer, but closed in winter to protect the bats that spend the winter here.

Obermarchtal and its lush surroundings are visible from the lookout point from the ruins of Hohwart in Rechtenstein. The 12th century Burg Hohwart has been a ruin since the early 18th century. This picturesque bend in the Danube also has the Brauselhau nature preserve with its old creeks and protruding cliffs. The Schelmental and its bizarre rock formations are a short hike away.

Turn right into **Brühlhofstraße** ⌇ follow this street out of Rechten-

stein ⌇ after the railway crossing turn left onto a paved bicycle path, which turns to gravel after about 100 meters.

You take the partly unpaved cycle path through the nature reserve Lautermündung (mouth of the small river Lauter) and along the rail track ⌇ after the bridge you reach Untermarchtal riding on **Bergstraße**.

Untermarchtal

prefix: 07393

- ℹ **Infozentrum (information centre)**, Bahnhofstr. 4, ☎ 917383, @ avo425
- 🏛 **Kalkofenmuseum (lime kiln museum)**, Bannbühl 1, ☎ 917383 ⊖ ⊙ The operational and original plant illustrates the phases of early industrial lime production - crushing, burning and discharging. @ wjr872
- ✿ **GenerationenAktivPark Garten Eden (GenerationsActivePark Garden Eden)**, Freiherrvon-Speth-Str. 9, ☎ 30446, ☎ 917383. The garden is dedicated to young and old and offers a lot of variety with its different zones (zoo, sensory and therapeutic garden, move-

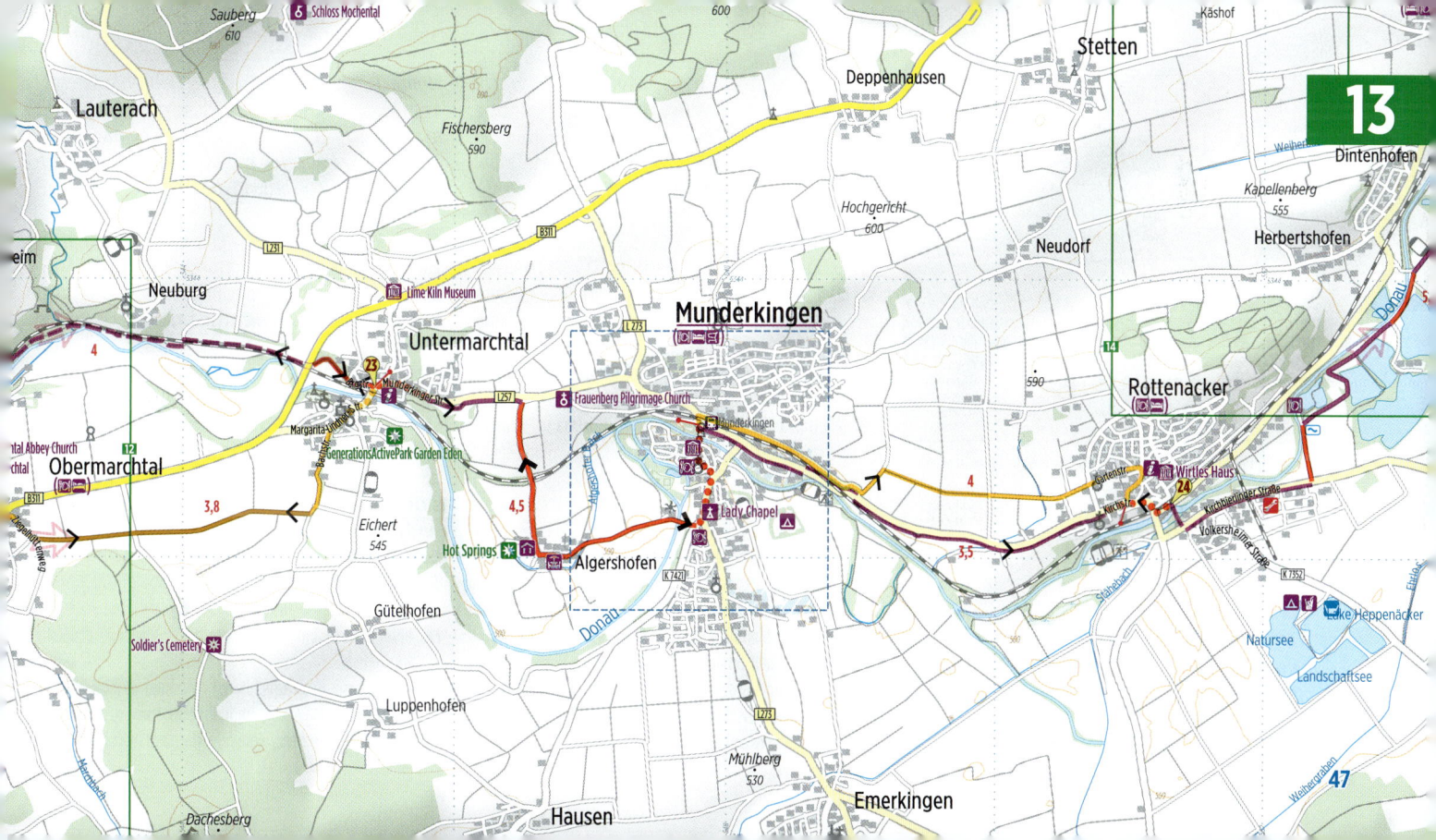

Sauberg
610

Schloss Mochental

Käshof

Stetten

600

Deppenhausen

Dintenhofen

Lauterach

Fischersberg
590

Kapellenberg
555

Herbertshofen

Neudorf

B311

Hochgericht
600

L1251

Neuburg

Lime Kiln Museum

13

Munderkingen

590

Untermarchtal

L273

Rottenacker

23

L257

Frauenberg Pilgrimage Church

Munderkingen

Margarita

GenerationsActivePark Garden Eden

Wirtles Haus

ntal Abbey Church
hltal

Obermarchtal

12

Lady Chapel

4,5

Eichert
545

24

4

Volkersheimer Straße

Hot Springs

Algershofen

K 742

3,5

B311

Gütelhofen

590

K 7352

Lake Heppenäcker

Soldier's Cemetery

Natursee

Landschaftsee

Luppenhofen

580

Danube

L273

Mühlberg
530

Hausen

Emerkingen

Near Ehingen

ment garden, forest experience area, active children's island). @ emj373

Follow the street to the T-intersection ⌁ **23** turn left onto the busy **L 257** ⌁ as you leave Untermarchtal, ride onto the paved field road along the right side of the **L 257** ⌁ after a slight climb turn right towards Algershofen ⌁ ride through Algershofen.

Algershofen (Munderkingen)

❀ **Warme Quellen (hot springs)**. The springs, which originate from a depth of 170 m, contain sulphur and radon and have a temperature of 16° C in winter. @ xkb561

Take the tree-lined avenue towards Munderkingen ⌁ after crossing the Danube, keep left at both intersections ⌁ follow the main street past the cemetery ⌁ turn left into **Martinstraße** ⌁ left into **Kirchgasse**.

Munderkingen
prefix: 07393

ℹ️ **Tourist-Information**, Alter Schulhof 2, 📞 9534581, @ hun765

🏛️ **Städtisches Museum (town museum)**, Schulhof 3, in the former „Heilig-Geist-Spital", 📞 2856 ☺ Topic: Local finds, life from the time of the Romans and Alemanni (bronze Mercury statuettes), city and church history, brush production, dolls and dollhouses and much more. @ fgg155

⛪ **Wallfahrtskirche Frauenberg (pilgrimage church)**, Marchtaler Str., 📞 2282. The baroque pilgrimage church was built on the site of an Alemannic spring sanctuary. @ gkp127

🏛️ **Marienkapelle (Lady chapel)**, Schillerstr./Erzbergerstr. The chapel is said to be one of the oldest buildings in the city. The rectangular blocks on the west wall were probably built during the Staufer period (11th-13th centuries). @ xpt677

✳️ **Historischer Stadtkern (historic town centre)**, 📞 9534581 🅺 Magnificent half-timbered houses such as the Mochentaler Hof and the Pfründhaus, baroque buildings and the town hall from 1563 bear witness to 1200 years of town history and form a harmonious ensemble. @ upp332

Munderkingen was one of the Habsburg possessions west of Austria. The picturesque old city with its many gabled roofs, churches and narrow streets is surrounded on three sides by the Danube, which makes a tight loop around the city.

Munderkingen to Ehingen   12,6 km

Beside St. Dionysius church turn right into the narrow lane ⌁ continue straight into **Donaustraße** and over the bridge across the Danube ⌁ turn right onto the bicycle path along the **L 257** ⌁ cross the intersection with **Angerweg** ⌁ after 500 m the path changes to the other side of the street ⌁ after the railway crossing, follow the bicycle path across the side street and back to the right side of the **L 257** ⌁ in Rottenacker the bike path ends at the church ⌁ ride on the main street through the village.

Rottenacker
prefix: 07393

ℹ️ **Bürgermeisteramt (mayor´s office)**, Bühlstr. 7, 📞 95040, @ ubx666

🏛️ **Heimatmuseum „Wirtles Haus" (museum of local history)**, Bühlstr., 📞 95040 ☺ ⌚ On four floors, the focus is on stock keeping, living culture, working life around 1900, local history with its personalities and the cultural and economic influence of the Danube. @ nen735

❊ **Sehenswerte Ortsmitte (worth seeing town centre).** Awarded twice in 2005.

🛏 **Badesee Heppenäcker (swimming lake),** ☎ 0173/2316308, @ lsc673

Ride onto the bridge over the railway line ～ turn left into **Bahnhofstraße** (L 255) before crossing the river ～ **24** after 100 m turn right onto the old pedestrian and bicycle bridge across the Danube ～ turn left on the bike path on **Kirchbierlinger Straße** (L 257) ～ after one kilometre turn left ～ keep right after the wastewater treatment plant and continue towards Dettingen ～ keep right by the first bridge over the Danube ～ continue between fields over the bridge into Dettingen.

Dettingen (Ehingen (Donau))

Cross the railroad tracks ～ **25** at Rottenacker Straße turn right ～ on the cycle paths beside the main roads you reach the city of Ehingen ～ cross the **B 465** at the

pedestrian lights and follow the cycle path signs to the market square of Ehingen.

Ehingen (Donau)
prefix: 07391

ℹ **Tourist-Info,** Marktpl. 1, ☎ 503216, @ jaj436

🏛 **Städt. Museum und Spitalkapelle (city museum and hospital chapel),** Am Viehmarkt 1, ☎ 503531, ☎ 75065 ➣ Around 1340 foundation of the hospital, testimonies of the history of the former Upper Austrian town, Geopark infopoint, chapel built around 1493 with impressive murals. @ vuo128

🏛 **Städtische Galerie Ehingen (town gallery),** Tränkberg 9, ☎ 503505, ☎ 503503 ➣ Nöth Collection in the former „Speth'scher Hof". @ hdx446

⛪ **Herz-Jesu-Kirche (Sacred Heart of Jesus church).** Built in 1719, after 1825 royal Württemberg, later episcopal convict.

⛪ **Liebfrauenkirche.** In the baroque pilgrimage church, whose origin dates back to 1239, stands a stone graven image (1440) of the Multscher School.

⛪ **Stadtpfarrkirche St. Blasius (city parish church),** ☎ 8088. Still has 14th c. building structure. @ ubl718

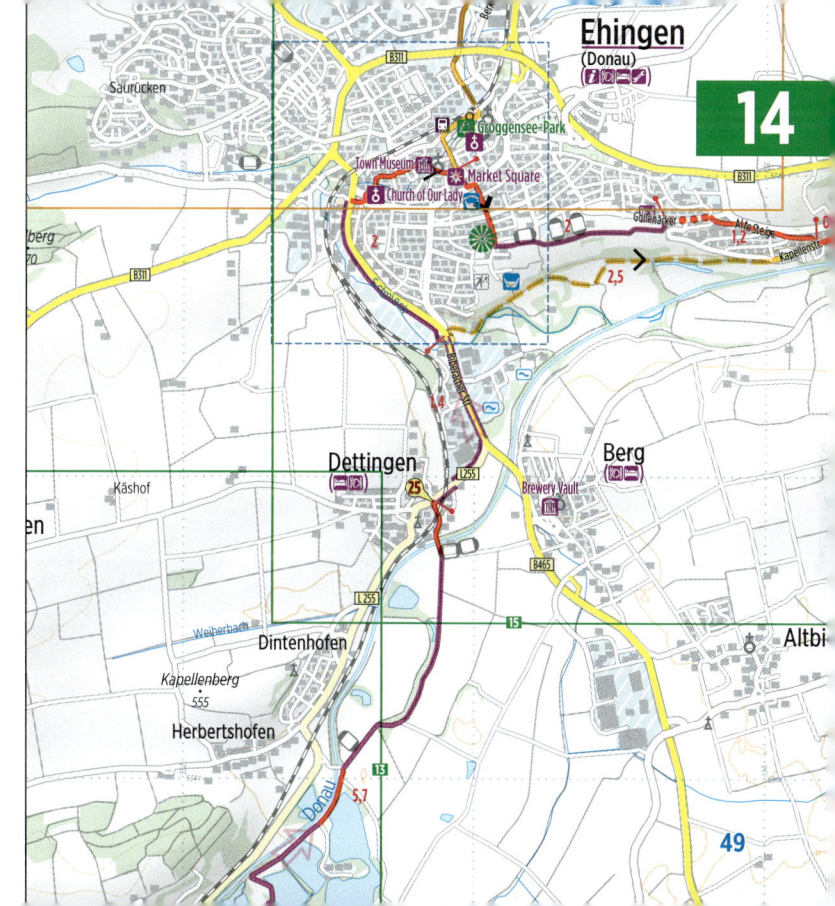

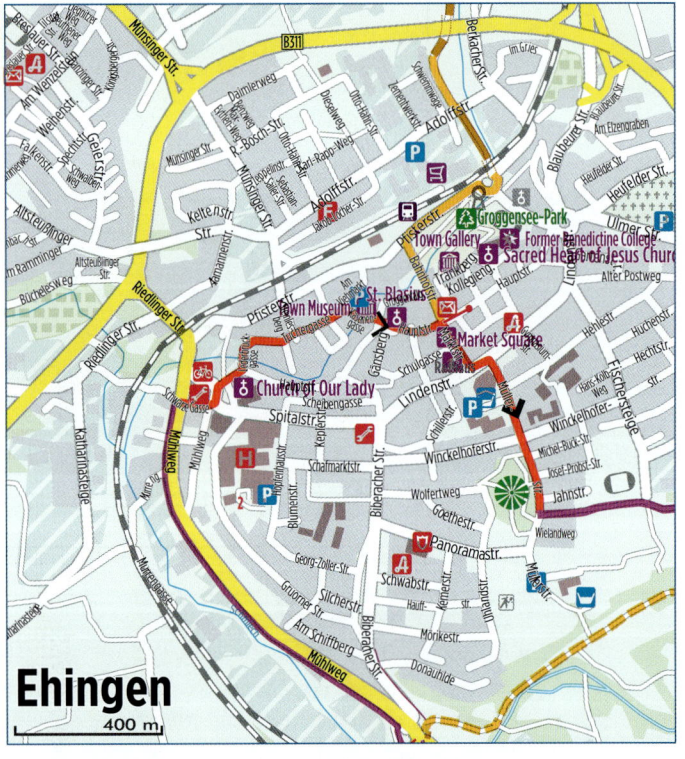

Ehingen

400 m

Wolfertturm (tower), Müllerstr., ☎ 5030 ⓒ From the tower built in 1891 you have a wonderful panoramic view up to the Alps. @ wdc453

Bierwanderweg (beer hiking trail), ☎ 503216. A unique culinary adventure hike for all age groups. The 14 km long certified city hike takes you along the Danube to the Berg district. @ kwj116

E-Bike-Tour, meeting point: Brauerei Wirtschaft Berg, ☎ 503216. The mountain beer tour leads on 112 km by the most beautiful river valleys and the biosphere area Swabian Alb. @ ikv742

Ehemaliges Benediktinerkolleg (former Benedictine college), Kollegieng. From 1698 to 1709 the mighty building was erected by the Vorarlberg master builder Franz Beer on behalf of Zwiefalten Abbey.

Ehinger Musiksommer (summer of music), Spitalstr. 30, ☎ 503503. Open Air Filmfestival, Aug., Ehinger Jazztage, Oct., more information at the Tourist-Info. @ llw242

Marktplatz (market place) 24 With historical town hall (1713), small castle, former Ständehaus, market fountain.

Groggensee-Park, Pfisterstr. 24 Sculptures by the Basel artist Stefan Hübscher can be seen in the magnificent park. @ mro617

Freibad (outdoor pool), Müllerstr. 35, ☎ 770150, @ fys133

ALTERNATIVE
In Ehingen you are faced with a tough choice. Either you stay on the main route along the Danube to Ulm or you take an alternative route through the idyllic (Blautal) Blau valley to Blaubeuren and the famous Blautopf. Those interested in history will also get their money's worth in Blaubeuren: the world's oldest finds from the Late Palaeolithic are on display in the Urmu in Blaubeuren and you can also visit the „Hohle Fels" cave near Schelklingen!

Blautal alternative   42.7 km

Ehinger to Blaubeuren   21 km

TIP
The Blautal alternative begins at the **Marktplatz** in Ehingen. The route is posted with signs that say Donau Radweg, Alternative Blautal and leads first to the train station.

Schelklingen, Besichtigung Hohle Fels

In front of the train station go right 〰 at the roundabout turn left into the cycle path and go under the railway bridge 〰 continue along the stream 〰 cross the main road straight ahead 〰 pass under the federal road 〰 cross the road and continue along the cycle path 〰 in front of the houses, the cycle path veers off to the right **A** 〰 the next village is Berkach 〰 turn right into **Allmendinger Straße**

and straight ahead 〰 on a quiet road to Allmendingen.

Allmendingen
prefix: 07391

🛈 **Gemeindeverwaltung (municipal office)**, Hauptstr. 16, 📞 70150, @ qmb573

🛏 **Waldfreibad (outdoor pool)**, Schwimmbadweg 32, 📞 5580, @ rgr831

Follow the **Bergstraße**, which becomes **Kleindorfer Straße** 〰 before the railway tracks turn left into **Katzensteige** 〰 at the next main road turn right and

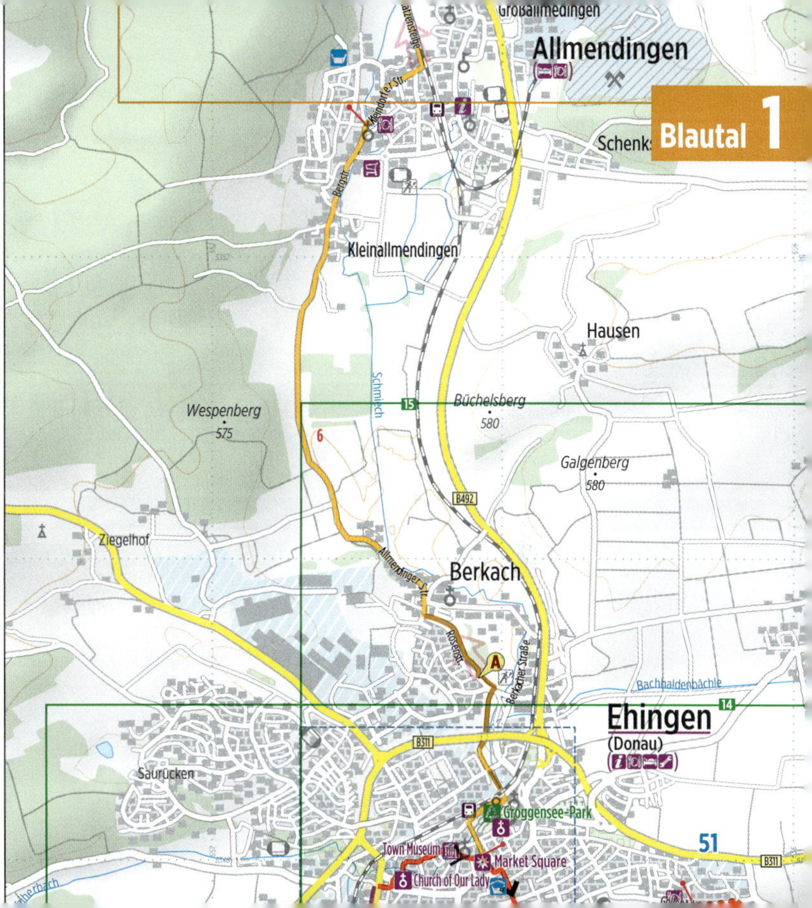

Blaubeuren, die Hammerschmiede am Blautopf

immediately left again **B** ~ follow the road toward **Schmiechen** ~ take the road right into Schmiechen ~ turn right on **K 7408** ~ follow the bike path along the left side of **B 492** ~ to the left towards Schelklingen.

Schelklingen
prefix: 07394

Schelklingen-Hütten (huts), Mühlstr. 5, ☎ 24817 ☺ ☺ The main topics in the information centre are among others: Archaeological finds, Alb water supply, Schmiechener lake, nature and landscape

of the Schmiechtal, railway. Many exhibits are from the temporal context around the „Venus of Hohle Fels". @ ift856

Stadtmuseum (town museum), Spitalg., in the former hospital, ☎ 1640 ☺ The Schelklingen pottery, geology and archaeology of the municipality are exhibited in the former municipal hospital, a half-timbered building from the 14th-16th c. @ clh131

Burgruine Schelklingen und Schlossturm (castle ruin and tower), ☎ 897. The tower offers a magnificent view of the Schelklingen river loop. @ ibd837

Steinzeithöhle „Hohle Fels" (stone age cave), ☎ 24817, ☎ 245832, ☎ 0151/23070962 ☺ In the cave, a plastic representation of a woman, the „Venus of the Hohle Fels"(Venus of the hollow rock), and the „Vulture Flute", a musical instrument, were found. They are both about 42,500 years old and thus the oldest figure and the oldest musical instrument in the world. @ vdc777

Freibad (outdoor pool), Hohler-Felsen-Weg, @ can845
Straight ahead into the village ~ **C** before the bridge over the Ach turn right into the

Hohle-Felsen-Weg 〜 past the Gasthof Hohle Felsen 〜 under the railway 〜 past the outdoor pool and the Stone Age cave „Hohler Fels" 〜 at the next crossing keep left 〜 in front of the railway line turn right to Weiler.

Weiler (Blaubeuren)
prefix: 07344

- ♂ **Günzelburg (castle ruin).** The ruin was already dilapidated at the end of the 15th c. Today some remains of the wall are still preserved.

- ⌂ **Brillenhöhle (spectacle cave)**, ☏ 92860 ⓒ The cave is an important, Late Palaeolithic site. It was probably mainly used in winter. @ mwu411

- ⌂ **Geißenklösterle**, Bruckfelsstr. 20 ⓐ The site about 500 metres above the cycle path is part of the UNESCO World Heritage „Caves and Ice Age Art of the Swabian Alb". @ rvg343

At the first houses cross the bridge 〜 go straight on along the main road into the village 〜 turn right into **Aachtalstraße** 〜 **D** turn right into **Wiesenweg** 〜 this turns into

a cycle path leading along the road to Blaubeuren.

At the big intersection cross the **B 28** with the help of the traffic lights 〜 you arrive at the turning point of **Weilerstraße** 〜 after the bend always follow the road 〜 **E** cross **Karlstraße**, cross **Aach** and continue on **Auf dem Graben** 〜 at the fourth possibility turn left into **Klosterhof** 〜 past Kloster 〜 at the T-crossing turn right into **Blautopfstraße** and again right into **Mühlweg** and you are already in front of the Blautopf spring.

Blaubeuren
prefix: 07344

- ℹ **Tourist-Information**, Kirchpl. 10, ☏ 966990, @ xuw177

- 🏛 **Urmu – Urgeschichtliches Museum (Prehistoric museum)**, Kirchpl. 10, ☏ 966990. The unique Palaeolithic finds of the region are exhibited in the Urmu. The most famous are the Venus of the Hollow Rock and an ivory flute, the oldest art and musical instrument in the world. @ drh324

Blautopf

Hammerschmiede am Blautopf (hammer smithy), Blautopf-str. 9, ✆ 921027 ⊗ The authentic mechanical workshop and former grinding mill is still used today for demonstrations and courses. @ jfi146

Heimatmuseum (local history museum), Klosterhof 11, ✆ 966990 ⊜ Accommodated in the „Bathhouse of the Monks". On three floors the multifaceted past between monastic and reformatory influence as well as laborious agricultural work is shown. @ ytq518

Kloster Blaubeuren (monastery), Klosterhof 2, ✆ 962625 ⊗ The high altar from 1493 including choir stalls in the former Benedictine monastery is a jewel of late Gothic art. The beautiful cloister and herb garden still invite you to linger. @ ead837

Badhaus der Mönche (bathhouse of monks), Klosterhof 11, ✆ 966990 ⊜ The only remaining bath house of monks with Seccopaintings worth seeing in the festiveroom. @ dvt826

Stadtführungen (city tours), ✆ 966990. City, costume and theme tours as well as Swabian tours. Further information can be obtained from the Tourist Information Office. @ nmf781

Blautopf, ✆ 921027. The mermaid „Schöne Lau" awaits you with a smile at the legendary Karst spring with its unique play of colours. @ vro862

Blauhöhlensystem (cave system). The film „Dark blue - The colour of eternal night" with spectacular underwater and sur-

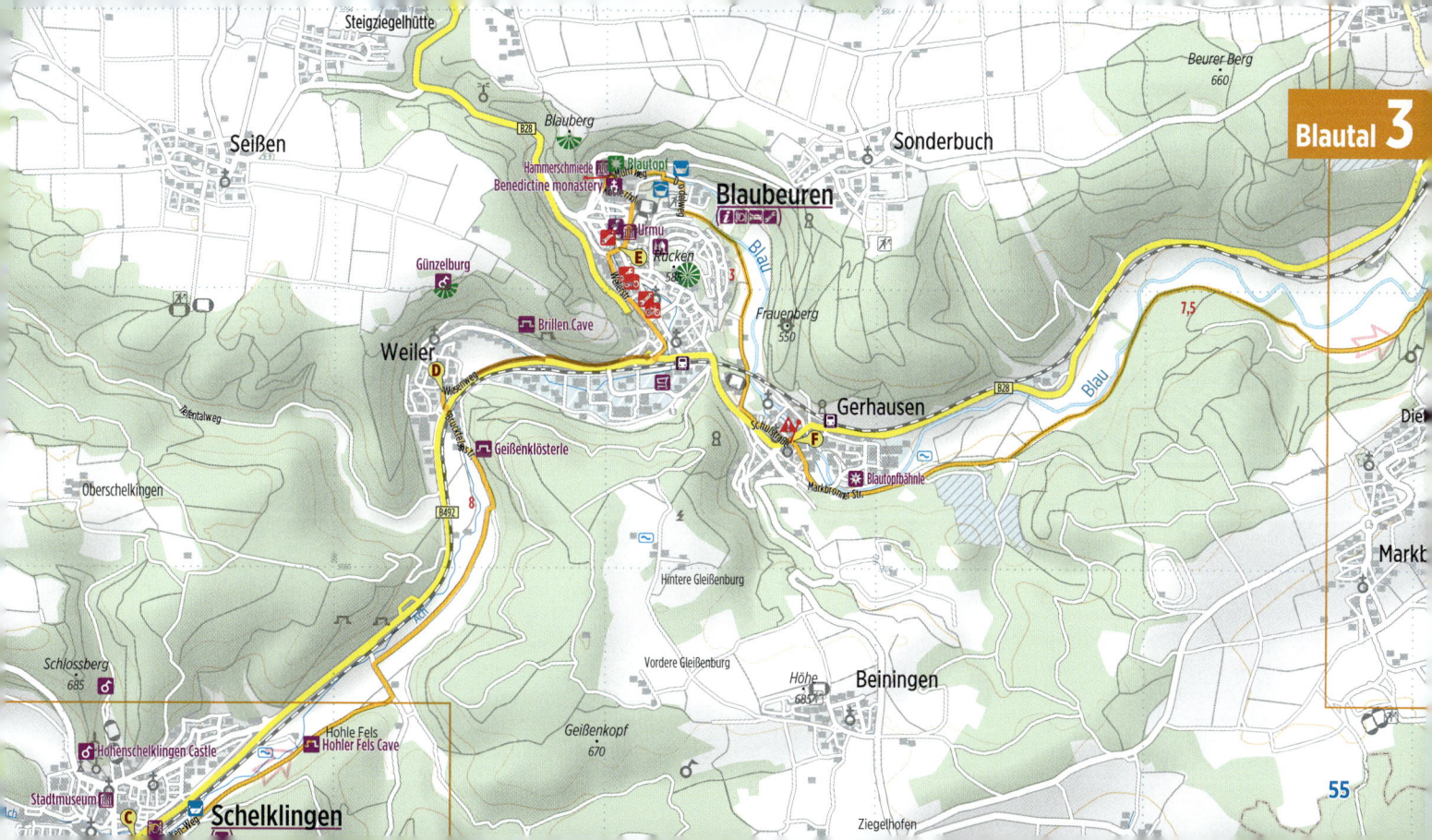

Steigziegelhütte

Seißen

Blauberg

Hammerschmiede
Benedictine monastery
Blautopf
Blaubeuren

Sonderbuch

Beurer Berg
660

Günzelburg

Urmü
Rucken
535

Blau

3

Frauenberg
550

7,5

Brillen Cave

Weiler
D

Blau

Gerhausen

B28

Geißenklösterle

Schulhaus
F

Blautopfbähnle

Markbronner Str.

Oberschelkingen

8
B492

Hintere Gleißenburg

Diei

Markt

Schlossberg
685

Vordere Gleißenburg

Höhe
685

Beiningen

Hohle Fels
Hohler Fels Cave

Geißenkopf
670

Hofenschelklingen Castle

Stadtmuseum

C

Schelklingen

Ziegelhofen

Near Blaustein

rounding shots from the blue cave system can be seen free of charge in the Urmu. @ cfa536

🏊 **Christian-Schmidbleicher-Freibad (outdoor pool)**, Mühlweg 16, ✆ 3956, @ sre785

🏊 **Hallenbad (indoor pool)**, Dodelweg 16, ✆ 7043, @ mgg115

Around Blaubeuren, in the Blautal, in the Aachtal and in the Lonetal, archaeological finds are steadily made. These rank among the oldest in Europe. Around 40,000 years of age is the „Venus vom Hohle Fels" and thus the oldest handcrafted figure in the world. Even the oldest musical instruments, two flutes made of bird bones, one even crafted of mammoth ivory, were found in these valleys. You can marvel at these finds in the Urmu. In the Ulm Museum you will also encounter the „Lion Man".

Blaubeuren to Ulm   21.7 km

From the Blautopf continue on the **Mühlweg** 〰 keep right at the fork and stay on the **Mühlweg** 〰 turn right before the outdoor pool over the Blau and left before the indoor pool 〰 follow the course of the **Dodelweg** 〰 after the tennis courts turn left onto a cycle and footpath 〰 this leads along the Blau to Gerhausen.

Gerhausen (Blaubeuren)
prefix: 07344

✳ **Blautopfbähnle (nostalgic train „Blautopfbähnle")**, Steingrubenstr. 13, ✆ 96300 〰 On various theme tours with the „nostalgic Blautopfbähnle" (nostalgic train) you can make wonderful trips in and around Blaubeuren. @ xui273

At the entrance to Gerhausen after the sports field turn left into **Brunnenweg** 〰 turn left into **Schulstraße**, be careful at the demarcated school yard, here you are only allowed to push the bike 〰 before you reach **Hauptstraße**, here turn left ⚠ 〰 **F** at the next possibility turn right, **Markbronner Straße** 〰 before the Blaubrücke turn right 〰 always right side of the Blau 〰 from now on always follow the valley to Arnegg.

Arnegg (Blaustein)

Right at the beginning of the village turn left into **Oberer Wiesenweg** 〰 turn left and cross the river to the path next to Blau 〰 continue to **Gerhauser Straße** 〰 turn right to Radweg and cross Blau again 〰 first opportunity turn left 〰 following the road past a parking lot 〰 on an unpaved road to Blaustein 〰 on the left is Herrlingen.

Herrlingen (Blaustein)

✳ **Villa Lindenhof**, Lindenhof 2 🕐 Art nouveau villa with park worth seeing.

Blaustein
prefix: 07304

ℹ **Tourist-Information**, Boschstr. 12, ✆ 802162, @ vcb475

ℹ **Stadtverwaltung (town office)**, Marktpl. 2, ✆ 8020, @ aqo166

🏊 **Bad Blau (indoor pool)**, Boschstr. 12, ✆ 802162, @ whi123

Blaustein is just outside Ulm where the Swabian Alb and Upper Swabia meet. Ulm is known for its university and cathedral and lies in a landscape of large forests and juniper heaths.

Wippingen

Oberherrlingen Palace

Oberherrlingen

Herrlingen

Villa Lindenhof

B28

Gerhauser Str.

Haupstr.

Obere Wiesenweg

Arnegg

Dietingen

Markbronn

Klingenstein Palace

Klingenstein

2,6

L1244

G

Bad Blau

Steinzeitdorf Ehrenstein

Blaustein

Botanik Gardens

Eselsberg

Ehrenstein

LK9915

LK9903

Ulm

Wilhelmsburg Citadel

Safra

B10

B10

Blaukanal

B28

8

Roter Berg

Dreierberg
590

Harthausen

Ermingen

Söflingen Monastery

Jägerstr.

Söflingen

Concentration Camp Memorial

18

L1079

B10

Bread and Art Museum

Ulm Hbf

Weststadt

Wagnerstr.

Metzger Tower

Gothic Cathedr

0,6

0,6

1

0,5

Glacis

Water tower

Federal Fortress

19

Donaubad

B10 B28

57

Klingenstein (Blaustein)

🏰 **Schloss Klingenstein (castle)**. Built in 1756 above the cellar vaults and on the foundations of the old north castle of Klingenstein. The castle is still inhabited. @ vcm264

As you near the edge of Klingenstein turn left over the bridge across the Blau ⌇ turn right after crossing the railway tracks ⌇ at the T-intersection turn right and immediately left into **Ehrensteiner Straße** ⌇ take the second left into **Josefweg** ⌇ at the end of the street keep right and follow the bicycle path along the river.

Ehrenstein (Blaustein)

prefix: 07304

🔲 **Steinzeitdorf Ehrenstein (Stone Age village)**, ✆ 802162. The Neolithic settlement is part of the UNESCO World Heritage „Prehistoric Lake Dwellings around the Alps" and originated about 6,000 years ago. Excavation finds can also be admired in the Blaustein Town Hall and the Ulm Museum. @ jdc834

The route further on runs parallel to the railway tracks ⌇ follow the tracks, passing under the **K 9915** and a short while later turning right ⌇ the cycle path leads to the **B 28** ⌇ pass under the **K 9903** and the **B 28** ⌇ onto the cycle path along the Blau ⌇ cross the Magirusstraße and turn left onto the Blau ⌇ pass under the **B 10** ⌇ then turn right onto the cycle path along the **B 10** ⌇ at the Ehinger Tor(gate) turn left onto the cycle path along the **Neue Straße**, on which you pass under the railway ⌇ after the underpass turn left in a loop up to the railway line ⌇ along the railway line and through a car park back to the Danube ⌇ there turn left onto the asphalted cycle path.

Ulm

see page 62

Ehingen to Ulm   **33.8 km**

Leave the market in Ehingen along the **Markt-straße** ⌇ turn left on **Lindenstraße** ⌇ immediately turn right on **Müllerstraße** ⌇ at the end of the climb turn left on the bicycle path ⌇ you get a nice view into the Danube valley as you pass the playing fields on the cycle track towards **Nasgenstadt** ⌇ turn right as you reach a street, the **Gollenäcker** ⌇ turn right again into the first side street and follow the right bend onto **Kapellenstraße** ⌇ this street leads you to the major road **L 259** ⌇ turn right and ride on the cycle path ⌇ you reach the first houses of Griesingen.

Griesingen

prefix: 07391

ℹ **Gemeindeverwaltung (municipal office)**, Alte Landstr. 51, ✆ 8748, @ sky488

Turn left at the intersection with the small road ⌇ turn right into the paved field road ⌇ at the T-intersection turn left and ride toward Öpfingen.

Öpfingen

prefix: 07391

ℹ **Gemeindeverwaltung (municipal office)**, Schlosshofstr. 10, ✆ 70840, @ urw131

Ersingen (Erbach)

prefix: 07305

ℹ **Ortsverwaltung (municipal office)**, Mittelstr. 11/1, ✆ 9262880, @ wdf577

✉ **Badesee (swimming lake)** @ tdm643

26 Turn right by the church ⌇ immediately left on **Seestraße** ⌇ continue straight ahead onto the path ⌇ turn left on the street between the playing fields ⌇ cross the main road and ride to the right on the paved lane ⌇ after 200 m turn left and follow the lane to the barrage on the Danube ⌇ from here you follow the paved path along the water towards Erbach.

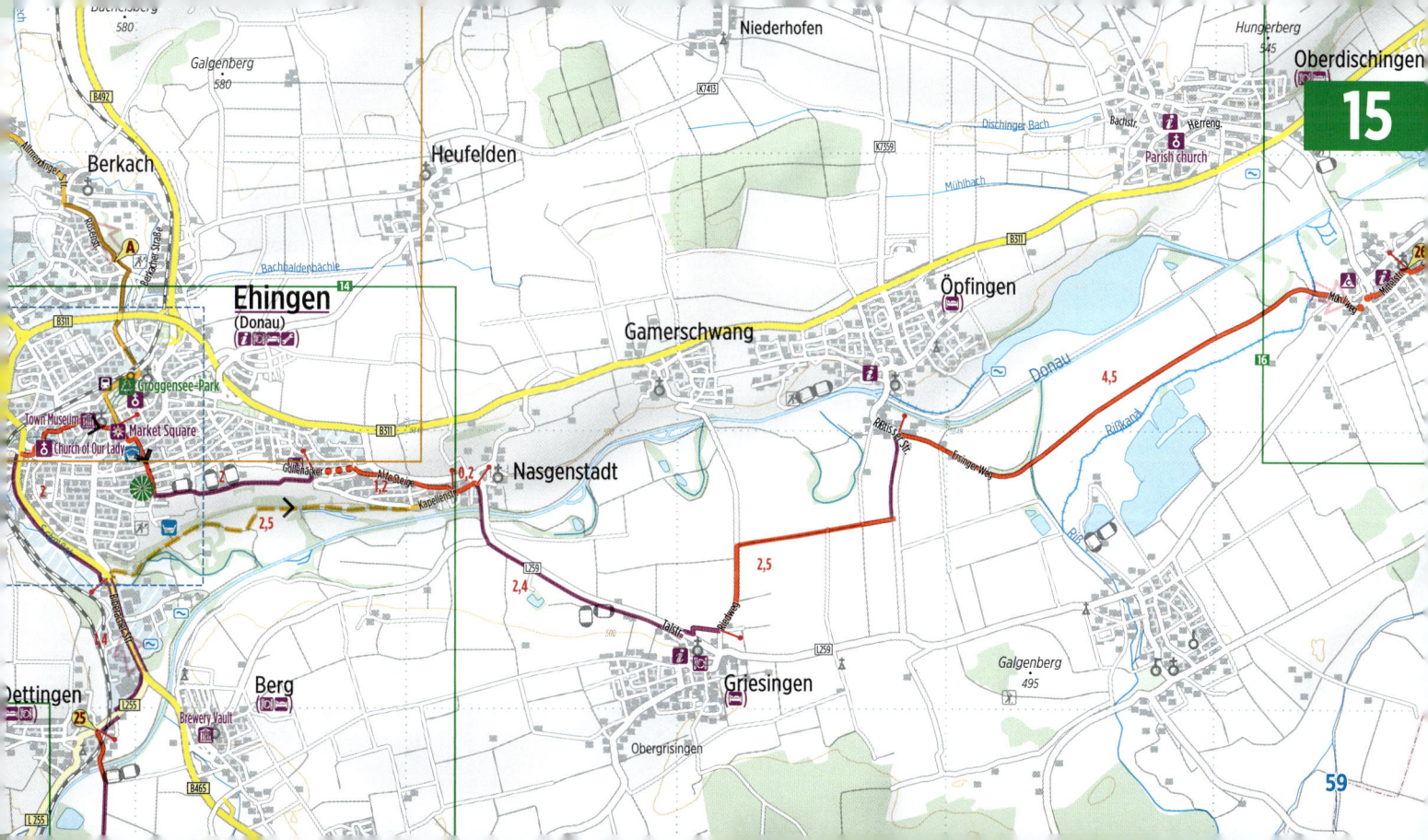

Niederhofen

Hungerberg
545

Oberdischingen

Dischinger Bach

Bachstr.
Herreng.

Parish church

Duchsberg
580

Galgenberg
580

B492

Berkach

A

Heufelden

K7413

K7359

Mühlbach

B311

Öpfingen

Gamerschwang

Donau

4,5

16

Bachbaldenbächle

Ehingen
(Donau)

14

Groggensee-Park

Town Museum

Market Square

Church of Our Lady

2

B311

Göllenacker

Alte Steige
1,7

0,2

Kapellenstr.

Nasgenstadt

2,5

2,4

L259

Birkhof-Str.

Erninger Weg

Riß

Rißkanal

2,5

Dettingen

Thurauer Bach

1,4

25

Berg

Brewery Vault

L255

B465

L255

Griesingen

Talstr.

L259

580

Obergrisingen

Galgenberg
495

26

Marktweg

Mühlstr.

59

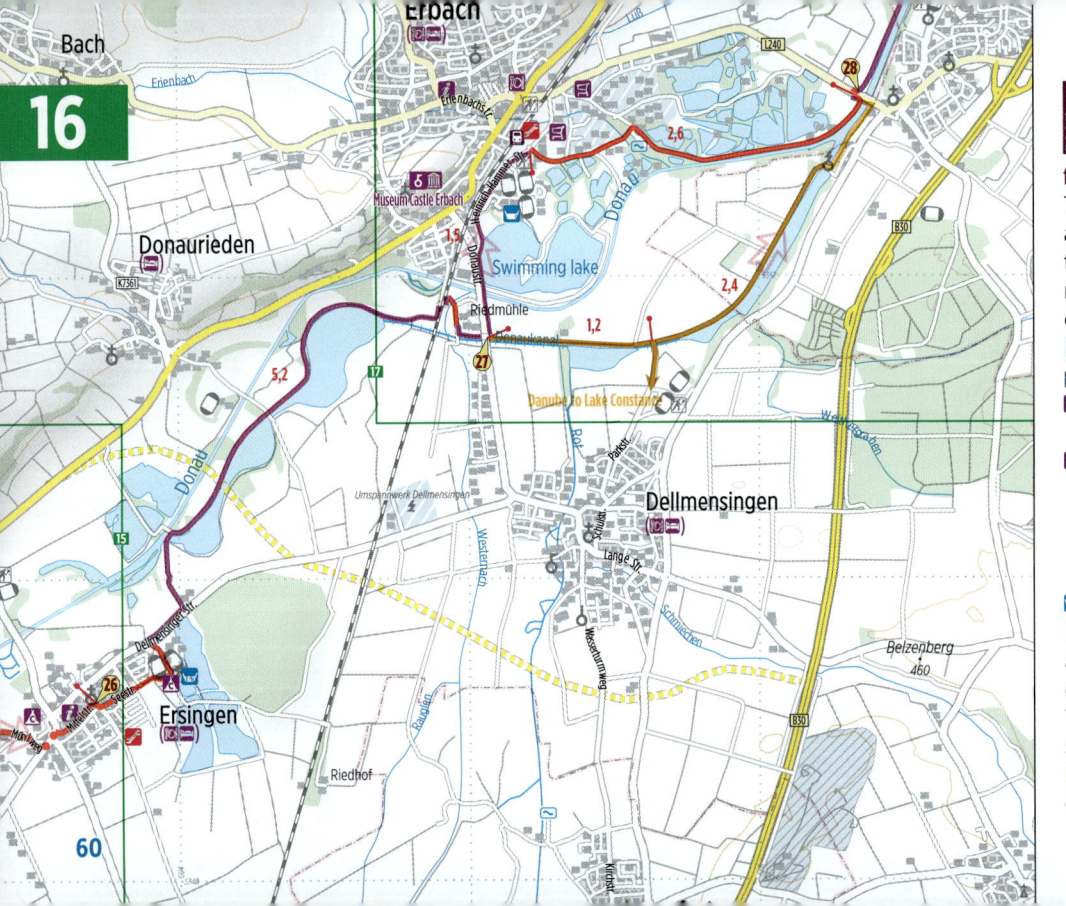

16

Danube to Lake Constance

FORK ▮ Those not wishing to ride via Erbach have the choice to take a shorter and much quieter alternative route to Donaustetten from here, following the narrow lake formed by the dam on the Danube Canal.

To follow the main route, **27** turn left immediately after passing under the bridge ⁓ follow the bicycle path along the **K 7375** ⁓ when you reach the intersection, turn right onto the bicycle path along the **Heinrich-Hammer-Straße.**

Erbach

prefix: 07305

🛈 **Stadtverwaltung (town office)**, Erlenbachstr. 50, ✆ 96760, @ ncv344

🏛 **Museum im Schloss Erbach (palace Erbach museum)**, Schloßberg 1, ✆ 4646 Ⓒ The Renaissance building is surrounded by mighty walls and a moat. Part of the rooms serves as a palace museum. Some of the rich furnishings date back to the time of its construction. @ jlo761

✉ **Strandbad am Badesee (outdoor pool)**, ✆ 3621, @ bve834

Follow the main route turn left onto cycle path along the **Donaustraße** ⁓ continue along the cycle path along Heinrich-Hammer-Straße. Turn right after the tennis courts and follow the street **Großes Wert** ⁓ in the sharp left bend by the wastewater treatment plant turn right ⁓ follow the paved lane past ponds and along the Danube until you reach the **L 240** across the river from Donaustetten.

Donaustetten

28 cross the road and continue along the paved field road beside the Danube ⌁ by **Gögglingen** cross the **K 9916** and turn left along the bicycle path ⌁ immediately turn right and continue on the path, at first along the Danube, then up to the street along the Donautal industrial zone ⌁ cross the street and turn right on the bicycle path along **Hans Lorenser Straße** ⌁ **29** turn right after the access road to the transformer station ⌁ you cross the Danube on a bicycle and pedestrian bridge through the Gronne nature reserve ⌁ turn left on the bike path along **Laupheimer Straße** ⌁ pass under the road bridge ⌁ turn left after 150 meters ⌁ turn right by the Danube and keep left at the fork in the path ⌁ follow the paved lane along the canal to the Wiblingen hydroelectric power station ⌁ cross the canal and the Danube and ride up to the railway line ⌁ turn right and follow the bicycle path along the railway line and the Danube towards Ulm ⌁ just after passing under a large road bridge you reach a small pedestrian and bicycle bridge.

Ulm

stinging in Ulm (every 4 years), Lichterserenade (Saturday before Schwörmontag)

- ✳ **Stadtführungen (city tours)**, ☏ 1612830 ⏱ Ask at the Tourist Information about the daily guided tours. @ kfx622
- ✳ **Zeughaus und Einstein-Brunnen (armoury and Einstein well)**, Am Zeughaus ㉔ It was first mentioned in a document in 1433. In the 16th and 17th cs it was extended and an impressive complex was built. Right next to it is the Einstein well, which pays tribute to the city's most famous son. @ bjf378
- 🌳 **Tiergarten Ulm (zoo)**, Friedrichsau 38, ☏ 1616742 ㊰ Located in the local recreation area Friedrichsau, you can admire native and exotic animals. @ oca861

One of the prettiest parts of Ulm must surely be the fisher and tanner quarter - a dense neighborhood of old half-timbered houses that have settled with age and lean over the narrow streets and the waters of the Blau. It takes no great fantasy to imagine the smells and sounds as fishermen and merchants traded plump carp, pike and other fresh fish caught in the nearby Danube. Ulm's rivermen made an important contribution to the city's prosperity, using their famous Ulm-barges to transport goods and settlers from Swabia down the Danube. When these simple vessels arrived in Vienna, they were taken apart and sold as firewood because dragging them back upstream would have cost too much time and money. As with many other crafts, industrialization brought the end of that way of life. Today the picturesque streets and the quadrennial Fischerstechen serve as reminders of that past. The Fischerstechen is a jousting competition in which contestants try to push each other into the water.

A short distance downstream one comes to the tilted Metzger tower. According to local legend, the tower started to lean when local butchers met there to plot how they would deny accusations that they were making their sausages smaller and smaller.

One tower that definitely does not lean is the tallest church steeple in the world: the soaring tower of Ulm's cathedral. It reaches 161.6 meters into the sky and has been Ulm's defining landmark since it was completed in 1890. Visitors who are not afraid of heights and narrow spaces can climb the 768 steps to the top of the spire. This energy-sapping endeavour is worth the effort, offering marvellous views across the region and to the Alps in the south.

Not quite so impressive was the elevation achieved by the Tailor of Ulm, Albrecht Berblinger, in 1811, when he attempted to fly with a self-built glider. He leapt from a riverside tower and promptly landed in the Danube. Nevertheless, his spirit of experimentation seems consistent with Ulm's claim that it is a city of science. Albert Einstein was born in Ulm, and the University's new "research city" on the Eselsberg is home to numerous important research institutes.

Less difficult to understand than the theory of relativity, but possibly just as important, is bread. This basic staple of human nutrition is the subject of the Museum of Bread near the cathedral. Other important sites in the city include the town hall built in 1370 at the end of the fisherman's quarter. It features an astronomical clock and murals that show an Ulm barge on the river. In 1810, Napoleon incorporated the city of Ulm into the kingdom of Württemberg and the Danube became the border with Bavaria, allowing Neu Ulm to develop as a separate city.

Ulm to Ingolstadt

157 km

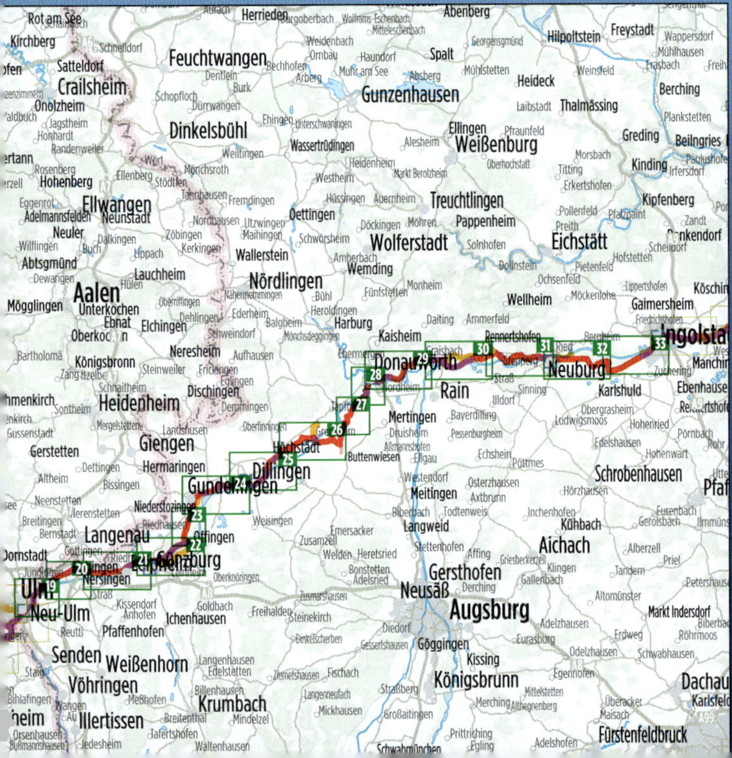

m/km: ↗ 2.6 (415m) ↘ 3.3 (521m) cycle path: 48 % unpaved: 29 % busy road: 8 %

The second stage of the tour covers the Danube valley between Ulm and Ingolstadt. A short distance past Ulm, riders cross into Bavaria, where the route remains for the rest of the distance to Passau. The landscape becomes flatter and you will pass inviting lakes and ride through wetland habitats, rich with plant and animal life, formed around the confluences of the Danube with numerous tributary rivers. The route passes through or near historic old cities like Günzburg, Dillingen and Höchstädt, where aristocratic families and the church built impressive baroque and renaissance edifices. Parts of the route between Donauwörth and Neuburg are hillier as they cross the foothills of the Franconian Alb, which extends down to the Danube from the north. In Neuburg, the rider is welcomed by the impressive palace and romantic townscape before reaching the end of the section in Ingolstadt.

The route follows bicycle paths, quiet country lanes and unpaved paths and field and forest roads. There are only a few short stretches with heavier traffic, and almost no difficult climbs to be conquered.

Ulm

see page 62

Ulm to Günzburg   26.6 km

When you cross the Danube in Ulm, you are also crossing the border between Baden-Württemberg and Bayern (Bavaria). The route will stay in the free state of Bavaria all the way to Passau, and you will become well accustomed to the beer, veal sausage (Weisswurst) and pretzel (Brezel) culture which has found such strong tradition here. Enjoy!

Neu-Ulm

prefix: 0731

🛈 **Tourist-Information**, Münsterpl. 50, Ulm, ✆ 1612830, @ nir673

🏛 **Edwin Scharff Museum**, Petruspl. 4, ✆ 70502555 🚻 With permanent collection and special exhibitions of the artist Edwin Scharff and his contemporaries, children's museum with adventure rooms. Recently renovated in 2017, @ vbw581

Neu-Ulm, Water lily pond in Glacis Park

🏛 **Museum Walther Collection**, Reichenauerstr. 21, ☎ 1769143 ☺ ☝ International private collection of contemporary photography and video art from Africa and Asia. @ coq738

⛪ **St. Johann-Baptist-Kirche (St. John Baptist Church)**. The church was built from 1922-26 in expressionist style. @ xjq812

⛪ **Wasserturm (water tower)**, Turmstr. 🕐 The landmark of the city was built in 1898 on the powder magazine belonging to the Federal Fortress. @ jat656

✳ **DAV-Kletterwelt**, Nelsonallee 17, ☎ 60307510 🛝 Indoor and Outdoor climbing, @ ynu783

✳ **Ecodrom**, Industriestr. 4, ☎ 2074840 🛝 Cart track with electric karts, two-storied, @ kal562

✳ **Oldtimerfabrik Classic (classic car factory)**, Lessingstr. 5, ☎ 70511844 🛝 Classic car fans have implemented this unique concept: Originally they wanted a place to store their cars, which developed into a mixture of museum, shopping centre for car enthusiasts and event location. @ jgt887

✴ **Glacis-Stadtpark (Glacis City Park)** 🕐 You might stroll here, but also enjoy a rich cultural programme in summer. @ xkn148

🏊 **Donaubad (indoor pool)**, Wiblinger Str. 55, ☎ 985990, @ evj247

At the beginning of the 19th c., Ulm became part of the Kingdom of Württemberg, the settlement on the right bank of the Danube remained in the Kingdom of Bavaria. In the middle of the 19th century, Neu-Ulm became a major a garrison town. Large ramparts surrounded the town. The garrison was dissolved after the First World War. The bombardments in the Second World War destroyed 80 percent of all buildings. Afterwards Neu-Ulm became a garrison town again. From 1951 to 1991 the US army was stationed here. Today, the former barracks site houses a new university building, a sports and leisure park, student residences, the tax office and restaurants. Part of the fortress and the water tower are located in the Glacis Park, which has been developed into a large leisure area with water games, children's playgrounds, a restaurant and a concert stage.

Continue along the river bank ⌇ **1** you pass below a road bridge, the Herdbrücke, and a little later another road bridge, the Gänstorbrücke, as you leave the centre of Ulm ⌇ as you follow the river you pass a large park, the **Friedrichsau** ⌇ after the park continue on the bicycle path next to **Thalfinger Uferstraße** ⌇ you pass a hydroelectric power station, the Donaukraftwerk Böfinger Halde.

After the power station the bicycle path continues along the river ⌇ you come to follow the **Thalfinger Uferstraße** once more as you near Thalfingen, the path eventually switching to the left side of the road ⌇ continue past the railway station and the playing field before turning left into the **Donaustraße** by the little white church ⌇ **2** cross the railway tracks into Thalfingen.

⛪ **St. Laurentius**. The frescoes of the magnificent Rococo church were designed by Joseph Wannenmacher. @ vgx784

Stay on **Donaustraße** ⌇ in the centre of town turn right at the post office onto **Elchinger Straße** ⌇ follow the wide bicycle path along the left side of **Elchinger Straße** out of the town.

Oberelchingen (Elchingen)

prefix: 07308

Pfarr- und Wallfahrtskirche St. Peter und Paul (parish and pilgrimage church), Klosterhof, ✆ 264362. Between 1773-84 the nave was redesigned in the style of early classicism and the choir in rococo style. The church still bears witness to the size of the former imperial abbey, which was founded in the 12th century and abandoned in 1802. @ yuw816

Lauschtour „Napoleon in Elchingen" (Eavesdropping tour) ㉔ Around the monastery church Napoleon defeated the Austrian army on 14 Oct. 1805. Since then, Elchingen has also been immortalized on the Arc de Triomphe in Paris. The battle comes to life again at the original locations during the eavesdropping tour on the subject of „monastery silence and cannon thunder". @ fco774

Martinstor der ehem. Klosteranlage (Martinsdoor of the former monastery) ㉔ West gate of the former monastery complex.

Klostergarten (monastery garden), Klosterhof, ✆ 0731/264362 ℭ Following the historical model with plants of medieval monastic medicine and modern medicinal plants. In addition, a viewing platform next to the garden offers a wonderful view of the Danube valley and the Ulm cathedral, and even as far as the Alps when the foehn is blowing. @ ugh368

Hallenbad (indoor pool), Am Bildstöckle 1, ✆ 0731/7261

⚠ Be careful at the busy intersection when entering Oberelchingen ⤳ continue along the

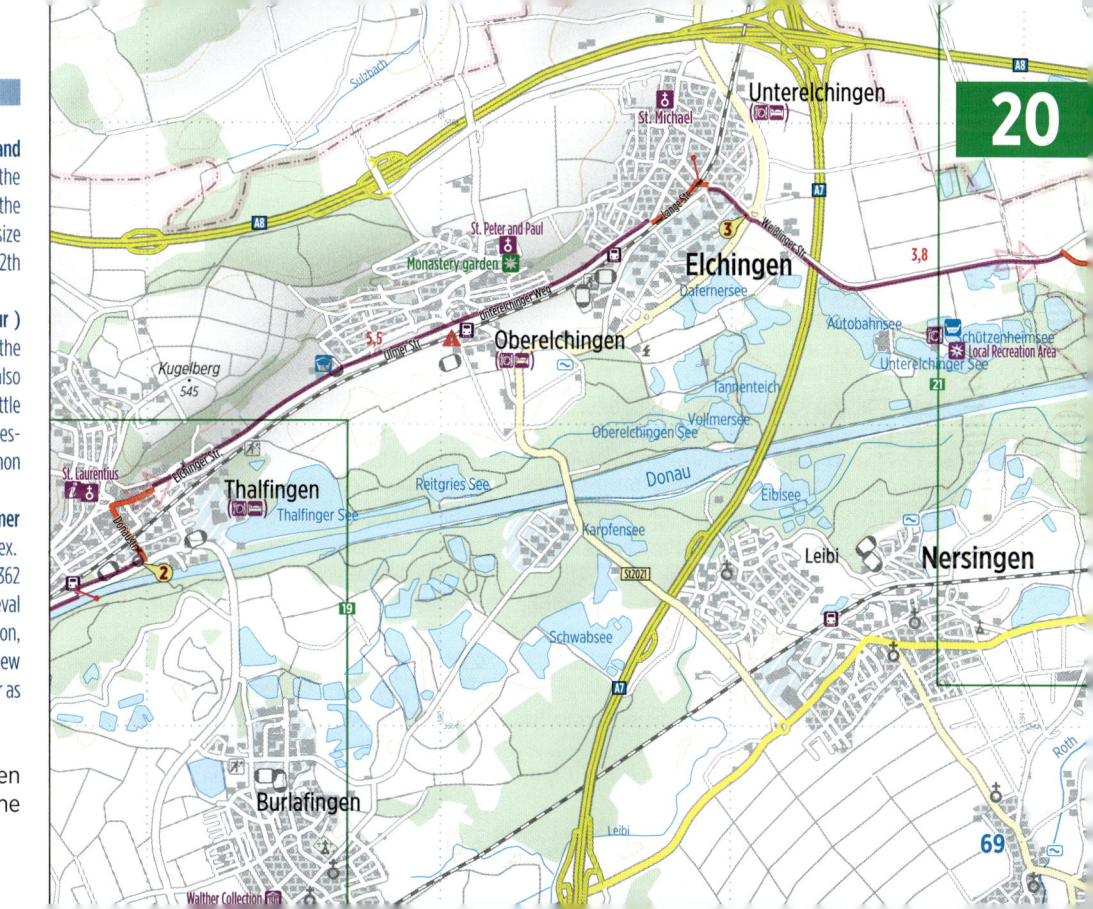

bicycle path to Unterelchingen ∿ the path ends just past the railway station.

Unterelchingen (Elchingen)

St. Michael. The high altar was designed by Joseph Feuchtmayer in 1743, the stucco work by Georg Eitele.

200 m after the railway station turn right onto **Lange Straße** ∿ ride parallel with the train tracks ∿ at the next railway crossing turn right on **Hauptstraße** ∿ keep left after crossing the tracks and continue on the bicycle path along the right side of **Weißinger Straße** ∿ **3** proceed straight at the roundabout ∿ and across the bridge over the **A 7** freeway ∿ continue parallel to the **Weißinger Straße** to Weißingen.

Weißingen (Leipheim)

As you enter the village turn right into the first side street, **Ortsstraße** ∿ in the centre of the village keep right and take the wide, straight gravel path into the forest, the „Weißinger Hölzle" ∿ 1 km after the underpass under the A 8 freeway the route returns to the Danube ∿ ride under the road bridge.

CENTRE Here you can use the bridge to get you across the river into Leipheim.

Leipheim

prefix: 08221

Tourist-Information, Schloßpl. 1, Günzburg, ☎ 200444, @ ibi643

Stadtverwaltung (municipal office), Marktstr. 5, ☎ 7070, @ oyj633

Heimat- und Bauernkriegsmuseum Blaue Ente (local history and peasant war museum), Stadtberg 1, ☎ 70721 ☺ City history and interesting facts about the peasant war and mill technology. @ vai375

Pfarrkirche St. Veit (parish church). The Evangelical Lutheran parish church was extended in the 14th c. @ uum774

Schloss (castle). The present castle was built in the 16th c. Parts of the ground floor and the foundation walls date back to the 11th c.

Stadtmauer und Stadtbrunnen (city wall and fountain), in the old town ㉔ The rectangular wall from the 14th c. is still 80% intact and currently being renovated. @ nsk285

Gartenhallenbad (indoor pool), Günzburger Str. 68, ☎ 71979, @ tej447

A bridge guarded by a castle at the current site of Leipheim gave the town regional importance as early as 1063. In 1453 the city and its inhabitants were sold to Ulm for 23,200 gulden. On the second weekend of July, the city celebrates a children's festival, which was first held in 1818 to celebrate a good harvest after years of war, famine and hardship.

Another noteworthy site is a 600-year old linden, or lime, tree on the Lindenweg near the cemetery.

The route from Leipheim to Günzburg continues along the north bank of the Danube but away from the river ∿ at first along the street **Weidlenweg** ∿ turn right before the fields and the creek and follow the track through the riparian forests ∿ you cross a bridge over a small tributary, the Nau, before coming to a T-intersection at the edge of the forest ∿ turn right ∿ cross to the other side of **Heidenheimer Straße** and turn right on the bicycle path along the left side of the street.

FORK You now have the choice between two signposted routes. One route follows a flat gravel path along the Danube and bypasses both Günzburg and Offingen. The other passes through Günzburg and over the heights to Offingen, where the two routes reconnect. The Günzburg route is 2.5 km longer and has several mild climbs.

branches off where the street makes a sharp turn to the right ∿ between fields turn left ∿ at the next intersection turn right and follow the gravel path through the forest. The gravel path becomes a road of two paved tracks ∿ at the intersection turn right on the paved street ∿ in the distance you can now see the cooling towers of the Gundremmingen nuclear power plant ∿ after about 2 km you reach Offingen.

Offingen
prefix: 08224

ℹ Verwaltungsgemeinschaft (administrative community), Marktstr. 19, ✆ 96970, @ Iny475
At the T-intersection turn left on **Hauptstraße** ∿ continue past the church ∿ turn right by the cemetery on **Donaustraße** ∿ you pass below the railway line and continue to the intersection with the main road ∿ turn left onto the bike path on the left side of the road ∿ after crossing the Danube

turn left on the paved side street ∿ **6** after 150 m the two routes rejoin, the north bank route coming from the left.

Günzburg
to Gundelfingen 13.9 km

From the city centre return to Waypoint **5** on the already familiar route
After the sports and tennis courts, turn right into the city forest ∿ past the Günzburg outdoor swimming pool ∿ after the pool turn left over the bridge, crossing the Nau once again ∿ keep right and follow the track down to the Danube ∿ for the next 8 km you will ride on the gravel path directly beside the Danube ∿ pass under the B 16 main road ∿ by the bridge to Reisensburg, where you have the option of crossing to the south bank, you must cross the road before continuing along the river.

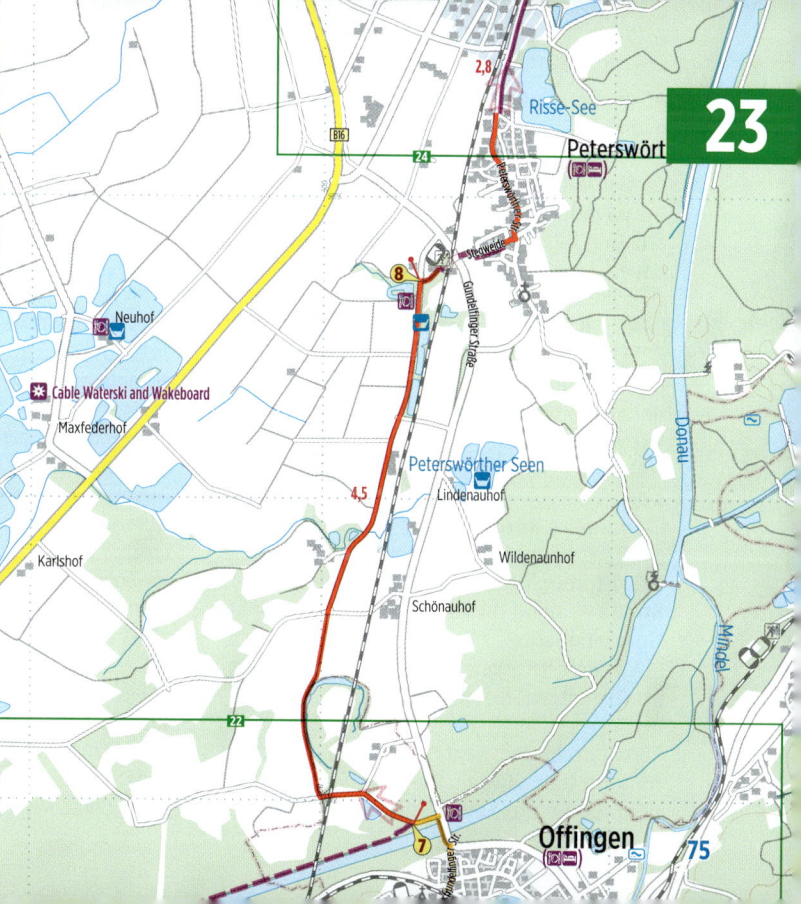

After a long ride beside the river you pass a hydroelectric power station ⁓ after passing under a railway bridge you come to an intersection with a paved lane ⁓ **7** continue along the paved street towards Peterswörth ⁓ after crossing the railway tracks turn right into the paved lane between the fields ⁓ continue straight until you pass an inn and bathing lake ⁓ **8** turn right before the playing fields ⁓ keep right by the tennis courts and follow the bicycle path under the railway line and under the main road ⁓ in Peterswörth turn left where the path ends by the street.

Peterswörth (Gundelfingen an der Donau)
prefix: 09073

❊ **Wasserski- u. Wakeboard-Seilbahn**, Haldenweg 10, ✆ 920690 ⊜ Wakeboard and water ski courses, fun park, @ cqr546

Drive through the village on **Peterswörther Straße** ⁓ along the tracks in the direction of Gundelfingen.

A shorter alternative route to Echenbrunn begins here to the right on Stadionstraße.

Turn left at the next side street and ride through the railway underpass ⁓ follow the right bend on **Xaver-Schwarz-Straße** and afterwards the left bend by the railway station onto **Bahnhofstraße** into the centre of Gundelfingen ⁓ after crossing three bridges, turn left onto **Prof.-Bamann-Straße** and ride through the town gate ⁓ turn right on **Hauptstraße**

Gundelfingen an der Donau
prefix: 09073

ℹ **Kulturamt im Rathaus**, Prof.-Bamann-Str. 22, ✆ 999118, @ kpu551

🏛 **Automobil-Museum Gundelfingen (automobile museum)**, Bächinger Str. 68, ✆ 2575 🕖 Lovers of classic cars will get their money's worth here, models from lesser known manufacturers are also exhibited here.

❊ **Romantische Innenstadt (Romantic city centre)**. Parish church St. Martin, hospital church, town hall, Schlachtegg castle, gate tower, city wall, etc.

Gundelfingen is a romantic small city that is also sometimes called the city of gardners. With three arms of the river flowing through its centre, Gundelfingen lies between the meadows and flood plains of the Danube valley.

Gundelfingen apparently grew out of an outpost on the Roman road that passed here. The name seems to come from Gundolf, a local ruler in the third century after Christ. Remnants of the old city walls and archaeological finds dating to the 6th and 7th cs AD bear testament to the small city's long history.

Gundelfingen to Dillingen — 12 km

Turn right again on **Lauinger Straße** ⁓ follow the bicycle path along the Lauinger Straße ⁓ after crossing the railway line you reach Echenbrunn

Faimingen (Lauingen (Donau))

🏛 **Apollo-Grannus-Tempel**, Tempelweg 🕘 Remains of a Roman temple from the 2nd c. @ gwc216

In Faimingen, a district of Lauingen, you can visit the remains of the carefully reconstructed Apollo Grannus Temple. It belongs to a fort that once served as a supply depot for soldiers on the Roman border.

After the Roman Temple make a left and right turn, then continue along **Kastellstraße** ⁓ at the next intersection turn left out to the main road, where you turn right onto the bicycle path along the **Gundelfinger Straße** through Lauingen.

Lauingen (Donau)
prefix: 09072

ℹ **Stadtverwaltung (town office)**, Herzog-Georg-Str. 17, ✆ 9980, @ rnt168

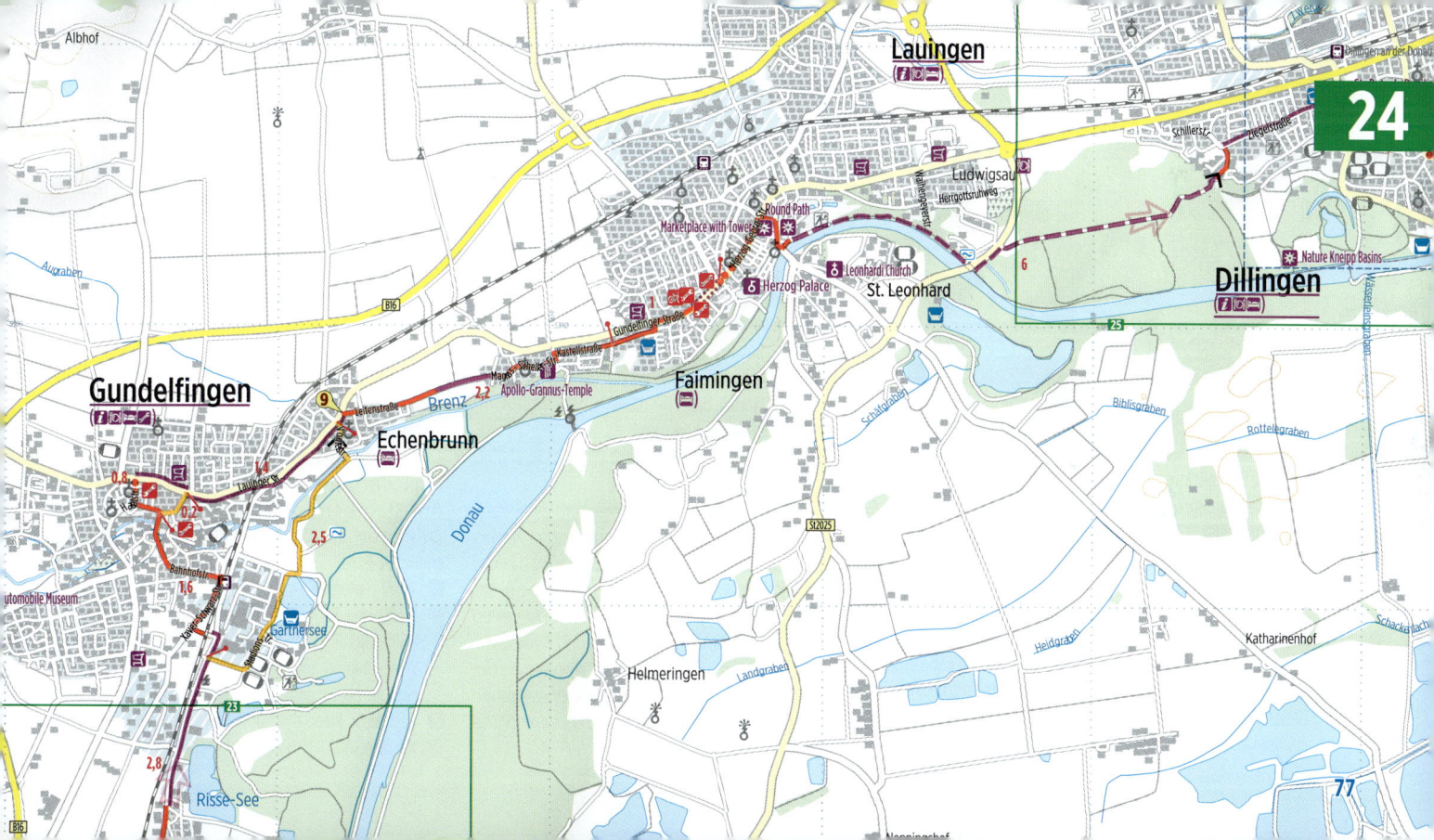

Lauingen

Albhof

Augraben

B16

Gundelfingen

Echenbrunn

Brenz

Gartensee

Risse-See

Automobile Museum

Bahnhofstr.

Lauinger Str.

Leitenstraße

Gundelfinger Straße

Kastellstraße

Magg-Scheiz-Str.

Apollo-Grannus-Temple

Faimingen

Donau

Helmeringen

Landgraben

Heidgraben

Schätzgraben

St2025

Ludwigsau

Herrgottsruhweg

Round Path

Marketplace with Tower

Herzog Palace

Leonhardi Church

St. Leonhard

Dillingen

Dillingen an der Donau

Nature Kneipp Basins

Biblisgraben

Rottelegraben

Katharinenhof

Schackerlach

Schillerstr.

Ziegelstraße

6

25

24

0,8

0,2

1,6

1,4

2,5

2,8

2,2

9

1

23

77

Schloss Dillingen

🏛 **Heinz Piontek Museum**, Brüderstr. 10, 📞 91044 🕐 The museum presents the life and work of the Georg–Büchner–Prizewinner Heinz Piontek, focusing above all on his years in Lauingen and Dillingen. @ qwj862

⛪ **Leonhardikirche (church)**. The today's church was built in the 18th c. @ rls656

⛪ **Herzogschloss (ducal palace)**, Schlossstr. In its eventful history, the palace was not only the seat of the sovereign, but also the widow's residence of the Palatine Countess Elisabeth (1559-63), a hospital and some of the rooms were also used as a gymnasium or museum. @ jit168

⛪ **Schimmelturm (white horse tower)**, Herzog-Georg-Str. 17. The former watchtower was completed in 1478 and shows the pride of the citizens of Lauingen through its magnificent outer facade. @ bvp316

✳ **Marktplatz mit klassizistischem Rathaus (market square with classicistic town hall)** 24 Lauinger market square is often described as one of the most beautiful market squares in Swabia.

✳ **Stadtführungen (city tours)**, Herzog-Georg-Str. 17, 📞 998132 🕐, @ epi335

✳ **Wehrgang mit Tränktor (round path)**. On the square with the city wall, the Tränktor, the hospital church and an old half-timbered building arises the feeling as if you had been transported back to ancient times. @ mki813

🏖 **Auwaldsee (alluvial lake)** @ rcq275

🏊 **Kreishallenbad (indoor pool)**, Friedrich-Ebert-Str. 10, 📞 6566, @ rlk538

Lauingen has one of the prettiest markets in Swabia, with its classicist town hall and monument for Albertus Magnus. Born in Lauingen in 1193, Magnus was a Dominican friar who is considered one of the great medieval philosophers of Germany. He advocated the peaceful coexistence of science and theology. Faimingen, a suburb of Lauingen that also lies on the cycle route, contains interesting ruins of a Roman fortress, including the carefully restored ruins of the Apollo Grannus temple.

Cross the market square and turn right into **Albertusstraße** 〰 at the next crossing turn right into **Donaustraße** 〰 follow the street until you reach the Danube 〰 before the bridge turn left into **Segrepromenade** 〰 on this street along the banks of the Danube 〰 after 1.3 km pass the sewage treatment plant 〰 go under the bypass road 〰 turn left on the gravel road along the bypass road 〰 after 250 m turn right on the gravel road through a quiet piece of forest 〰 cross two bridges to Dillingen 〰 turn left uphill on the asphalted road to the first houses 〰 turn right on the accompanying cycle path to **Ziegelstraße** 〰 into the historic centre of the town 〰 after the town gate at the main road turn right into **Am Stadtberg** street **10**.

Dillingen a.d.Donau
prefix: 09071

ℹ **Tourist-Information**, Königstr. 37/38, 📞 540, @ jmg435

🏛 **Stadt- und Hochstiftmuseum (city and bishopric museum)**, Hafenmarkt 11, 📞 4400 🕐 Prehistory, Roman times, craftsmanship, university and military history department, blacksmith's shop for hooves and wagons. @ jhs444

⛪ **Basilika St. Peter**, 📞 4050. St. Peter's is the second basilica of the diocese of Augsburg. In 1979 Pope St. Peter raised it to the

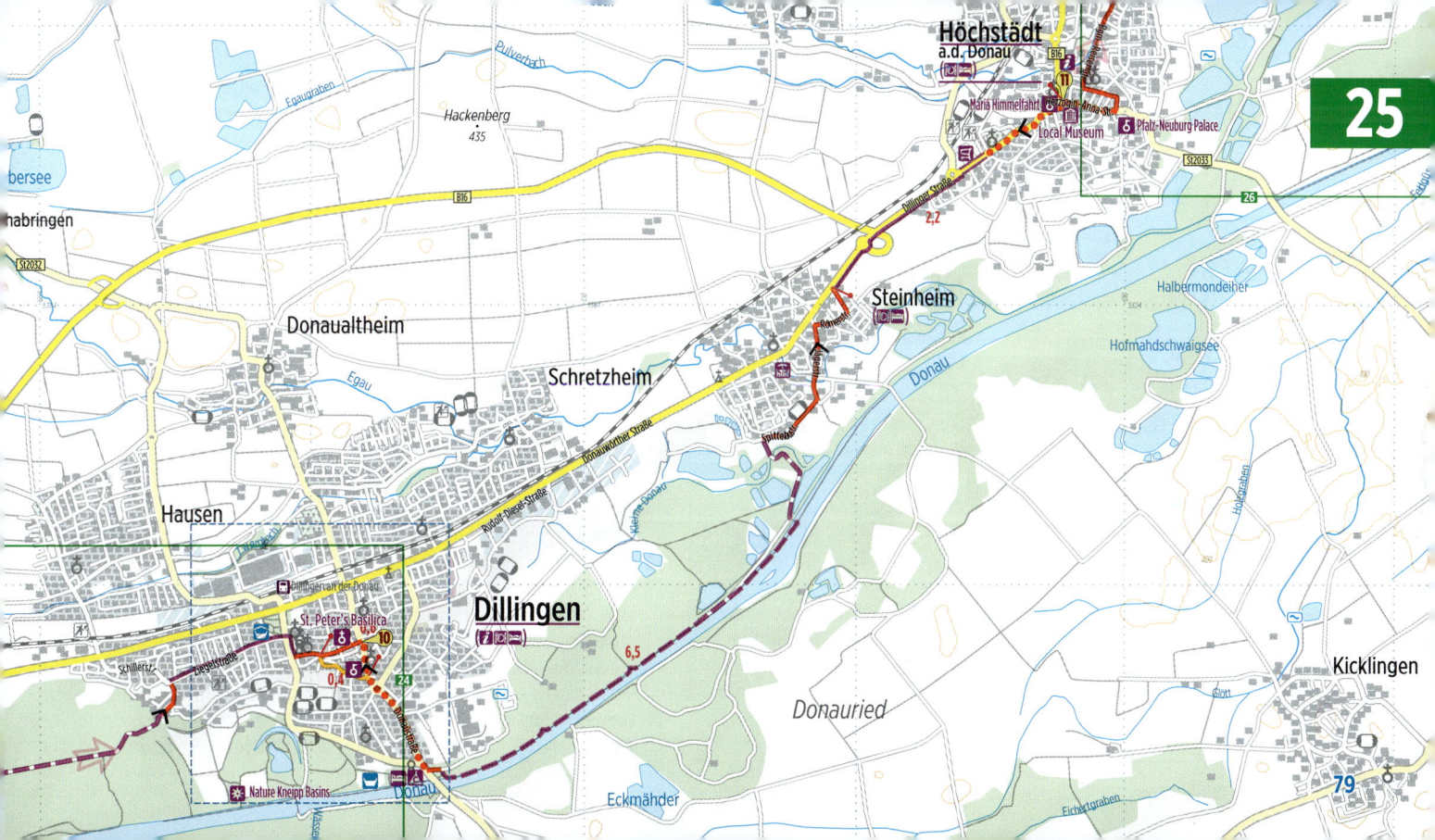

Pulverbach

Höchstädt
a.d. Donau

B16

Maria Himmelfahrt

Local Museum

Pfalz-Neuburg Palace

St2035

Egaugraben

Hackenberg
435

B16

26

habringen

St2032

Halbermondeiher

Donaualtheim

Steinheim

Hofmahdschwaigsee

Schretzheim

Egau

Donau

Donauwörther Straße

Rudolf-Diesel-Straße

Kleine Donau

Hausen

Dillingen an der Donau

St. Peter's Basilica

10

24

6,5

Donauried

Nature Kneipp Basins

Donau

Eckmähder

Kicklingen

Glott

Eichelgraben

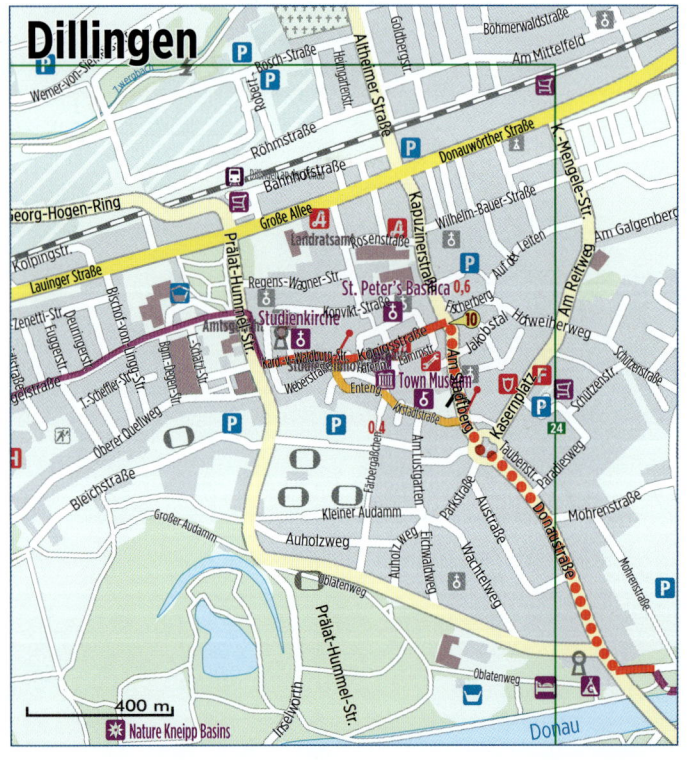

Dillingen

Nature Kneipp Basins

status of „Basilica minor" (smaller basilica). @ spj157

Studienkirche (university church), ☎ 4050. The former university church was built at the beginning of the 17th c. as part of the Jesuit College.). @ lxf484

Dillinger Schloss (Dillinger palace). Former prince-bishop's residence. @ nev443

Altstadt (old town), ☎ 54208. During a city tour you will discover the city's sights: town hall, Wilhelm Bauer Fountain, Marientor, City and Hochstift Museum, Franziskus Fountain, Study Church, Ulrich Monument and many more. @ gfn866

Goldener Saal (golden hall), Kardinal-von-Waldburg-Str. 6, ☎ 54211 ⊖ The magnificent auditorium of the former university impresses with its rococo furnishings.

Natur-Kneipp-Anlage (Nature Kneipp basins) ㉔ Very idyllic Kneipp facility in a tributary of the Danube. Sebastian Kneipp lived and studied temporarily in Dillingen. It was here that he tested his famous hydrotherapeutic treatment on himself for the first time.

Eichwaldbad (outdoor pool), Oblatenweg 10, ☎ 71582, @ heu667

Hallenbad (indoor pool), Ziegelstr. 10, ☎ 703701, @ geo452

Dillingen was shaped by the presence of senior clerics and church intellectuals. It was the seat of power for the prince-bishops of Augsburg who ruled a large territory. The establishment of a university by Jesuits added to the city's influence. It is also one of the few German cities that did not suffer damage during World War Two.

It was in Dillingen that the clerical scholar Sebastian Kneipp invented the cold-water therapy that bears his name. He claimed that regular dips in the cold Danube helped cure a lung ailment.

Dillingen to Höchstädt   8.7 km

At the roundabout turn left (3rd exit) onto the street **Kasernplatz** ～ turn right into the street **Am Galgenberg** ～ continue to the commercial area, where you turn left on **Gutenbergstraße** ～ at the T-intersection turn right on **Rudolf-Diesel-Straße** ～ at the

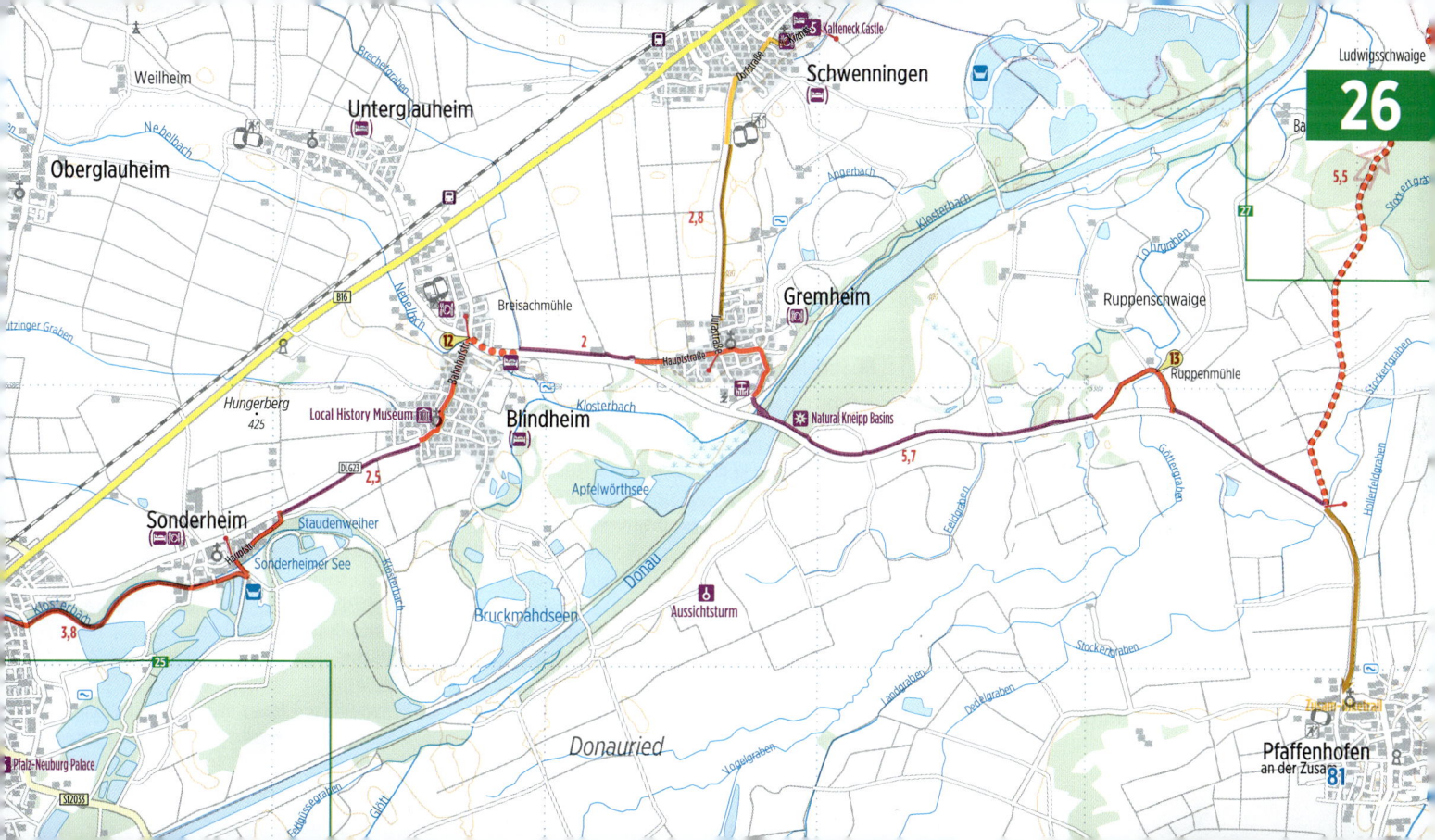

Ludwigsschwaige

26

Weilheim

Oberglauheim

Unterglauheim

Nebelbach

Brechtelgraben

Schwenningen

Kalteneck Castle

Angerbach

Klosterbach

Ruppenschwaige

B16

Breisachmühle

Gremheim

Hauptstraße

2

2,8

Hungerberg
425

Local History Museum

Blindheim

Klosterbach

Natural Kneipp Basins

Ruppenmühle

13

5,7

DLG23

2,5

Sonderheim

Staudenweiher

Sonderheimer See

Apfelwörthsee

Donau

Bruckmahdseen

Aussichtsturm

Klosterbach

3,8

25

Pfalz-Neuburg Palace

ST2033

Donauried

Glött

Pfaffenhofen
an der Zusam

81

5,5

Stockertgraben

LD-Graben

Güttingraben

Feldgraben

Hollerfeldgraben

Stockergraben

Landgraben

Dedelgraben

Vogelgraben

Fastgrasgraben

Schloss Höchstädt

end of the street change to the bicycle path along the main road (**B 16**) to Steinheim.

Steinheim (Dillingen a.d.Donau)

🏠 **RadlerOase**, An der Egau 9. Rest area with water, tables, air pump, shelter. @ rdx634

Continue along the main road through the town ∼ a bicycle path begins again on the right side of the road as you leave Steinheim, where you are rejoined by the route along the Danube from Dillingen ∼ continue along the main road to the **Marktplatz** (market square) in Höchstädt.

Turn right into **Römerstraße** ∼ turn left into **Markomannenstraße** ∼ turn right onto the cycle path along the **B 16** to Höchstädt.

Höchstädt a. d. Donau
prefix: 09074

🛈 **Bürgerservicebüro (public service office)**, Herzog-Philipp-Ludwig-Str. 10, ☎ 440, @ ffg448

🏛 **Heimatmuseum (local history museum)**, Marktpl. 7, ☎ 4412, ☎ 5262 ◔ ◑ Particularly worth seeing is the pewter figure diorama of the Battle of Höchstädt-Blindheim with over 9,000 hand-painted figures. @ mxy476

⛪ **Stadtpfarrkirche Mariä Himmelfahrt (city parish curch)**. Late Gothic hall church (1442), choir stalls, sacrament house, baptismal font, @ qst647

🏛 **Schloss der Pfalzgrafen von Pfalz-Neuburg (palace of the Palatine earls of Pfalz-Neuburg)**, Herzogin-Anna-Str. 52, ☎ 9585700 ◉ Four-winged Renaissance building, exhibition on the battle of 1704, museum of German faiences, temporary exhibitions of the Forum of Swabian History, castle chapel with interesting ceiling paintings, cultural events. @ cmp613

✱ **Denkmalweg (memorial path)**. „In the footsteps of 1704", 29 km cycle route, offers the opportunity to observe the significant battle in its scenic context.

✱ **Stadtführungen (city tours)**, ☎ 4412 ◔ meeting point: palace, @ ipp556

The picturesque old city of Höchstädt is famous for the decisive battle fought here during the War of the Spanish Succession. Allied armies led by Prince Eugene of Savoy and the Duke of Marlborough defeated a French-Bavarian army that was seeking to capture Vienna and force an end to the war. English speaking peoples call this the Battle of Blenheim.

Höchstädt to Donauwörth   28 km

11 The route branches off at the market square to the right onto **Herzogin-Anna-Straße** ∼ turn left into **Geigergasse**, then right into **Bürgermeister-Reiser-Straße** ∼ follow the path along the Klosterbach stream ∼ past ponds to Sonderheim ∼ turn left at the T-junction, then left again into the town.

Sonderheim (Höchstädt a. d. Donau)

In Sonderheim turn right at the T-intersection ∼ after leaving the village, keep left ∼ turn right and follow the bicycle path beside the road to Blindheim ∼ the path ends as you reach the first houses.

Blindheim
prefix: 09074

🏛 **Heimathaus (local history museum)**, Weiherbrunnenstr. 9, ☎ 3239 ◔ Worth seeing this Heimathaus with a statue from the year 1704. The former farmhouse, which is under a preservation order, now houses a museum dealing with work and live in the countryside. @ kse621

Blindheim saw much of the action in what was the costliest battle in the War of the Spanish Succession. The "Book of History" monument on the town square stands as a reminder and call for peace.

Follow the main street, at first called **Höchstädter Straße**, then **Bahnhofstraße**, through Blindheim 〜 **12** turn right on **Mühlstraße** 〜 a bicycle path begins on the left side after 300 m 〜 keep left on the **Hauptstraße** as you reach Gremheim.

Gremheim (Schwenningen (Donau))

❄ Natur-Kneippanlage (Nature Kneipp facility), am Donau-Radweg ㉔, @ tlv464

EXCURSION To reach the Kalteneck water palace in Schwenningen, turn left into the **Jurastraße**.

Schwenningen (Donau)
prefix: 09070

🏰 **Schloss Kalteneck (castle)**, Kirchstr. 26b, ☎ 909940, ☎ 0175/3308280. The oldest surviving parts of the orignal water castle date from before 1140, possibly as early as 950. The castle was rebuilt as a water palace in Renaissance style around 1570.

Follow the **Hauptstraße** through Gremheim 〜 after two right bends you leave the village 〜 turn left on the paved bicycle path before reaching the main road 〜 follow the path up to and over the bridge across the Danube 〜 continue on the bicycle path along the main road until it comes to an end 〜 turn left onto a small road 〜 **13** keep right as you pass the **Ruppenmühle** 〜 you return to the main road 〜 turn left and follow the bicycle path along the main road once again 〜 after 1.3 km you reach a side road, where you turn left towards Donauwörth 〜 follow this road for the next 10 km between fields to Rettingen.

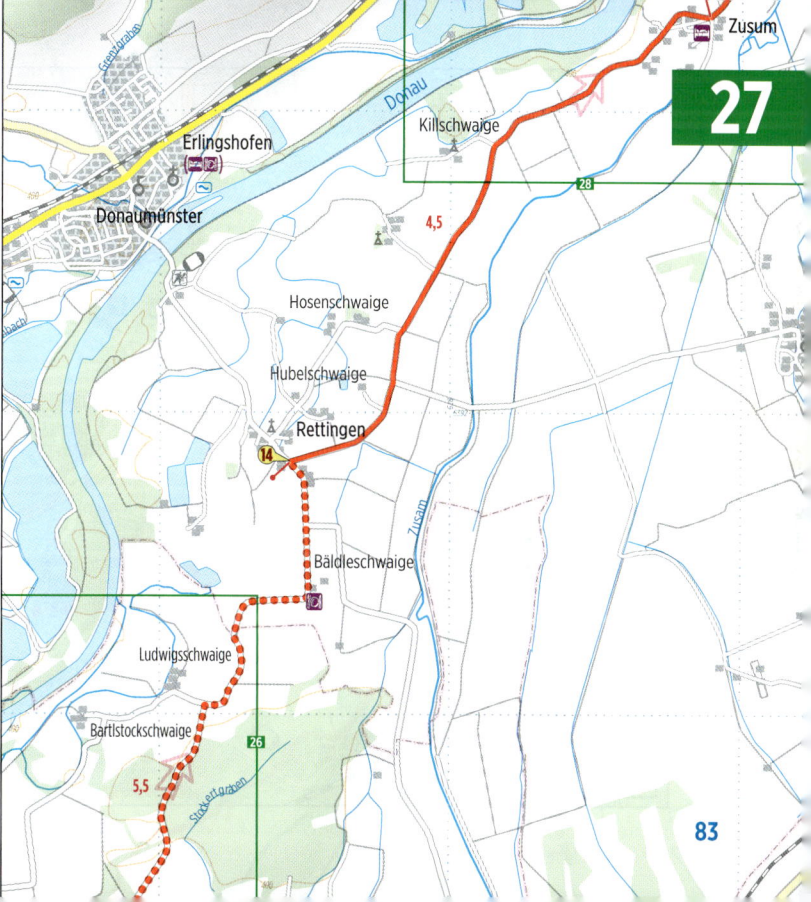

after being awarded the protectorate of the town.

A barracks for soldiers built near the city wall in 1715 is open to the public today. Other surviving remnants of the city wall include the Riedertor, the last of four main entrance gates to the city, and the Färbertor, one of the 38 towers that once guarded the wall.

Among the stories associated with the Holy Cross Abbey is one related to the relic of the holy cross which Graf Mangold I. brought from Byzantium. He had gone to Byzantium for a bride for the Emperor's son, a mission he was unable to fulfil.

Donauwörth to Bertoldsheim   21.7 km

Take the Promenade through the park

From the promenade the bike trail of the Via Claudia Augusta detours. The Romantic Road cycle path runs parallel to the Danube cycle path.

At the end of the park turn left onto the busy **Zirgesheimer Straße** in the industrial estate turn right onto the **Schützenring**, turn left onto **Amorellenwörth** and left onto **Im Weichselwörth** turn right onto **Zirgesheimer Straße** and pass under the large road bridge as you leave Donauwörth a bicycle path along the right side of the road takes you to **Zirgesheim**

As you pass Zirgesheim the bicycle path switches to the left side of the road just before **Altisheim** the path ends follow **Gartenstraße** to the left into the village keep right back down to the main road, where you turn left and continue to Leitheim a bicycle path begins on the right hand side.

Leitheim (Kaisheim)
prefix: 09097

Schloss Leitheim (castle), Schlossstr. 1, ☎ 485980. Once the castle was used as a summer residence for the abbots of Kaisheim, today it is a hotel.

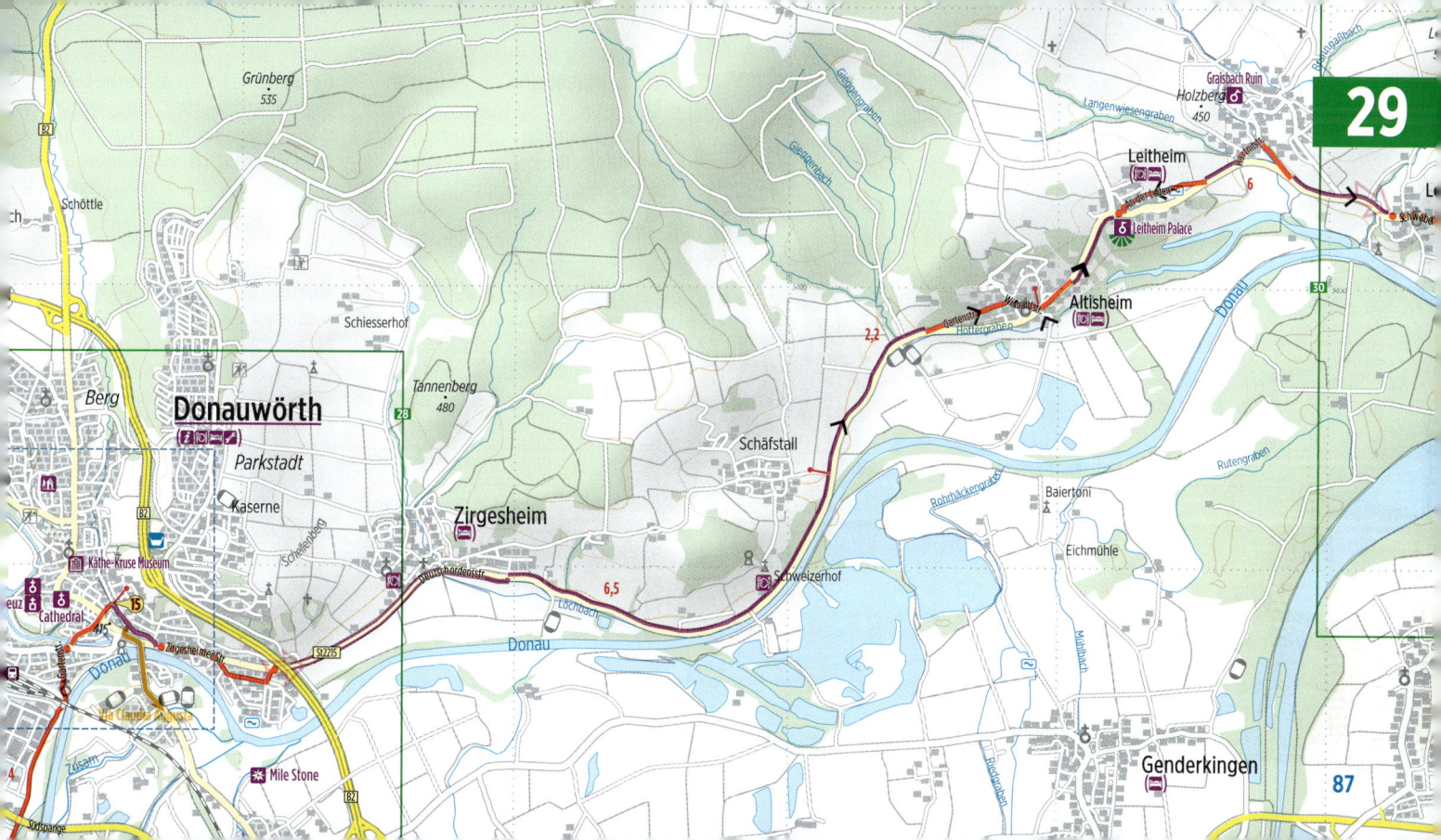

Grünberg
535

Schöttle

B2

Berg

Donauwörth

Parkstadt

Kaserne

Schiesserhof

Tännenberg
480

28

Zirgesheim

Schäfstall

Katre-Kruse Museum

Cathedral

15

Zirgesheimer Str.

St2215

Weintschbordensstr.

B2

Mile Stone

2,2

6,5

Donau

Löchbach

Schweizerhof

Donau

Graisbach Ruin

Holzberg
450

Langenwiesengraben

Leitheim

Leitheim Palace

Altisheim

Waldwirtst.

Gartenstr.

Hollergraben

Baiertoni

Eichmühle

Robrhäckengraben

Rutengraben

Mühlbach

Genderkingen

Donau

6

30

29

87

Schloss Leitheim

On **Schloßstraße** into the village and after a few meters turn left into **Jurastraße** ~ turn right into **An der Leiten**.

Graisbach (Marxheim)

⚔ **Burgruine Graisbach (castle ruin)** ⓦ Presumably constructed around 1130, it was dismantled during the 18th c.

Turn left from the **St 2215** into the **Hartnitstraße** ~ turn right into the **Graf-Reisach-Straße** ~ again along the **St 2215** to **Lechsend**. Follow the main road through the village, then onto the bicycle path along the right side of the main road to Marxheim while enjoying the wonderful view over the Danube valley

Marxheim

ALTERNATIVE If you want to avoid the unpaved bank along the Danube, you have the possibility to drive straight ahead on the asphalted road to Bertoldsheim.

16 Turn right towards Bruck just after the church ~ turn left as you reach Bruck ~ pass the playing field and keep left after the tennis courts ~ follow the unpaved path beside the dike along the Danube until you reach a recreational area with a small jetty ~ keep left here and follow the paved lane into Bertoldsheim ~ straight ahead onto **Seestraße**.

Bertoldsheim (Rennertshofen)

prefix: 08434

ℹ **Markt Rennertshofen (municipal office)**, Marktstr. 18, Rennertshofen, ✆ 94070, @ xmx636

⛪ **Pfarrkirche St. Michael (parish church)**. The Gothic building houses frescoes from around 1430 and is therefore considered to be the oldest in the district. @ nvq731

⛪ **Barockschloss (baroque castle)**. The three-winged castle was built from 1718-30 by Gabriel de Gabrieli, a master builder from Eichstätt. @ hpr227

✳ **Segelsee (sailing lake)**. The Danube dammed near Bertoldsheim is a popular recreational area and the „lake" is used for sailing. @ ipw223

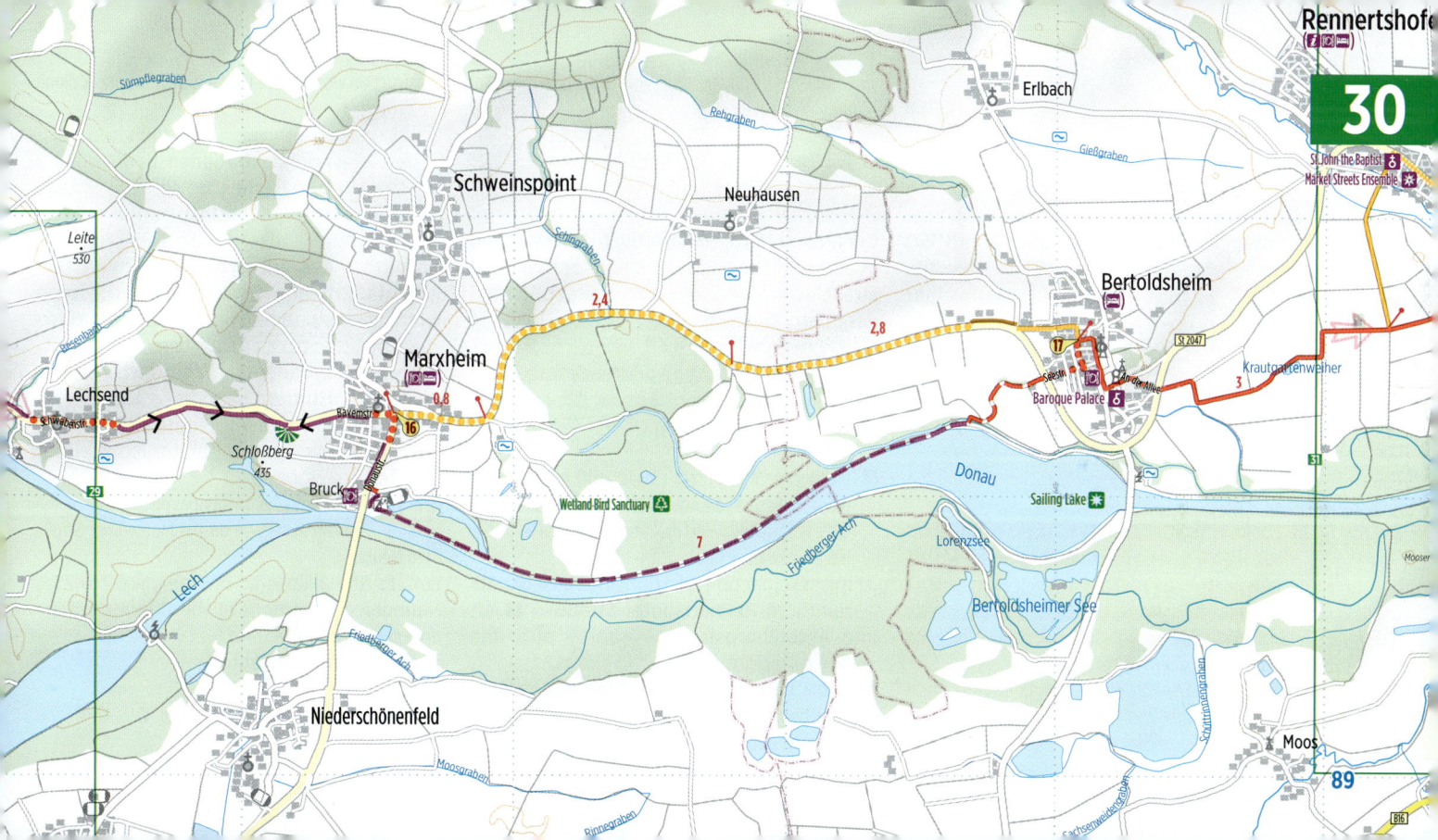

Bertoldsheim to Neuburg   16.7 km

In Bertoldsheim turn left at the next major junction into **Burgheimer Straße** ~ **17** turn right into **Bräuhausstraße** ~ turn right into **Marxheimer Straße** and ride straight past the church ~ turn left and after about 150 m turn right into **An der Allee** ~ cross the St 2047 ~ past the **Krautgartenweiher** pond.

EXCURSION Here you have the opportunity to make an excursion to Rennertshofen.

Rennertshofen

prefix: 08434

ℹ **Markt Rennertshofen (municipal office)**, Marktstr. 18, ✆ 94070, @ xmx636

⛪ **Pfarrkirche St. Johannes der Täufer (parish church)**, Praun-eckg. 4, ✆ 241. The beautiful baroque church dates back to 1702, the tower dates back to 1300 and was heightened in the 18th c.

✳ **Historischer Rundgang (historical tour)**. The tour begins at the kindergarten (Marktstr. 26), is signposted and leads to the most important monuments. @ ymp556

✳ **Marktstraßen-Ensemble (market street)**. Bordered by the Swedish Gate in the West and the Market Gate in the East, you will find houses on Marktstraße that are all listed buildings: the Baroque parish church, the Renaissance town hall (1st half of the 16th c.) and the historic market wall with well preserved gate towers. @ pyf512

✳ **Renaissance-Rathaus (Renaissance town hall)**, Marktstr. 18. Built around 1530 by the Augsburg master builder Sebolt Schönmacher. @ ubf556

Continue along the main route to **Hatzenhofen** ~ at the football pitch turn right onto **Egloff-straße**, which becomes **Hatzenhofer Straße.**

Stepperg (Rennertshofen)

⛪ **Wallfahrtskirche St. Anton und St. Anna (pilgrimage church)**. The small pilgrimage church is picturesquely situated on the Antoniberg, directly above the Danube. With tomb (1676), preserved frescoes and ceiling paintings. Client was baron Dominikus von Servi. @ bap318

⛪ **Dreiflügeliges Schloss (three-winged castle)**. In the 16th c. the people of Wels had the main building built, around 1805 the castle was given its present appearance by the addition of two wings. @ krr425

At the next junction turn right into **Usselstraße** ~ right into **Rennertshofer Straße** ~ **18** left into **Antonibergstraße** ~ shortly after the village turn right.

TIP On the Danube, construction measures for flood protection between Stepperg and Riedensheim will be carried out and will last until 2019. Due to these construction works there may arise disturbances along the cycle route.

Continue zigzag through meadows and fields ~ past a few ponds to **Riedensheim.**

On the **Weberstraße** through the village ~ parallel to the **St 2214** through a small forest, shortly afterwards turn right ~ through the **nature reserve Finkenstein** with its stunning wilderness ~ the path winds its way under magnificent old trees ~ at the edge of the forest turn right to **Bit-tenbrunn** ~ follow the **Weingartenstraße** up to the **Hüldernweg**, here right ~ at the T-junction left into the **Eulatalstraße** ~ after a few meters on the **Monheimer Straße** turn right.

ALTERNATIVE If you want to avoid the unpaved section of the route, you can also cycle on the Monheimer Straße to Neuburg.

Left to the dike and on the dike towards Neuburg ~ turn right at the Danube bridge and cross the river.

Neuburg an der Donau

prefix: 08431

ℹ **Tourist-Information**, Ottheinrichpl. A 118, ✆ 55240, ✆ 55241, @ aka722

Neuburg

🏛 **Schlossmuseum (palace museum)**, Residenzstr. 2, ✆ 64430 ♿ Part of the Bavarian state collection of paintings, Flemish baroque paintings, baroque tombs in the garden, prehistory museum, religious tradition. @ kpx667

🏛 **Stadtmuseum (town museum)**, Amalienstr. A19, ✆ 539053 ♿ In the baroque aristocratic palace from 1517 the history of the city is exhibited on three floors. @ bjd585

⛪ **Studienkirche und Studienseminar (study church and study seminar)**, ✆ 5000. The former Ursuline monastery with its monastery church dating from 1700 now houses a day nursery. @ uyj843

⛪ **Die Münz (former mint)**. Castle from 1200 built on a prehistoric Celtic defensive position. Served as a mint in the 16th c. Restored in 1989.

⛪ **Residenzschloss (residential palace)**, Residenzstr. 2. The mighty Renaissance chateau from the beginning of the 16th c. was built by Count Palatine Ottheinrich as a residence. The baroque east wing with its striking round towers visible from afar was added in the 1660s. Particularly worth seeing is the courtyard façade decorated with sgraffito towers.

Also worth seeing are the castle chapel, the oldest Protestant church in the world, the castle museum and the state gallery.

✳ **Hofapotheke (court pharmacy)**, Karlspl. 52. The baroque building from the 18th c. now houses a jazz club in the vaulted cellar.

✳ **Provinzialbibliothek (provincial library)**. Early Rococo structure from the 18th c. designed by F. M. v. Loew, Baroque chamber in the upper floor. Library since 1803. @ wrh688

✳ **Rathaus (town hall)**. The Renaissance building from the beginning of the 17th c. houses the municipal art gallery on the ground floor.

✳ **Weveldhaus**, Amalienstr. A19. The aristocratic palace with Renaissance and Baroque features and magnificent stucco rooms now houses the town museum.

🏊 **Freibad Brandlbad (outdoor pool)**, Unterer Brandl 1, ✆ 538-497, @ qlh445

🏊 **Parkbad (indoor pool)**, Ludwig-Thoma-Pl. 1, ✆ 61980, @ enl441

From 742 to 801 Neuburg was a bishopric seat. It first became part of Bavaria in 1247, and then became the residential seat of the principality of Palatinate-Neuburg in 1505. In 1777 it returned to

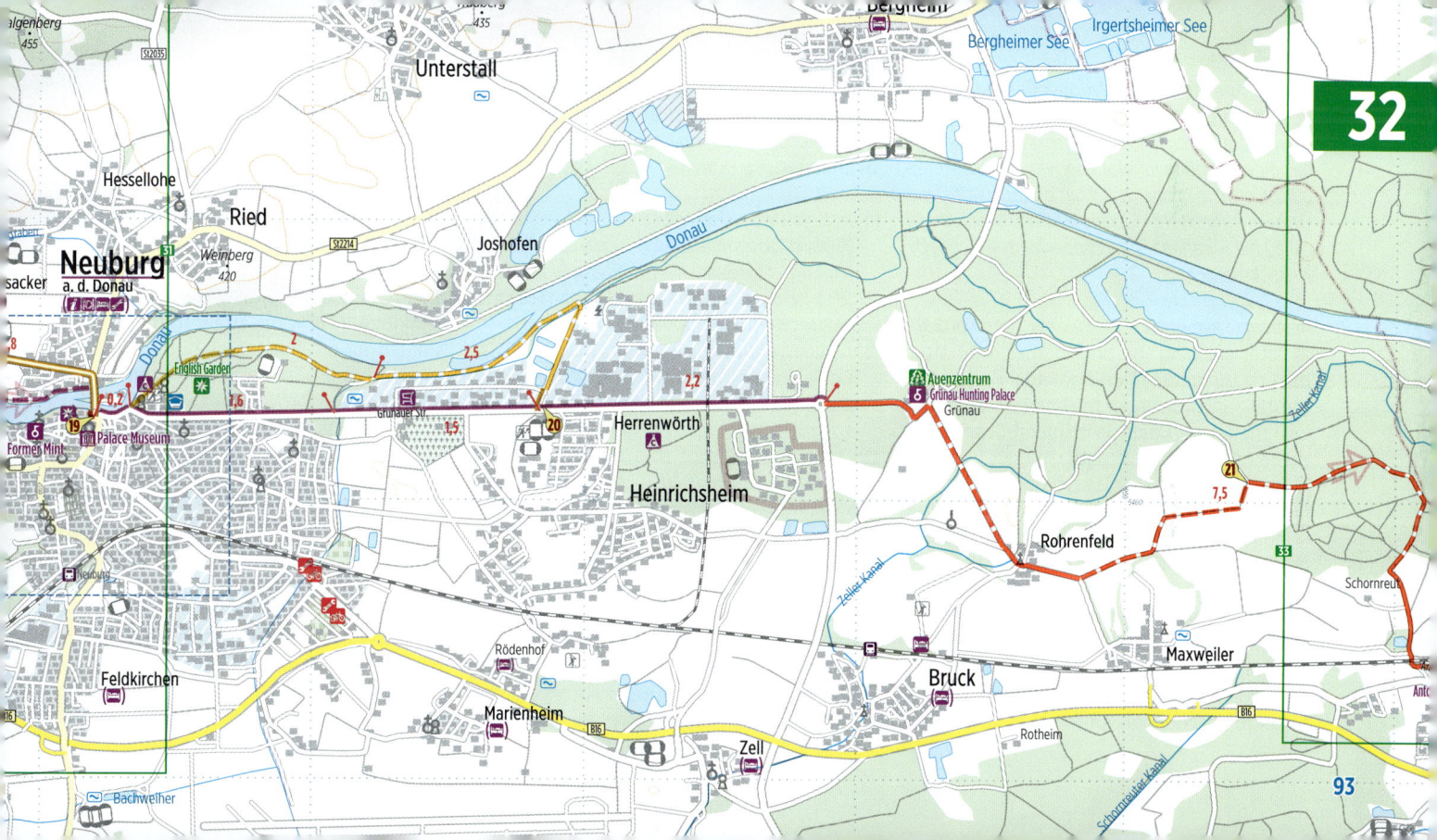

Bavaria. The most distinctive structure in the small city is the large Neuburg palace, which some call the most beautiful renaissance palace on the Danube. It has an enchanting interior courtyard with 2-storey balconies. The chapel was built on orders of Duke Ottheinrich between 1530 and 1550 and is sometimes called the Bavarian Sistine chapel for its frescoes by H. Bocksberger.

Neuburg to Ingolstadt   24.9 km

19 After crossing the bridge, turn right after the first building ～ turn right again in front of the gate and ride under the bridge ～ continue into the street **Oskar Wittmann Straße** and ride along the bicycle path.

For all those who prefer to cycle directly along the Danube, we can recommend a side route. Turn left at the Donau Ruderclub/Camping Donau Ruderclub and cycle along the Danube behind the dam. After the old branch of the Danube turn right over the bridge onto the **Ochsengründlweg**, follow this until you reach Grünauer Straße, where you come back to the main route.

20 Continue straight on the bicycle path past the industrial area ～ ride straight ahead through the roundabout towards the Grünau Palace.

The Au (wetland) begins east of this roundabout. The royal hunting lodge Grünau and is located less than a kilometer past the main road.

Grünau (Neuburg an der Donau)
prefix: 08431

🛏 **Jagdschloss Grünau (hunting lodge)**, ✆ 647590. Count Palatine Ottheinrich had this romantic palace complex built around 1530 in the style of the early German Renaissance for his wife Susanna. The exhibition of the wetland information centre is located on the ground floor. @ hjq435

🏛 **Auenzentrum Neuburg/Donau (wetland centre)**, ✆ 6475920. Various exhibitions, theme trails and educational offerings provide information about the habitats, development and significance of the floodplains. @ wjs233

On the other side of the palace turn right and ride to Rohrenfeld ～ keep left at the fork and ride out of the village ～ in the right bend turn left into the gravel lane, which you follow between fields ～ **21** at the beginning of the village left onto **Am Anger** ～ at the first possibility left across the Ach stream ～ immediately after the bridge straight on **Achstraße**.

Weichering

🛏 **St. Vitus**, Kirchweg 2. After the medieval predecessor church had been repeatedly destroyed by wars and storms over the centuries, it was decided at the beginning of the 20th c. to build

a new church. The present neo-Romanesque church, built with red clinker bricks, was finally consecrated in 1903.

🏛 **Antoniuskapelle (chapel)**. The small chapel was erected a few years after the new St. Vitus church was built on the site of the old main church.

✳ **Naherholungsgebiet „Niederforst" Weichering (local recreation area)**. The two bathing lakes are remnants of the gravel mining of the 1970s and 1980s. Restaurant, kiosk, toilets, etc.

You pass under the railway line and proceed straight ～ follow the street to the left over a small bridge ～ immediately turn right onto a paved lane ～ continue straight onto the unpaved path through the wooded floodplain until you pass a house next to the track **22**.

Here you have access to an unpaved path that follows the river into the city. You rejoin the main route by the park after the barrage.

Continue straight on the bicycle path along the dike into Ingolstadt ～ you ride past the Glacisbrücke and then the Konrad-Adenauer-Brücke.

The historic centre of Ingolstadt on the other bank of the river can be easily reached across the Konrad-Adenauer-Brücke.

Ingolstadt
prefix: 0841

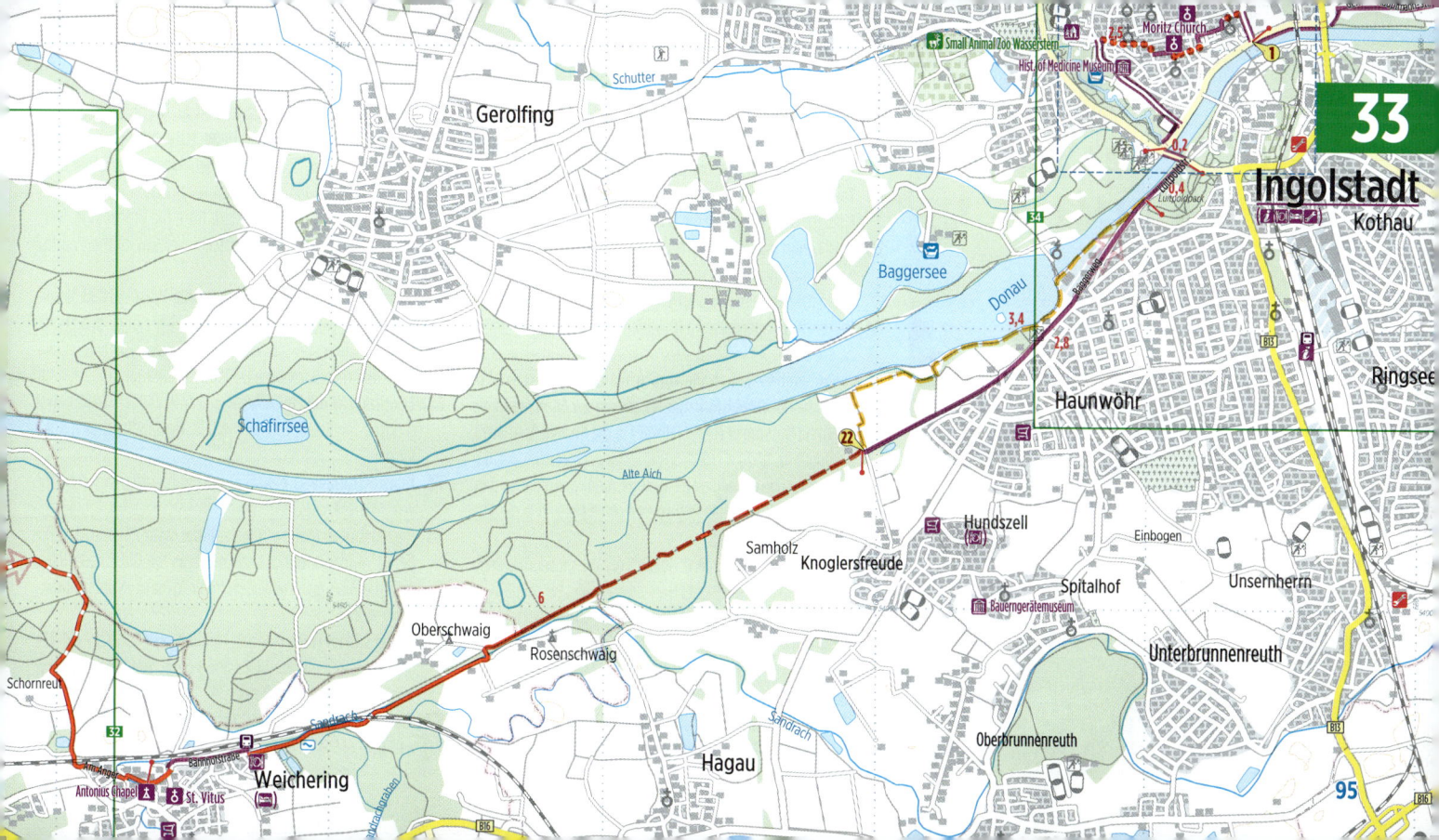

33

Gerolfing

Schutter

🦌 Small Animal Zoo Wasserstein

Hist. of Medicine Museum

Moritz Church

2.5

1

0.2

Ingolstadt

Kothau

34

Baggersee

Donau

3,4

2.8

Haunwöhr

Ringsee

B16

22

Schafirrsee

Alte Aich

Hundszell

Einbogen

Samholz

Knoglersfreude

Spitalhof

Unsernherrn

Bauerngerätemuseum

6

Oberschwaig

Rosenschwäig

Unterbrunnenreuth

Sandrach

Oberbrunnenreuth

Schornreut

Sandrach

32

Hagau

Bahnhofstraße

Weichering

Antonius Chapel

St. Vitus

B16

B16

Ingolstadt

ℹ Tourist Information im Ingolstadt Outlet Shopping Village, Otto-Hahn Str. 1, ☎ 8863100, @ cec211

ℹ Tourist-Information am Hauptbahnhof (tourist information at the main station), Elisabethstr. 3, ☎ 3053005, @ ghh744

ℹ Tourist-Information am Rathausplatz (at the town hall square), Moritzstr. 19, ☎ 3053030, @ bco258

🏛 Audi Forum Ingolstadt, Auto-Union Str. 1, ☎ 2834444 ♿ How has automotive engineering and Audi developed? You can find out in the museum. @ pqg176

🏛 Bayerisches Armeemuseum (Bavarian Army Museum), Paradepl. 4, ☎ 93770 ♿ Topics: Bavaria's military history in a European context from the late Middle Ages to modern times. @ wna357

🏛 Deutsches Medizinhistorisches Museum in der Alten Anatomie (German Museum of Medical History in the Ancient Anatomy), Anatomiestr. 18-20, ☎ 3052860 ♿ History of medicine, permanent exhibition on medical technology, medicinal plant garden, museum café and changing special exhibitions in a medical context. @ hqh614

🏛 Fleißhaus, Kupferstr. 18, ☎ 3051885 ♿ The museum is dedicated to the Ingolstadt poet Marieluise Fleißer. @ dmd817

🏛 Museum für Konkrete Kunst (museum of concrete art), Tränktorstr. 6-8, ☎ 3051871 ♿ How diverse Concrete Art has developed since its beginnings can be discovered through the exhibits of the museum. @ gcw874

🏛 Spielzeugmuseum (toy museum), Auf der Schanz 45, ☎ 3051881, ☎ 3051885 ♿ The museum is sure to make the hearts of the young and young-at-heart beat faster: a wide variety of toys from 1900 to the present day are on display here. @ bur261

🏛 Stadtmuseum im Kavalier Hepp (city museum), Auf der Schanz 45, ☎ 3051885, ☎ 3051881 ♿ Ingolstadt's history is not only rich in cars and oil, also some important archaeological finds, such as an amber necklace from the Bronze Age, were made here. The museum offers an overview of the eventful history of the city. @ gdq562

⛪ Asamkirche Maria de Victoria, Neubaustr. 11/2, ☎ 934150. Simple and inconspicuous from the outside, since not even a church tower announces the sacred building, the splendour only unfolds inside the church from the 1730s. @ hos267

⛪♿ Moritzkirche mit Pfeifturm, Moritzstr. 2, ☎ 934150. The oldest church in Ingolstadt was built in 1234. Next to the church is the former Gothic watchtower.

⛪ Münster (cathedral), ☎ 934150. Late Gothic hall church from the year 1425. @ svr133

⛪ Herzogskasten (palas of the medieval castle), Hallstr. 2-4. The Gothic secular building, also known as the Old Palace, dates from the 13th c. and is nowadays home to the city's public library, @ fxo686

⛪ Neues Schloss (new palace), Paradepl. 4, ☎ 9377222 ♿ The castle was built in the 1430s and houses the Bavarian Army Museum in these days. @ hnq361

✳ Kreuztor (cross gate). The Cross Gate (1385) is the only medieval gate of the second city wall still preserved.

- 🏞 **Kleinzoo Wasserstern (small animal zoo)**, Gerolfinger Str./Aloisweg 19, 📞 86421, 📞 0176/43002631 📅 Various animal species are at home in the small zoo: monkeys, reptiles, birds, etc. @ hik135
- 🌳 **Klenzepark**, Brückenkopf 4 📅 The park, situated next to the Danube, was built in the 19th c. as part of the fortress, there is also a beautiful rose garden. @ cjb666
- 🏊 **Freibad (outdoor pool)**, Jahnstr. 27, 📞 804550, @ hvy633
- 🏊 **Naherholungsgebiet Baggersee (local recreation area quarry pond)**, Mitterschüttweg. Water playground, game park, miniature golf, Kneipp facility, kiosk, etc. @ vcf318
- 🏊 **Donautherme Wonnemar (thermal bath)**, Südliche Ringstr. 63, 📞 379110, @ aku882
- 🏊 **Hallenbad (indoor pool)**, Lindberghstr. 71, 📞 804540, @ inh561

Ingolstadt (pop. 120,000) offers something for just about every visitor, but especially for anyone interested in art and history.

The earliest known record of the city documents that it already existed in 806. Ingolstadt gained city status in 1250. The most significant structures in the city include the large late gothic cathedral, the Neues Schloss, and the rococo Maria de Victoria church, which contains the so-called Lepanto monstrace. Created by the Augsburg goldsmith Johann Zeckel over the course of 30 years, it depicts the victory over the Turkish fleet at Lepanto in 1571.

Fans of horror stories can pursue the legend of Frankenstein's monster. Mary Shelley set her novel "Frankenstein, or, The Modern Prometheus" in Ingolstadt. For hot and tired cyclists looking for refreshment, what could be more welcome than a stein of Bavarian beer? It was in Ingolstadt that the famous Bavarian "Reinheitsgebot" or "purity law" was first drafted in 1516 to assure the quality of beer. The city once boasted 25 breweries. Today only four remain, but the product they brew is considered some of the best beer in the world.

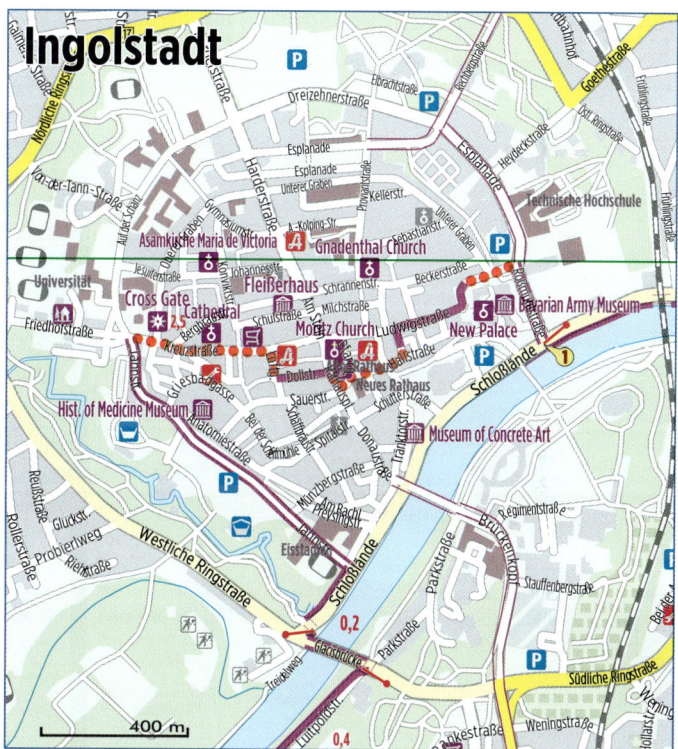

Ingolstadt to Regensburg

92 km

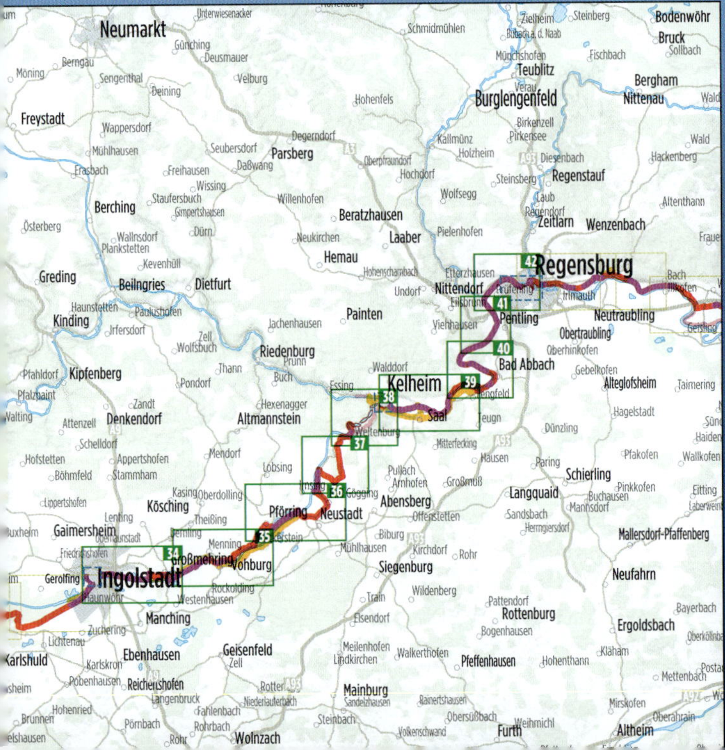

m/km: ↗ 2.4 (221m) ↘ 2.8 (255m) cycle path: 58 % unpaved: 41 % busy road: 11 %

The third stage of your ride begins in Ingolstadt. The first kilometers follow the still-placid Danube to the small city of Vohburg with its city walls and gates that have witnessed some 1200 years of history. The Danube then enters a more dramatic stretch, as it enters the narrow gorge where the river's waters have forced their way through the Franconian Jura mountains between Weltenburg and Kelheim. We recommend taking a boat for this short stretch, which is much more relaxing and enjoyable than the route over the hills, and offers spectacular views of the breathtaking scenery. After Kelheim the river makes another couple of bends before reaching its northern most point in Regensburg. This spectacular city offers everything a tourists heart desires.

Most of this stage follows quiet country lanes, car-free bicycle paths and paths along the river. There are, however, several short stretches with heavier traffic and a few brief climbs.

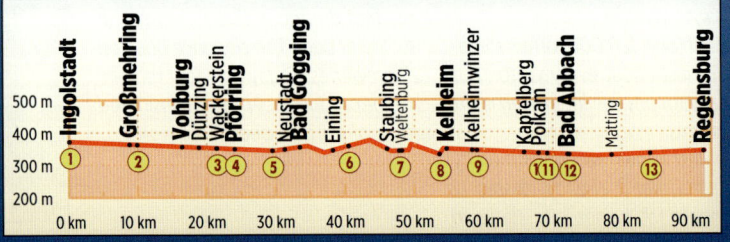

Ingolstadt, Kreuztor

Ingolstadt see page 94

Ingolstadt to Vohburg 16.5 km

1 You leave Ingolstadt on the cycle path along the **Schlosslände** ～ cross under the railway and Schiller bridges ～ follow the unpaved path on the dam.

ALTERNATIVE Before the route enters Kleinmehring it passes over a very narrow bridge, which is difficult to pass when towing a trailer. Those who wish can therefore continue straight ahead along the dike to Großmehring or even as far as the barrage at Vohburg, which bypasses the busy bridge by Großmehring!

Turn left after the power station ～ by the main road turn left ～ follow the trail, keeping right ～ turn right as you reach a street, then immediately left into the narrow path ～ turn right and pass under the main road ～ continue along **Nibelungenstraße** ～ keep right into **Uferstraße** ～ at the end of the street you reach the **Donaustraße**, the centre of Großmehring lies to the left.

Großmehring

prefix: 08407

ℹ **Gemeinde Großmehring (municipal office)**, Marienpl. 7, ✆ 92940, @ qpy271

8 **Pfarrkriche Unserer Lieben Frau (parish church)**, Regensburger Str. 5. The parish church with the steep roof dates back to the 1st half of the 13th c., although several conversions were carried out in the following centuries: The new choir was added in the late Gothic period, the tower superstructure in the Baroque period. A common entrance hall connects the church with the new St. Wolfgang's Church next door.

Turn right and immediately right again into a small street over a bridge.

ALTERNATIVE To stay on the north bank, turn left after the small bridge, then right after the underpass and through another underpass to the track along the river.

Otherwise continue straight ahead and make your way up to the bridge and cross the Danube ～ continue on the unpaved trail along the river bank ～ keep right by the barrage, where the route along the north bank rejoins the main route from the left ～ after crossing a small bridge take the next turn to the left onto the path along the top of the dike ～ follow the dike into Vohburg ～ **2** on the south bank turn left onto the unpaved Danube dam ～ in the left bend and at the Danube turn right and now directly along the river to Vohburg.

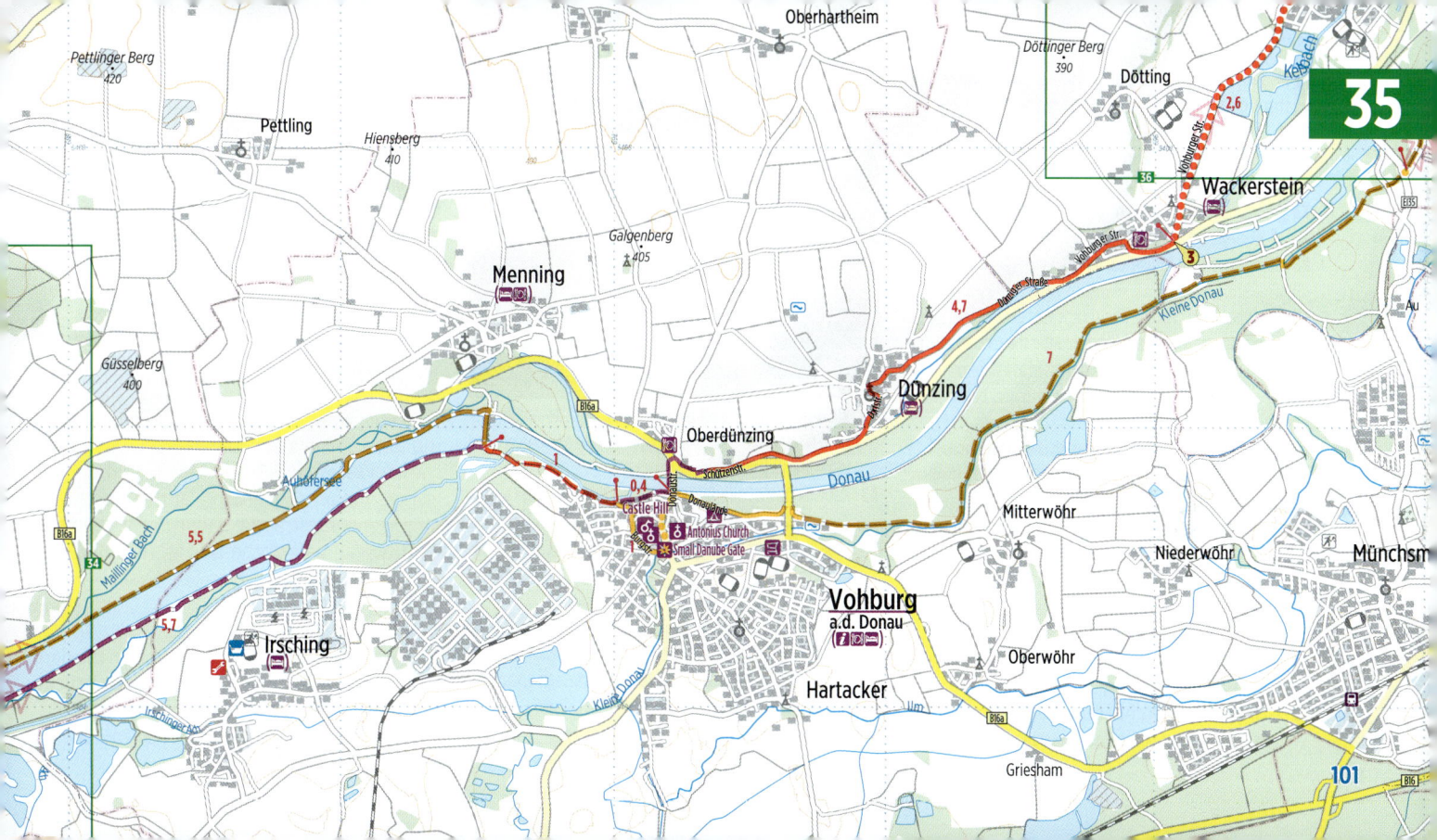

Oberhartheim

Döttinger Berg
390

Dötting

Pettlinger Berg
420

Pettling

Hiensberg
410

Galgenberg
405

Menning

Gusselberg
400

B16a

Oberdünzing

Dünzing

Wackerstein

36

3

Kleine Donau

Au

E355

2,6

4,7

7

Donau

Mitterwöhr

Niederwöhr

Münchsm

Schützenstr.

Castle Hill

Antonius Church

Small Danube Gate

Irsching

Vohburg
a.d. Donau

Hartacker

Oberwöhr

Griesham

34

Maillinger Bach

Auhöfersee

Kleine Donau

Ilm

B16a

B16

101

5,5

5,7

0,4

1

35

In Vohburg you can also take a short round trip through the city centre by following **Auertorstraße** to **Burgstraße** and **Donaustraße**.

Vohburg an der Donau

prefix: 08457

- ℹ️ **Tourismusbüro (tourism office)**, Agnes-Bernauer-Str. 1, ☎ 9369700, @ nnn833
- ℹ️ **Stadtverwaltung (municipal office)**, Ulrich-Steinberger-Pl. 12, ☎ 92920, @ nch578
- **Antoniuskirche**, Stadtpl. The church was built in 1727 by the Franciscans as a monastery church. After the secularisation of the monastery, the building was first used as a storeroom, then as a theatre hall and finally as a horse stable, before it was returned to the church in 1880.
- **Stadtpfarrkirche St. Peter (city parish church)** @ emf684
- **Burgberg (castle hill)**. The only remains of the former medieval castle complex are the renovated circular walls, the gate and a semi-circular tower. The interior of the complex has been used as a municipal cemetery for many years.
- **Wasserturm (watertower)**. At the top of the castle hill is the mighty water tower from 1959, which serves as a water tank and holds around 200 m³.
- ✳️ **Auertor (gate)**. The massive, simple Gothic gate from the 15th c. is located in the west of the city.
- ✳️ **Groß-Donau-Tor (Large Danube gate)**. The city gate in the north near the river dates back to the 15th century.

The boat Kelheim in the Danube gorge

- ✳️ **Klein-Donau-Tor (small Danube gate)**. The late-Gothic gate from 1471 forms the southern entrance to the town square and is the town's landmark.
- ✳️ **Rathaus (town hall)**, Donaustr. 15, ☎ 92920. From the former Andreaskirche of 1270, a modern town hall has developed. The church was used for religious purposes until 1880, when it was profaned and temporarily used as a warehouse, fire station or gymnasium. In 2007 the town hall moved in.

From the very beginning, the castle hill formed the centre of origin and development of this town on the Danube. Findings from the 1970s indicate that the mountain was already inhabited in 1500 BC.

From Vohburg you now have a choice of two routes to Neustadt a. d. Donau. The main route takes you via Pförring along the north bank, the alternative route takes you on mostly unpaved paths directly along the dike on the south bank, but it is not signposted.

South Bank alternative   13 km

For the alternative on the path on the dam to **Donaustraße** ～ cross the road straight ahead and onto the **Donaulände** ～ pass under the bridge ～ straight ahead and along the Kleine Donau ～ turn right at the **Wackerstein training area** and cross the Kleine Donau ～ after the bridge immediately turn left ～ cross EI 35 ～ pass **manor Giesenau** ～ at the crossroads at the manor straight ahead ～ at the dam continue ～ before the bridge (B 299) keep right ～ immediately turn left again ～ cross the B 299 ～ take a right turn ～ straight ahead onto the cycle path **5**.

On the main route cycle on the path on the dam to **Donaustraße** ～ left over the **Donaubrücke bridge** ～ then right into **Schützenstraße** ～ onto the bike path next to the road to Dünzing

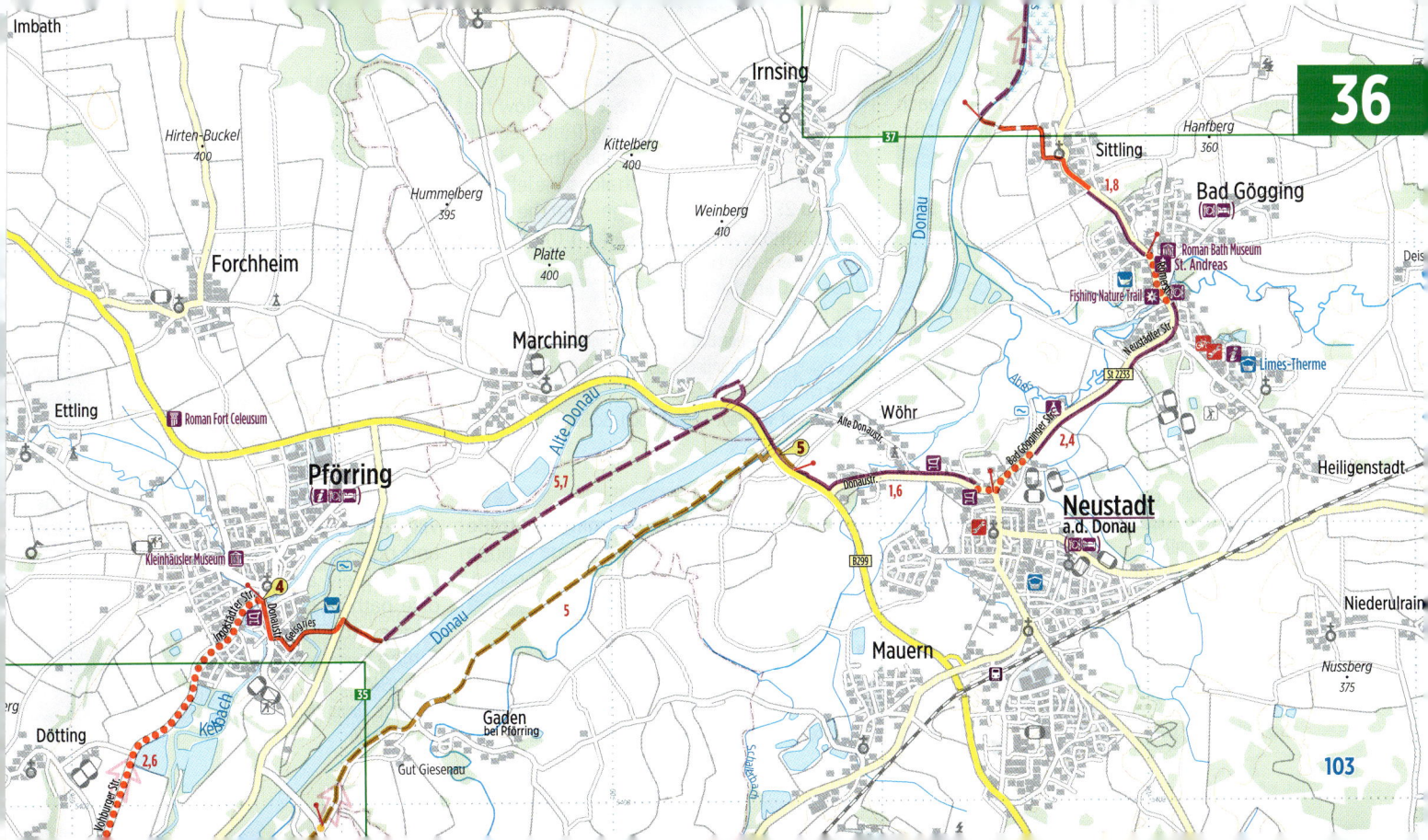

Imbath

Irnsing

Hirten-Buckel
400

Kittelberg
400

Hummelberg
395

Weinberg
410

Forchheim

Platte
400

Marching

Donau

Ettling

Roman Fort Celeusum

Alte Donau

Pförring

5,7

Wöhr

Alte Donau str.

Donaustr.

1,6

5

Kleinhäusler Museum

4

Donaustr.

Donau

5

Gaden
bei Pförring

Dötting

Keibach

2,6

Volburger Str.

Gut Giesenau

Schergenh.

Mauern

B299

B299

36

Hanfberg
360

Sittling

1,8

Bad Gögging

Roman Bath Museum
St. Andreas

Fishing Nature Trail

Neustädter Str.

Abfa

St. 2233

Limes-Therme

Bad Gögginger Str.

2,4

Deis

Heiligenstadt

Neustadt
a.d. Donau

Niederulrain

Nussberg
375

Weltenburg monastery

Weltenburg (Kelheim)

prefix: 09441

Zillen, ☎ 701234 🛥 As an alternative to the ships, small barges travel between Weltenburg and Kelheim. @ eon123

Schiffsverkehr zwischen Weltenburg und Kelheim (shipping traffic), pier at Weltenburg Monastery, ☎ 5858 🛥, @ dqf623

Kloster Weltenburg (monastery), Asamstr. 32, ☎ 6757500. The oldest monastery in Bavaria was founded around 617. In the 18th c. the monastery church was given its present form by the Asam brothers. The monastery brewery, founded in 1050, houses a brewery museum and offers daily guided tours. @ tdu686

The magnificent Weltenburg Abbey is believed to be the oldest monastery in Bavaria. The ceiling frescoes in the abbey church of the venerable old complex were created by the brothers Cosmas Damian and Egid Quirin Asam and are considered masterworks of baroque design. It depicts a heavenly Jerusalem soaring above the church nave and is so perfectly executed that the viewer cannot see transitions in the decoration.

TIP If you are travelling outside shipping hours, you can cycle to Kelheim on an unpaved forest path with a steep gradient.

The Danube gorge

The boat that shuttles between Weltenburg and Kelheim passes through a narrow valley of overwhelming beauty. It has taken eons for the river to carve this narrow path through the Franconian Jura ridge. The result is a winding narrow gorge of white cliffs that rise from beneath the river's surface to heights of almost 100 meters, and reduce the river's width to less than 70 meters.

The way in which the bizarre shapes of the rocks seem to push and shove each other and change shapes as the boat passes has inspired river travellers to give them names and invent fantastic stories about the gorge. There are the "three brothers" who turned to stone when two of them attempted to drown the third in the Danube's waters. There is the "stone pulpit" from which Luther is said to have preached to the fishermen, plus a "Bavarian lion" and the "pious bishop" who prays for the souls of the monks at Weltenburg.

In addition to these nature-made spectacles, the gorge offers cultural highlights, especially Weltenburg Abbey, which is said to be the oldest in Bavaria. It was founded in the year 610 by Columban monks. The brothers Cosmas Damian and Egid Quirin Asam helped build the current structures and painted the famous ceiling frescoes in the abbey church.

Hall of liberation

At the end of the spectacular ride through the gorge there is another impressive edifice on a bluff above the river just upstream from Kelheim. It is the Hall of Liberation, or Befreiungshalle, commissioned by King Ludwig I and built by Leo von Klenze, who was also responsible for the Hall of Fame, or Walhalla, a few kilometers further downstream. The Befreiungshalle was erected in memory of those who contributed to Germany's liberation from Napoleon's rule. Inside the circular structure stand eighteen oversized winged angels holding hands.

Kelheim, Hall of liberation

In the lower Altmühl valley between Kelheim and Dietfurt you can experience an exciting journey through time in Bavaria's largest archaeological park. Numerous sculptures and replicas in 18 different places can be explored by bike or on foot. Detailed information is available at the Tourist Information Kelheim. In map 38 you will find the stations marked as violet dots with the corresponding number (dot **1** in Kelheim).

1 Kelheim Old Town

In the town's Archaeological Museum you will find information about the archaeological park and you can also visit finds from the last millennia in the Gothic „Zehnthof".

2 Kelheim-Michelsberg

Behind the Liberation Hall an early Celtic post slotted wall was reconstructed–dating from around 450 BC.

3 Kelheim-Gronsdorf

Immediately close to the Gronsdorfer lock you can admire a wooden city gate with wall remains from the Celtic period. About 2.100 years ago, the city could only be entered through such a gate.

Kelheim

prefix: 09441

- **Tourist-Information**, Ludwigspl. 1, ✆ 701-234, @ bjj537
- **Personenschifffahrt auf der Donau (Passenger navigation on the Danube)**, ✆ 5858 Regular service between Kelheim and Weltenburg, additionally regular service through the Altmühltal and on the Main-Danube Canal, excursions. @ aka756
- **Personenschifffahrt im Altmühltal (passenger shipping in the Altmühltal valley)**, ✆ 5858. Regular service between Kelheim, Essing and Riedenburg between May and Oct. @ hxw374
- **Archäologisches Museum (archeological museum)**, Ledererg. 11, ✆ 10409, ✆ 10492 Permanent exhibition on the settlement history of the Danube and Altmühl valleys. Presentation of the city history „Kelheim - city in the river". Annual special exhibitions. @ oct635
- **Befreiungshalle Kelheim (liberation hall)**, Befreiungshallestr. 3, ✆ 682070 The imposing building is reminiscent of the Napoleonic Wars of Liberation 1813-1815. 34 larger-than-life marble goddesses of victory form a circle in the 48m high cupola hall. 174 steps lead over the colonnade gallery on the upper floor to the viewing platform, from which you have a fantastic view over the Danube city. @ yfr837
- **Orgelmuseum in der Franziskanerkirche (organ museum)**, Am Kirchensteig 4, ✆ 7750 The monastery church is decorated with Gothic and Baroque frescoes from 1471-1803. The

Regensburg

station the Danube cycle path continues along the Danube

ALTERNATIVE Here you have the opportunity to change to the route along the south bank, thus avoiding the heavy traffic along the main road by Kapfelberg and Poikam.

To take the main route along the north bank from Kelheimwinzer, **9** continue straight along the dike past the pumping station ⤳ turn right after passing under the bridge and follow the

gravel path along the Danube to Hermsaal ⤳ keep right by the houses, then right again at the T-intersection ⤳ after a short distance turn right and continue on the path along the river bank until you reach the main road ⤳ here you must ride with the traffic to Kapfelberg ⤳ turn right after the playing field onto **Am Yachthafen** ⤳ follow the road past the Marina and along the Danube to Poikam.

Poikam

After the left bend you reach an intersection by the railway underpass **10** ⤳ turn right into **Dorfstraße** and ride through the underpass ⤳ continue to the next 4-way intersection. Turn right and ride to the main road ⤳ turn right again and ride over the bridge across the Danube ⤳ turn right at the end of the bridge ⤳ then right again to pass under the bridge ⤳ **11** a bicycle path begins to the right immediately after the bridge ⤳ turn right into the paved path to the underpass under the main road, then turn left onto Kaiser-Karl-V.-Allee ⤳ ride through the pedestrian zone.

Bad Abbach
prefix: 09405

🛈 **Kurverwaltung / Tourist-Information**, Kaiser-Karl-V.-Allee 5, ✆ 95990, @ ipc435

🏛 **Heinrichsturm (Heinrich tower)**, Schlossberg, ✆ 95990, 🕐 can only be viewed from the outside. It is one of the oldest round towers in southern Germany and the landmark of Bad Abbach. @ xgx722

✳ **Kurpark (spa gardens)**, Kaier-Karl-V.-Allee 🕐 In the spa park there is an animal enclosure, the healing water hall, a Kneipp facility, a miniature golf course, and much more. @ rvh821

✉ **Inselbad (outdoor pool)**, Inselstr. 2a, ✆ 940623, @ lab766

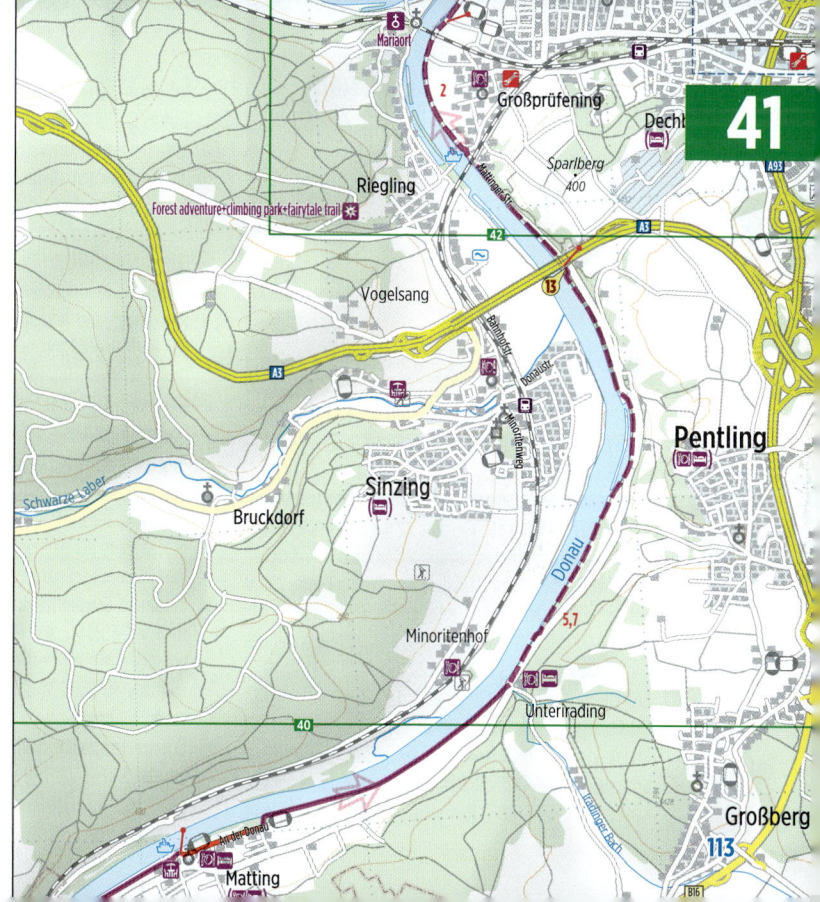

Kaiser-Therme (hot springs), Kurallee 4, ✆ 95170, @ sly552

Bad Abbach to Regensburg   19.5 km

In the right bend of Kaiser-Heinrich-II.-Straße/Regensburger Straße follow straight on the Oberndorfer Straße ~ 12 past the pedestrian and bicycle bridge ~ at the first houses turn left into the gravel path along the dike past Oberndorf.

Oberndorf (Bad Abbach)
prefix: 09405

❀ **Historisches Bauernhaus (historical farmhouse)**, Donaustr. 56, ✆ 957808. The oldest remains of the wall date back to around 1150, probably a wooden farm had already stood on the site of the house. Today you can even stay overnight in the oldest farm, in the former barn there is a guesthouse. @ wbo444

By the main road continue on the paved bicycle path, which takes you along the bank of the Danube to Matting.

Matting (Pentling)
prefix: 09405

⛴ **Historische Gierseilfähre (historical yaw ferry)**, ✆ 92082-13 🚲, @ scx356

Continue on the path along the river bank ~ 13 you pass below a road bridge ~ the cycle path takes you directly to Regensburg.

█ You are now in the centre of one of the most impressive cities of Europe. Take time to explore the medieval streets and alleys of Regensburg's extensive historic centre, which boasts a great variety of impressive historic architecture.

Regensburg
prefix: 0941

ℹ **Tourist-Information Altes Rathaus (Tourist information old town hall)**, Rathauspl. 4, ✆ 507-4410, ✆ 507-4411, @ wyr155

ℹ **Zentrale Zimmervermittlung (central accommodation service)**, Rathauspl. 4, ✆ 5074410

ℹ **Tourismusbüro Landkreis Regensburg (Tourist office)**, Altmühlstr. 3, ✆ 4009495, @ qoe638

⛴ **Donauschifffahrt Wurm + Noé (Danube shipping)**, Osteng. 3, ✆ 50277880. „Strudelrund-

The East Gate at Blue Hour

fahrt" (swirl ride) and various theme tours, Walhalla tour with the Crystal Fleet from historical „Wurstkuchl Nr. 3" / Steinerne Brücke. @ ide615

🚢 **Regensburger Personenschifffahrt Klinger GmbH (passenger shipping)**, Thundorfer Str., ☎ 52104. swirl and lock rides on the Danube and Walhalla rides from the Steinerne Brücke. @ cfp627

🏛 **Besucherzentrum Welterbe Regensburg (Visitor Centre World Heritage Regensburg)**, Weisse-Lamm G. 1, ☎ 5075410 ® Impressive exhibits and objects as well as interactive play stations and media installations await you on two floors. @ gyp451

🏛 **Brückturm-Museum**, Weiße-Lamm-G. 1, ☎ 5075410, ☎ 5075888 ® Objects and information about the history of the Stone Bridge and the Danube navigation. @ jne744

🏛 **document Kepler-Gedächtnishaus (Kepler memorial house)**, Keplerstr. 5, ☎ 5073442 ☺ Here you can learn everything about the life and work of the astronomer and mathematician Johannes Kepler (1571-1630). @ yps438

🏛 **document Neupfarrplatz**, Neupfarrpl. 1, ☎ 5071442. Underground showrooms at Neupfarrplatz (Roman period, medieval Jewish quarter, early modern period and National Socialist period). Access only with guided tour. Ticket sales at Tabak Götz, Dompl. 6. @ her177

🏛 **document Niedermünster**, Niedermünsterg. 4, ☎ 5971662. Registration and Info: Information Centre DOMPLATZ 5, Tel. 597-1660: One of the largest archaeological excavations in Germany is opening under the 12th c. Romanesque Niedermünster Church. @ xyo442

🏛 **document Reichstag**, Altes Rathaus, ☎ 5074410 © Historical Reichssaal in the Old Town Hall with Reichstag Museum. Here you will find documents on the history of the Reichsversammlung and the Reichstag in Regensburg. There are several guided tours per day, only with advance reservation due to limited number of participants. @ dkm723

🏛 **document Schnupftabakfabrik (snuff factory)**, Gesandtenstr. 3-5, ☎ 5073442. Authentic impression of the art of tobacco production in a medieval residential palace. Access by guided tour only: Fri-Sun 2.30 p.m., ticket sale at Café Anna, Gesandtenstr. 5. @ bcf561

🏛 **Domschatzmuseum (Cathedral treasure Museum)**, Krauterermarkt 3, ☎ 5972575 ® On display are works of goldsmith's art and paraments from the 11th to the 20th c. @ erv138

🏛 **Donau-Schifffahrtsmuseum (Danube navigation museum)**, Marc-Aurel-Ufer 1, ☎ 5075888 ⊜ The museum is located on board of two historic Danube ships: the steam paddle tug Ruthof (built 1922/23) and the motor tug Freudenau (built 1942). @ ecp715

🏛 **Fürst Thurn und Taxis Schlossmuseum mit Kreuzgang (Thurn und Taxis palace with cloister)**, Emmeramspl. 5, ☎ 5048133 ® The focus is on furnishings from the former Palais in Brussels and the residence in Frankfurt. The staterooms, including the 190 m² large and 7 m high ballroom, are particularly worth seeing. @ rhn528

🏛 **Fürstliche Schatzkammer und Marstall (Princely Treasury and Royal Stables)**, Emmeramspl. 5, ☎ 5048133 ® Exquisite furniture, finest porcelain, exclusive gold and silverware, a unique collection of valuable snuffboxes and numerous other precious items bear witness to the splendour of one of the leading dynasties of the European aristocracy. The Marstallmuseum, which is amongst the best carriage museums in Europe, houses an extensive collection of carriages, sleighs, sedan chairs and carrying chairs of the 18th and 19th century. @ tmi636

🏛 **Golfmuseum**, Tändlerg. 3, ☎ 51074 ⊜ Discover seven centuries of golf history in this museum. @ mhk221

🏛 **Historisches Museum (Museum of history)**, Dachaupl. 2-4, ☎ 507-2448 ⊜ The museum offers comprehensive information about the art and cultural history of Regensburg and Eastern Bavaria. @ akw276

- **Kunstforum Ostdeutsche Galerie (Artforum Eastern German Gallery)**, Dr.-Johann-Maier Str. 5, ☎ 297140 🖂 Paintings, graphics and sculptures of the 19th and 20th cs by artists from Eastern Europe are shown. @ gcr247
- **Museum der Bayerischen Geschichte**, Donaumarkt 1, ☎ 0821/32950 🖂 The Museum of Bavarian History shows the origin of modern Bavaria on more than 2,500 m². A multimedia and experience-oriented exhibition presents the history of Bavaria from the kingdom to the present day. @ nqd147
- **Museum Obermünster**, Emmeramspl. 1, ☎ 5972530 ☉ Topics: religious graphics, contemporary Christian art and folk art; additional public library and photo archive. @ hka412
- **Naturkundemuseum Ostbayern (natural history museum)**, Am Prebrunntor 4, ☎ 5073443 🖂 Permanent exhibitions on landscapes and the geological history of Eastern Bavaria. @ yry566
- **Städtische Galerie im „Leeren Beutel" (Municipal Gallery in the „Empty Bag")**, Bertold Str. 9, ☎ 5072440 🖂 Art of the 20th c. in Eastern Bavaria, special exhibitions of modern art. @ gak846
- **Dom St. Peter**, Infozentrum: Dompl. 5, ☎ 5971662 🕖 With bishop's grave, cloister and All Saints chapel. incl. ticket for cathedral treasure museum (cloister and All Saints chapel closed for renovation until 2020). @ fwr823
- **document Legionslagermauer (legionary camp wall)**, Parkhaus am Dachaupl., ☎ 5074410 🕙 Discover the traces of Roman buildings below ground. @ hky482

- **document Porta Praetoria**, Unter den Schwibbögen, ☎ 5074410 ⓗ Oldest city gate, built by the Romans around 179 AD, the only surviving legionary storage gate north of the Alps. The „Porta Praetoria" with an age of almost 2000 years is one of the oldest still preserved buildings in Regensburg. @ ikk843
- ✿ **Steinerne Brücke mit Brücktor (stone bridge with bridge gate)** ⓗ The stone building is one of the city's landmarks. Construction began in 1135, making it the oldest preserved bridge in Germany. At the time of its opening it was the only Danube bridge between Ulm and Vienna.
- ✿ **Geführte Radtouren (Guided bike tours)**, Wahlenstr. 17, ☎ 5073417. 2-hour guided tour with max. 12 persons. @ dxd715
- ✿ **Ostentor (East Gate)**, Ostengasse 37. The East Gate was erected in 1284 by members of the Regensburg Dombauhütte on the eastern edge of the so-called „East Suburb". The respective emperor entered – coming from the city of Vienna – through this east facing gate. The representative five-storey building is one of the best preserved Gothic city gates in Germany.
- ✿ **Botanischer Garten (Botanical Garden)**, Universitätsstr. 31, ☎ 9433295 ⊟, @ sxs112
- ✉⛱ **Westbad (Western bath)**, Messerschmittstr. 4, ☎ 6012944, @ hne713

Regensburg is an interesting city. Its history goes back more than 2,000 years, and few old cities can boast as many surviving medieval buildings and structures. The Steinerne Brücke, or Stone Bridge, for instance,

is not only the oldest functioning bridge over the Danube, but the oldest bridge in Germany. It was commissioned by Duke Henry the Proud and built in the first half of the 12th century.

Johann Wolfgang Goethe observed that in Regensburg "churches stand upon churches", but there are

Regensburg, Porta Praetoria

many other significant buildings as well. The old city with its narrow cobbled streets and impressive old homes, church buildings and the Thurn und Taxis palace has been designated a world heritage site by UNESCO. Numerous city squares, alleyways and markets, the colourful houses and old towers and gates give Regensburg a certain Mediterranean flair, which is why the city on the Danube is sometimes referred to as "the northernmost city of Italy."

The city's most distinctive landmark is the cathedral. The earliest parts of the church date to the 8th century and in 1255 the city began erecting a gothic structure. Construction was halted due to a lack of funds in 1525, and the cathedral was not completed until the 19th century. The northside of the building includes the so-called Eselsturm (donkey's tower), a romanesque element.

Regensburg was also the hometown of the astronomer and mathematician Johannes Kepler. The house at Keplerstraße 5, where he lived and died, has been converted into a museum. While Galileo Galilei was being forced to recant his theories about the motions of the planets, Kepler was allowed to publish his works unhindered – even though his mother had been accused of witchcraft.

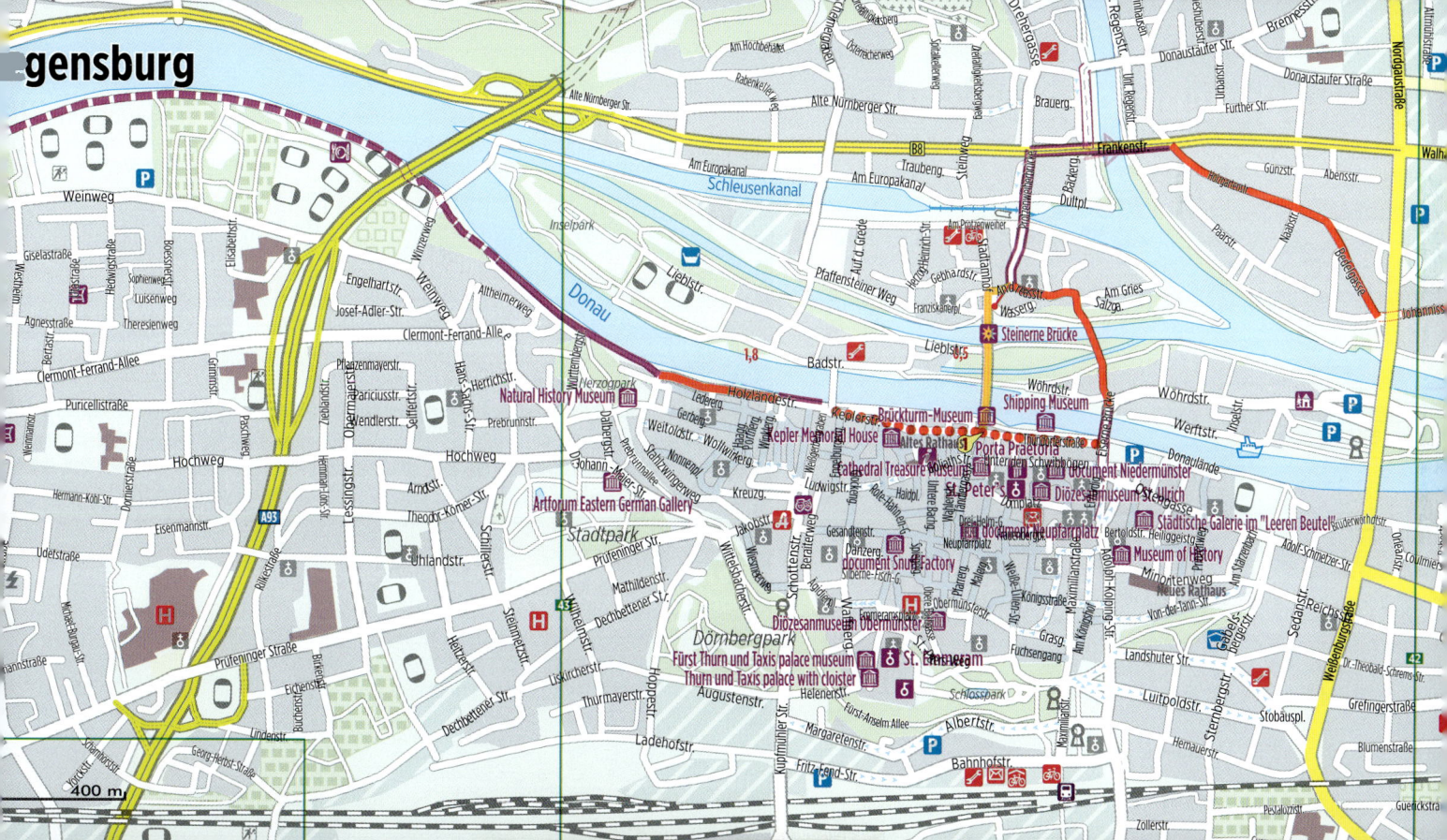

Regensburg to Passau

146 km

m/km: ⬈ 1.3 (196m) ⬊ 1.6 (233m) **cycle path:** 49 % **unpaved:** 12 % **busy road:** 4 %

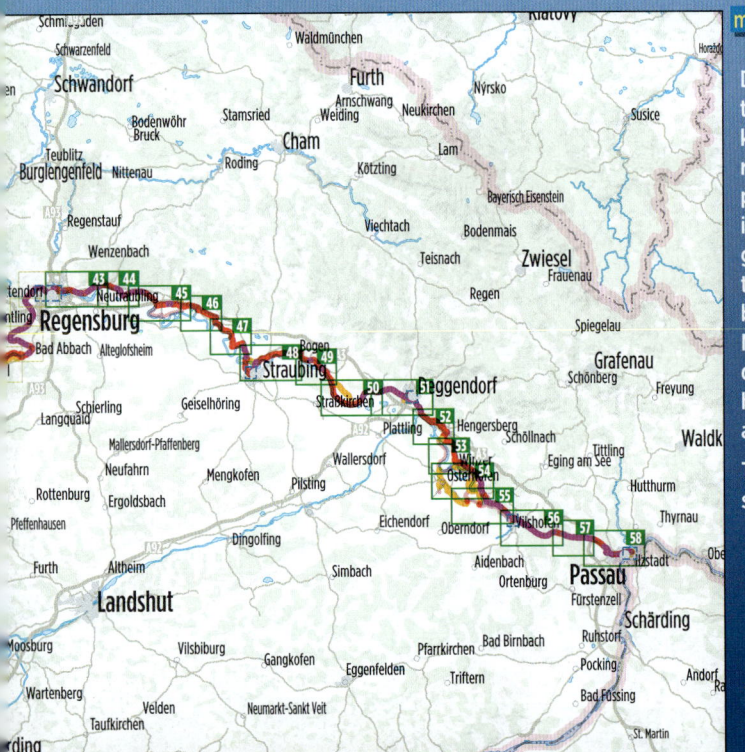

Downstream from Regensburg the Bohemian mountains force the Danube to turn to the southeast. The river passes along the northern edge of the fertile plain known in Germany as the Gäuboden while the foothills of the Bavarian Forest reach down to the river from the north. The river has grown in stature at this point and teems with ship traffic. The bike route heads downstream to Straubing, long considered the capital of the Gäuboden. The river meanders through graceful curves across the landscape until it reaches Deggendorf, gateway to the Bavarian Forest and the ancient rounded hills that rise towards the Czech border. The Danube bike route through Germany ends in "the Venice of the North," as the three-rivers city Passau likes to call itself. The city has a great deal to offer, ranging from the cathedral and catholic university to the old town hall, the pretty baroque city centre and the fortress standing guard on the bluff across the Danube.

The route follows mostly quiet country roads and bicycle paths, with only a few short stretches on busy roads.

› Regensburg   see page 113

Regensburg to Wörth   27.6 km

1 From the **Steinerne Brücke** go straight on the bike path on the left side of **Thundorfer Straße** ⁓ cross the Danube over the next bridge, the Eiserne Brücke ⁓ in the right bend, continue straight into **Proskestraße** and across the narrow bridge **Grieser Steg** ⁓ follow the **Andreasstraße** past the church ⁓ turn right at the T-intersection and cross the bridge **Protzenweiherbrücke** ⁓ at the next intersection turn right onto the bicycle path along **Frankenstraße** ⁓ after the bridge turn right into the first side street, **Holzgartenstraße** ⁓ after 500 m right on **Bedelgasse** ⁓ at the end of the narrow lane turn left under the road bridge and continue along **Johannisstraße**

turn left into **Gärtnerstraße** ⁓ immediately right again onto **Schwabelweiser Weg,** turn left and immediately right and follow the street away from the houses ⁓ you continue along the Danube to Schwabelweis ⁓ then along the dam to Tegernheim.

Tegernheim

✳ **Geopfad (geological path),** in the gorge of Tegernheim 🚴 Circular path through three large geological units of different ages, which meet at Tegernheim. @ aub517

Continue along a pleasant road to Donaustauf ⁓ **2** at the turn-off straight ahead.

> **EXCURSION** To reach Walhalla by bicycle you must make a long and steep climb. It is much easier to park your bicycle and use the footpath, which starts 500 m past the St. Salvator church and leads steeply up through the woods.

Donaustauf
prefix: 09403

ℹ **Tourist-Information,** Maxstr. 24, ✆ 9552929, @ anh561

⚑ **Wallfahrtskirche St. Salvator (pilgrimage church),** Wallhallastr. Built in Gothic style in the 15th c., then converted to baroque style before Leo von Klenze modified it in 1843 to complement Walhalla. @ gnx162

♜ **Burgruine Donaustauf (Donaustauf ruin)** ㉔ The castle was built as a fortress around 914 AD and was destroyed by the Swedes in the Thirty Years' War in 1634.

⚑ **Chinesischer Turm (Chinese Tower)** ↻ Around 1900, the Chinese Tower was moved from the Princely Garden of the Donaustaufer castle to the Prüfening castle garden in Regensburg. In 1999 it was removed from the Princely Garden. The sponsoring association „Chinesischer Turm" organizes concerts, exhibitions, etc. at and in the tower. @ tdx332

✳ **Historischer Ortskern (historic town centre).** The centre of the village, which consists mainly of late classicist buildings, stretches around the castle hill like an uninterrupted curved ribbon.

✳ **Walhalla,** Walhalla Str. 48, ✆ 961680 🚴 Temple in Doric style built by Leo von Klenze on behalf of King Ludwig I in the years 1830-42 on the Bräuberg. The most important classical building of the 19th c. @ ckr685

Donaustauf is a picturesque little town that wraps around the

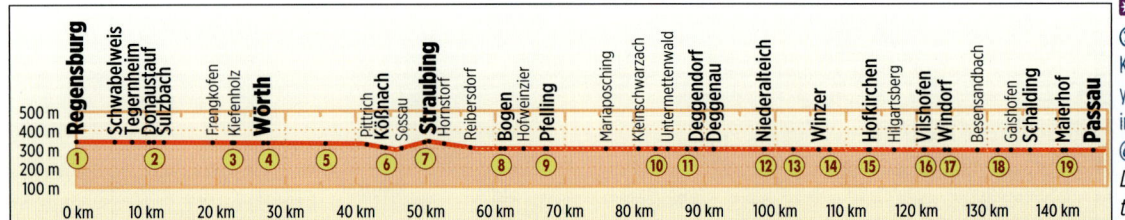

Walhalla

base of a small mountain under the ruins of the old castle. It emerged as a market town in the middle ages under the protection of the then mighty fortifications.

Walhalla

Even as Bavarian crown prince at the age of 20, Ludwig I wanted to build a temple to honor great Germans. But he had to wait 19 years before he could lay the cornerstone for Walhalla on the Bräuberg near Donaustauf not far from Regensburg. He had already commissioned 60 marble busts for the site. When it finally opened in October 1842, there

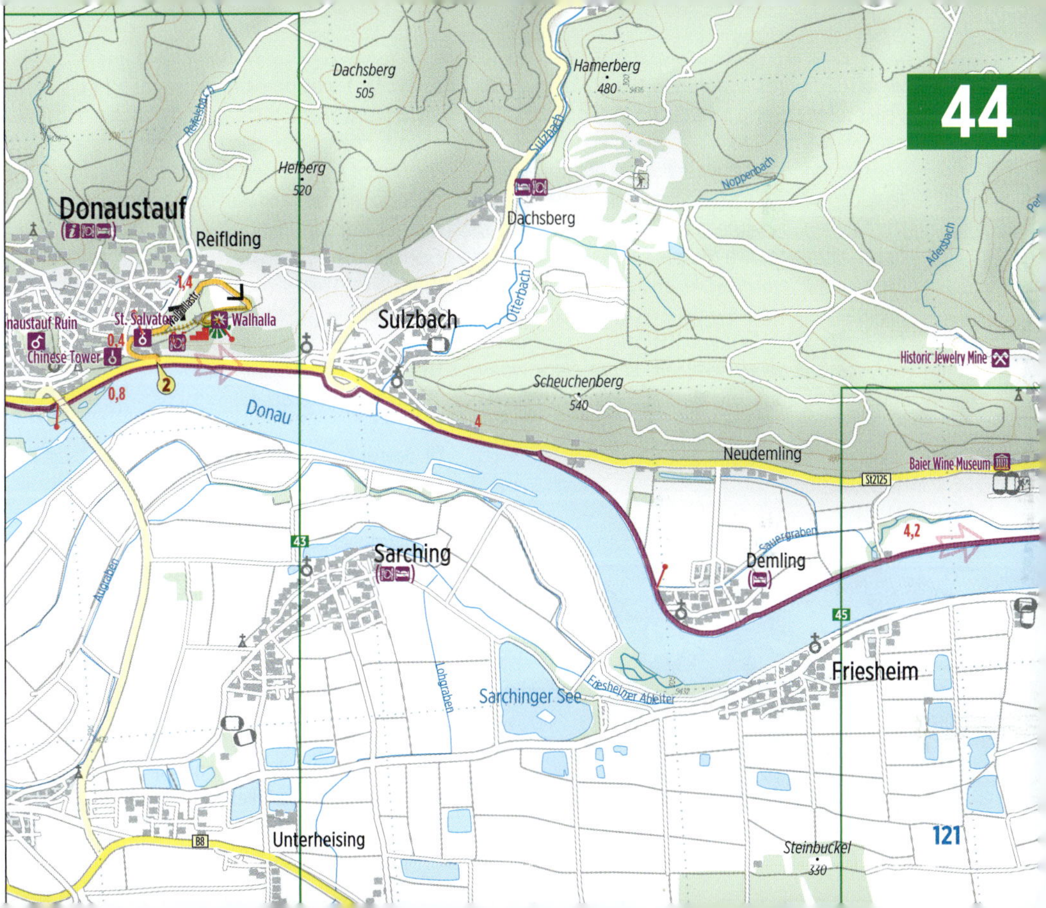

44

Dachsberg
505

Hamerberg
480

Helberg
520

Donaustauf

Reiflding

Dachsberg

Sulzbach

St. Salvator · Walhalla

Donaustauf Ruin

Chinese Tower

1,4

0,4

0,8

2

Scheuchenberg
540

Donau

4

Historic Jewelry Mine

Neudemling

Baier Wine Museum

St2125

4,2

43

Sarching

Demling

45

Friesheim

Auwanaer

Langraben

Sarchinger See

Frieshelzer Ableiter

Steinbuckel
330

Unterheising

B8

121

were 162 figures honored in the building. A few years later Ludwig I. built the Hall of Liberation near Kelheim.

The two monuments were built by the same architect, Leo von Klenze, who modelled Walhalla on the Parthenon in Athens. 348 marble steps lead up to the entrance. The temple's walls and columns are also made of marble, and the dimensions of the interior spaces almost exactly match those of the Parthenon. The name Walhalla comes from an old Nordic legend. "Walhall" is the place where the God of Gods and Battles, Odin (also known

Wörth Palace

as Wotan) welcomes fallen heroes to his table. In his last will and testament, Ludwig left instructions for new deserving Germans to be added to the Hall of Fame when fitting. It is a wish that the state government of Bavaria has honored at least 9 times since 1945.

Continue beside the main road past **Sulzbach** at the end of the path turn right and continue along the river bank past **Demling** to Bach, which lies to the left away from the river.

Bach an der Donau
prefix: 09403

- 🏛 **Baierweinmuseum (Bavarian wine museum)**, Hauptstr. 1b, ☎ 95020 ☺ Historic wine press house from the 14th c. and wine educational trail. @ ugv774
- ⚒ **Historisches Schmucksteinbergwerk (historic jewelry mine)**, Am Kittenrain, ☎ 0160/94958460 ☺ Experience 500 years of mining history on guided tours through mining caves and over underground lakes. @ rjp417

Continue along the river bank to Frengkofen you pass below a road bridge as you reach Kiefenholz.

FORK **3** Here the route divides. The southern route takes you along the Danube, partly on an unpaved path while the northern route takes you directly towards Wörth.

Along the Danube towards Wörth   9.7 km
To take the southern route turn right onto the unpaved path after passing under the freeway ride beside the Danube in the left bend after the sluices continue straight ahead into the upaved path you pass below another road bridge after another 4 km turn left opposite a wood **4** at the T-intersection the two routes rejoin.

Short route via Kiefenholz   5 km
To take the northern route, after passing under the freeway follow the street into **Kiefenholz** turn left opposite the church ride out of the village continue straight ahead through the roundabout, using the bicycle path along the left side of the road at the end of the cycle path take the side road keep right at th fork continue straight across the road and along the dike past Oberachdorf.

EXCURSION If you turn left at the following junction with the Auweg, you will reach Wörth an der Donau after crossing the motorway.

Wörth an der Donau
prefix: 09482

- ℹ **Tourist-Information**, Rathauspl. 1, ☎ 94030, @ kxk756

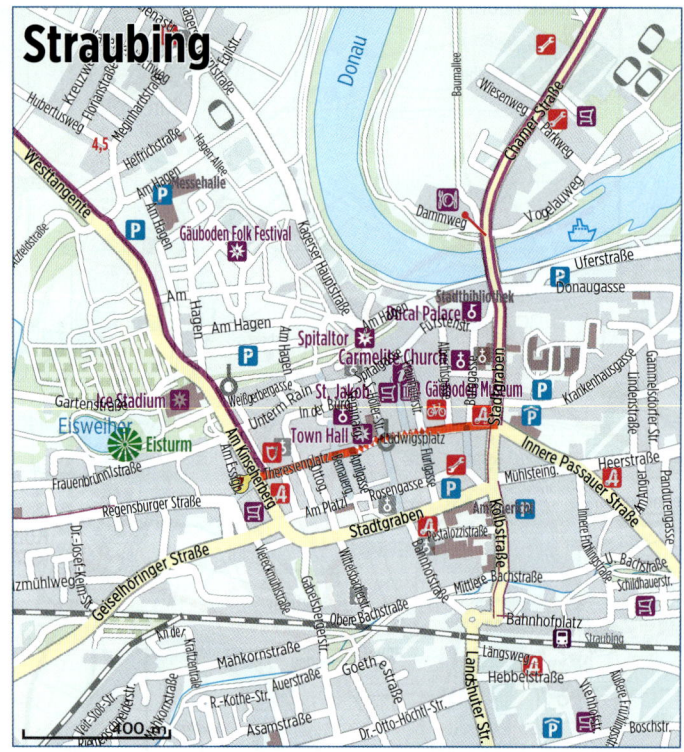

Straubing

barrage ~ straight ahead to the Straubinger Eisstadion ~ at the Eisstadion straight ahead ~ **7** at the second traffic light turn left onto the Theresienplatz ~ you are in the middle of the city centre. Straight ahead along the street to the bridge.

To ride through Straubing, turn right across the bridge, then left onto the bicycle path along the road ~ you cross the barrage on the Danube and come into Straubing ~ continue along the bicycle path past the **Straubinger Eisstadion ~ 7** by the second set of traffic lights turn left onto **Theresienplatz,** in the historic centre of the city.

Straubing
prefix: 09421

Tourist-Information, Fraunhoferstr. 27, ☏ 94460199, @ hyt173

Donau-Personenschifffahrt, Reederei Wurm, Passau (Danube passenger navigation), ☏ 0851/929292. Trips on the Straubing-Passau route. @ oxd858

Gäubodenmuseum, Fraunhoferstr. 23, ☏ 94463222 ☻ Includes the world-famous Straubing Roman treasure found in 1950 and items from the Bavarii, as well as local history and special exhibitions. @ gws255

Basilika St. Jakob, Pfarrpl., ☏ 999379. The late Gothic hall church from the 15th c. is one of the most important brick churches in Old Bavaria and houses the Moses window designed by Albrecht Dürer as a special treasure. The Kirchenbauförderverein offers guided tours on the 89 m high tower of the basilica. @ dgb882

Frauenbrünnl, Wallfahrtskirche „Unserer Lieben Frau" (Frauenbrünnl pilgrimage church „Our Dear Lady"), Frauenbrünnl-str. 117, ☏ 94460199 ☺ Baroque church built 1705-07. @ fwe711

Karmelitenkirche (Carmelite church), Albrechtsg. 34. The late Gothic hall church with monk's choir was redone in the baroque style around 1700 by Wolfgang Dientzenhofer., @ mug416

Ehem. Herzogsschloss (former ducal castle), Schloßpl. The construction of the irregular complex around a courtyard began under

126

Parkstetten

Scheftenmühle

Oberalteich

Fischerdorf

Thurasdorf

48

Bog

Unterzeitldorn

Reibersdorf

Alte Kinsach

Kinsach

Straubinger Str.

Bahnhofstr.

Sossau

Donau

Maria Himmelfahrt

Industriepark Sand

Sand

49

Hornstorf

1,8

Ziererstr.

Unteröbling

Asham

Hofstetten

Hunderdorf

Kagers

Donau

Gstütt

Oberöbling

Ittling

Moosdorf

St. Peter's Basilica

4,5

Ducal Palace

St. Jakob

Straubing

Ice Stadium

Timterer Moosgraben

B20

Roßeggergraben

Frauenbrünn

7

Straubing

Egisee

127

Straubing

Duke Albrecht I of Straubing-Holland in 1356. @ cfv632

🔹 **Stadtturm (city tower)**, Theresienpl., Ludwigspl. The medieval 68 m high landmark with the four corner towers and middle tower was built in 1316. Until the end of the 16th c. the tower was further extended.

✳ **Gäubodenvolksfest (Gäuboden folk festival)**, Am Hagen. The history of Bavaria's second largest folk festival goes back to 1812, the Gäubodenfest begins on the 2nd Saturday in August and lasts 11 days. The name derives from the Gäuboden, a geographically roughly defined area, in the centre of which lies Straubing. @ ahy457

✳ **Rathaus (town hall)**, Theresienpl. 2. The imposing Gothic main building has been used as a town hall since 1382 and was extended several times until the 19th c.

✳ **Spitaltor (hospital gate)**, Spitalg. The gate house from the late Middle Ages was given its present form in 1628.

✳ **Stadt- und Stadtturmführungen (city and city tower tours)**, Fraunhoferstr. 27, ☎ 94460199. Information and booking at the Tourist Information. @ nuy318

✳ **Trabrennbahn (Harness racing track)**, Ejadonstr. 45, ☎ 3777. Races take place regularly on East Bavaria's largest Harness racing track. @ kgq287

🔹 **Tiergarten (zoo)**, Am Tiergarten 3, ☎ 21277 ⌚ Eastern Bavaria's only zoo, with about 1,700 animals representing 200 species, and a unique aquarium for Danube aquatic life. @ qrf822

✉🏊 **AQUAtherm (indoor pool)**, Wittelsbacherhöhe 50/52, ☎ 864444, @ gvv311

The history of Straubing begins with a Celtic settlement called „Sorviodurum". It was followed by the Romans, who built several castra and a town. The Gäuboden museum displays numerous artefacts found in the region, of which the famous „Straubing Roman treasure" is especially noteworthy. Around 500 AD, a Bavarii clan, the „Strupinga" led by Strupo, moved into the settlement and gave it its current name. In 1218 Duke Ludwig der Kelheimer established the new city of Straubing. The city's oldest church is

St. Peters, a prime example of Bavarian Romanesque architecture. Its cemetery is also significant, with an extensive collection of gravestones representing every architectural style. In the 14th c. the city tower was built on the market square, which is lined with impressive middle-class and patrician city houses. The Ursuline church was built by Bavaria's great masters of the baroque, the brothers Asam.

Straubing also hosts the Gäubodenfest around the 15th of August each year. It is Bavaria's second biggest beer and amusement festival, following Munich's famous Octoberfest, and includes a regional country fair.

Straubing to Deggendorf   40 km

From Ludwigsplatz turn left onto the street Stadtgraben ～ cross the Danube and continue on the cycle path along Chamer Straße.

Hornstorf (Straubing)

After crossing the Old Danube on **Agnes Bernauer Bridge** turn right into **Ziererstraße** ～ follow this street to the left along the dike ～ go right on the quiet country road, which you follow to **Reibersdorf**.

Turn right and pass the church on the **Donaustraße** ～ turn right as you leave the village and follow the path along the dike to Bogen **8** after the playing fields turn right onto the path along the Kinsach river and over the bridge to **Straubinger Straße** turn right across the railway line along **Bahnhofstraße** to Stadtplatz.

Bogen
prefix: 09422

- **Stadt Bogen (town office)**, Stadtpl. 56, ☎ 5050, @ wht736
- **Kreismuseum Bogenberg (museum of the region)**, ehemaliger Pfarrhofstadel, old parish barn, ☎ 5786, ☎ 0160/97215810 ☎ Two main topics show the different stages of the Bavarian rhombuses and the history of the pilgrimage to the holy mountain of Lower Bavaria, the Bogenberg. @ bdo721
- **Pfarr- und Wallfahrtskirche Mariä Himmelfahrt (parish and pilgrimage church)**. Originally a proprietary church of the counts of Bogen, the structure came to be a pilgrimage church of the Assumption during the 12th and 13th c. @ afl524

49

Naturpark-Infostelle (nature park info point), Bahnhofstr. 26, ☎ 808855, ☎ 505109. Exhibition around the themes Danube, „Donaurandbruch" and Bogenberg. @ bft428

The history of Bogen can be traced back to the 8th century, when fishermen and traders started to settle at the mouth of the Bogenbach.

In 1104 an event occurred which would make the Bogenberg famous. At the foot of the small mountain local residents found a statue of Mary which had presumably washed ashore from a sunken ship. Count Aswin installed the statue in a castle chapel, whereupon so many pilgrims began making their way to the village that he donated his palace to Benedictine monks of Oberalteichen. In 1679 Pater Balthasar Regler had the statue undressed for scientific purposes and discovered that the statue depicted a pregnant Mary. This prompted many pregnant women to begin making pilgrimages to the church to pray for comfort and healing. The pregnant Madonna seen in the church today is not the original. Historic reports show that during the Thirty Years War the Swedes tossed the statue off the rocky cliff above the Danube. But the statue got caught in the undergrowth and was later retrieved. Some believe that a stone Madonna that stands in a niche to the right from the choir may be the original 13th century statue.

The Stadtplatz (city square) in Bogen is dominated by two rows of attached buildings. Almost the entire western half of the market burned to the ground in 1719, and another fire destroyed a number of houses on the uphill-side of the market in 1835 and 1836. Construction of the royal Bavarian state court in Bogen sparked a new period of prosperity in Bogen. As the population grew, new schools and a hospital were built and in 1895 the railroad reached the town. In 1952 Bogen attained city status and has since developed into a modern small city. Continue straight along Deggendorfer Straße out of Bogen 〜 at the intersection turn left into the small side street beside the main road, then continue on the bicycle path to Hofweinzier and further on to Pfelling.

Pfelling (Bogen)

9 Take the underpass under the main road 〜 turn left and follow the street past the houses 〜 continue straight ahead across the small stream at the end of the village and follow the road along the danube.

ALTERNATIVE The alternative route passing through Loham offers accommodation as well as shopping possibilities.

At this fork keep right into the paved lane beside the river, which you follow all the way to the ferry landing in Mariaposching 〜 continue along the river until the paved lane ends, where you can either continue on the gravel path along the top of the dike or ride with the traffic along the road until your reach Zeitldorf 〜 underpass the motorway 〜 **10** to the left there is the village of Metten 〜 past Mariaposching and Sommersdorf 〜 continue to the Danube bridge 〜 under the **A 3** 〜 continue along the **St 2125** 〜 Metten is on the left.

Metten
prefix: 0991

ⓘ Markt Metten, Krankenhausstr. 22, ☎ 998050, @ tya184

Benediktinerabtei Metten (Benedictine abbey), Abteistr. 3, ☎ 91080 ⊜ Established in 766, the abbey was expanded in 1726 with a library that now contains some 200,000 books. The abbey church with its dual towers was built 1712-29. @ hmj464

Prälatengarten (prelate garden), Egger Str. 2 ☎ The baroque garden with pavilion, fountain and Benedict column by the artist Josef Michael Neustifter was built in 2007 according to old models. @ xsl337

Freibad (outdoor pool), Jahnstr. 14, ☎ 9586, @ nsc267

Continue straight ahead along the river towards Deggendorf 〜 the path comes to follow the dike 〜 underpass the railway bridge **11**.

Deggendorf

CONNECTION Directly after the railway underpass you can cross the pedestrian and cyclist bridge to the other bank of the Danube, where the Via Danubia and the Isar cycle path meet.

Past the **Technische Hochschule** (university of engineering sciences) ⌁ turn left into **Edlmairstraße**, at the traffic lights turn right into **Hans-Krämer-Straße**.

CENTRE If you go straight ahead at the traffic lights and turn right into Veilchengasse, you will reach the centre of Deggendorf. Back on the Donau-Radweg (Danube Cycle Path) you go South via Luitpoldplatz and Pferdemarkt to the crossroads.

Deggendorf
prefix: 0991

🛈 **Tourist-Information**, Oberer Stadtpl. 1, ☎ 2960535, @ eun413

⛴ **Donauschifffahrt Wurm+Noé**, ☎ 0851/929292 ☺, @ qlr776

🏛 **Handwerksmuseum (craft museum)**, Maria-Ward-Pl. 1, ☎ 2960555 ☺ Cultural history of regional handicrafts. @ kxy533

🏛 **Schiffmeisterhaus „Info Hafen" (ship master's house)**, Schiffmeisterweg 10, ☎ 2504901 ☺ The approximately 400-year-old residential building has been used as an information and exhibition space since 2008. Here you can discover interesting facts about water, environment and health. @ nbh746

🏛 **Stadtmuseum (city museum)**, Östlicher Stadtgraben 28, ☎ 2960555 ☺ The cultural, economic and social development of the city and the region is displayed. @ ivv643

⛪ **Heilig-Grab-Kirche (Church of the Holy Sepulchre)**, Luitpoldpl. 25. The church was built in 1338, the baroque church tower dates from 1722-27.

⛪ **Pfarrkirche Mariä Himmelfahrt (parish church)** @ abt126

✳ **Altes Rathaus (old town hall)**, Oberer Stadtpl. 1. Building erected in 1535 with high stepped gables and the striking town hall tower. @ mvr855

Deggendorf's „pear-shaped" city limits reach way back to the middle-ages. Today a wide long market stretches down the middle of the city on two sides of the Old Rathaus with its imposing gothic

Isarmündung im Landkreis Deggendorf

tower. It is decorated with the crests of Bavaria and Deggendorf, with mythical animals and gargoyles, and with a medieval penal device, the „Schandkugeln" or „balls of dishonor", two stone balls connected by a length of chain. Heavy balls also figure in the Deggendorf dumpling legend, according to which the wife of one of the city's mayors was able to drive Bohemian invaders away with freshly-prepared dumplings.

In addition to the Rathaus, the two large parish churches, Maria Ascension and Church of the Holy Sepulchre, rank as the city's best known landmarks.

DETOUR Due to structural flood protection measures, the Seebach section via Niederalteich to Winzer is expected to be closed by September 2019. The Danube ferry and the village of Niederalteich can be reached. The diversion is signposted throughout and is temporarily the main route as shown in the map.

Deggendorf to Vilshofen an der Donau   34.7 km
Leave Deggendorf on the cycle path along the **Hengersberger Straße** ～ at the end of the village sign the route branches off to the

right ～ after 3.2 km you reach the detour on the asphalted road ～ here turn left, follow the signs to Niederalteich ～ **12** the Danube ferry is reachable on the right via the Hengersberger Straße, despite the detour.

Niederalteich
prefix: 09901

🛈 **Verkehrsamt (municipal office)**, Guntherweg 3, ✆ 93530, @ iln251

🚢 **Fußgänger- und Radlerfähre „Altaha" Thundorf-Niederalteich (Pedestrian and bicycle ferry)**, ✆ 0170/9252435 ☏, @ hmd843

🏛 **Flugzeugmuseum Gerhard Neumann (aircraft museum)**, Hengersberger Str. 5, ✆ 20270 ☉ Discover new and older models of combat aircraft. @ axv385

⛪ **Benediktinerabtei Niederaltaich (Benedictine abbey)**, Mauritiushof 1, ✆ 2080. The monastery was founded in 731 by the Bavarian Duke Odilo. Although the monastery burned down several times in the following centuries, Niederalteich was one of the most powerful monasteries in southern Germany until secularisation at the beginning of the 19th c. Since the beginning of the 20th c., the complex has again been used as a monastery. The monastery church is regarded as one of the earliest Gothic hall churches. Today only the outer portal testifies to the Gothic past, while the Baroque style of 1718 is clearly visible inside. @ ugr842

Duke Odilo established the Niederaltaich Benedictine abbey in 731 AD. In the following centuries the abbey suffered major fires a total of 13 different times. From outside, the main gate recalls the abbey's Gothic past while inside everything is done in the baroque style. It was here that the famous Bavarian tribal laws, the "Lex Baiuvariorum" were written down in the year 740.

FORK From Niederaltaich you also have a signposted route on along the right bank of the Danube as far as Vilshofen.

Left bank to Vilshofen   22.9 km

Leave Niederaltaich on **Hengersberger Straße** after the bridge over **Hengersberger Ohe** keep right and follow the cycle path along the small river near the village of Altenufer change to the right bank of the water course until you reach the official main route about 1 kilometre before getting to the small town of Winzer **13** at the main road, **Passauer Straße**, turn right into Winzer and cross it on the same road.

Winzer

prefix: 09901

Markt Winzer (municipal office), Schwanenkirchener Str. 2, 93570, @ miq783

52

Burgruine Oberwinzer (castle ruin). The castle was probably built in the 11th c. In Nov. 1744, during the War of the Austrian Succession, it was blown up and later used as a quarry. The remains of the walls are now listed as historical monuments.

Sternwarte (observatory), Pledlberg 1a, Every Friday observations take place in the planetarium. @ vbu765

Ride along the main street out of the town, where you ride along the bicycle path until it ends in the hamlet of Loh ⤳ **14** turn right opposite the houses of Loh ⤳ after 100 m turn left ⤳ ride straight along the paved field road to **Gries/Mitterndorf** ⤳ at the intersection by the houses in Gries turn right ⤳ keep left at the fork and ride past the houses ⤳ by the left bend, go straight out into the fields ⤳ follow the paved field road to a lake, where you turn left towards Sattling.

Sattling (Winzer)

Sattlinger Weiher @ rgh616

Stay right before the little bridge ⤳ follow the gravel field road, going straight at the next intersection ⤳ at the T-intersection by the next bridge keep right ⤳ turn left as you reach the dike and pump house by the Danube ⤳ follow the narrow path along the river into

Vilshofen an der Donau

Hofkirchen, where you continue along the street **Donaulände**.

Hofkirchen
prefix: 08545

- **Tourist-Information**, Rathausstr. 1, ☎ 97180, @ ufk668
- **Pfarrkirche Maria Himmelfahrt (parish church Mary assumption)**. Built around 1510 in its present form, also called the Cathedral of the Danube Valley.
- **Kreuzbergkapelle (chapel)**. In memory of the deceased of the plague at the end of the 30-year war, a place of prayer was built here, initially with 3 crosses and a wooden hut. In the 18th c. a brick chapel was built in honour of Our Lady of Sorrows. @ bsy844
- **Bienenlehrpfad (bee educational trail)** 24 First public bee nature trail in Lower Bavaria. In 30 showcases you will learn a lot of interesting facts about bees. You will also see the largest known hornet's nest, a large wasp's nest and can observe a colony of bees at work using a mirror. @ yod661
- **Kriegsgräberstätte (war gravesite)** 24 2,747 soldiers killed during the two world wars were laid to rest here by the German War Graves Commission. @ owu214
- **Freibad (outdoor pool)**, Schulg., ☎ 313, @ gqb656

Hofkirchen's existence can be traced back as far as the year 1005. It was granted market status in 1387 by Duke Albrecht the Younger. The city was an important landing station for the rafts and barge trains that plied the Danube until the mid-19th century. On October 18, 1745 Emperor Franz Stephan I spent the night in Hofkirchen as he travelled on his ship down the Danube after being crowned in Frankfurt.

15 Turn left into the street **Marktplatz** then right on **Vilshofener Straße** and take the bike path out of Hofkirchen after the playing fields turn right towards Unterschöllnach turn left before the wastewater treatment plant turn right after the bridge by **Unterschöllnach** follow the paved lane, which takes you along the Danube to Hilgartsberg.

Hilgartsberg (Hofkirchen)
prefix: 08545

- **Kreuzbergkapelle (Castle chapel)**, Hilgartsberg 44, ☎ 2303. The chapel is dedicated to St. George and, in contrast to the rest of the castle, well preserved. @ sxj832
- **Burgruine Hilgartsberg (castle ruin)**, Hilgartsberg 44, ☎ 2303. The castle was probably built in the 12th century and began to decay at the beginning of the 18th century. The Austrian War of Succession added to the already dilapidated castle: the Austro-Hungarian troops conquered it on 11th Nov. 1742 and set it on fire. Today various events take place in the old walls. @ mea434

Continue on the wide bicycle path along the Danube until you reach the road bridge across the Danube follow the bicycle path to the right past the marina after passing under the bridge turn left up to the bicycle path along the main road. **16**.

CENTRE To get to the centre of Vilshofen, turn left here, follow the cycle path across the bridge and on the other bank down to the bank in a narrow left loop. An underpass will take you to Obere Vorstadt and then turn left into Donaugasse and the old town.

55

Soldier's Cemetery

Aichet

Solla

Zaundorf

Langburg

Langkünzing

5,7

Maria Himmelfahrt

Hofkirchen

Herzogau

Lenau

15

Oberschöllnach

Ohetal-biketrail

1,2

Untermberg

Angerpoint

54

Kraftwerk Pleinting

Unterschöllnach

Hilgartsberg

Henhart

2,5

Bruck

Museum Quintana

2,4

Hilgartsberg Ruin
Castle Chapel

Pirka

Asing

Künzing

0,8

Haupts

6,5

Donau

Girching

Thannebergstr.

C

Pleinting

Einöd

56

Wallerdorf

Thannberg

Reisach

Unterbuch

Reifziehberg

Wimhof

Vilshofe

Zeitlarn

Daxlarn

6,5

Oberreith

Kohlstatt

Oberreith

Pleckental

Maria Hilf

Thannet

Alkofen

0,

139
bierUnterwelten

Vilshofen

prefix: 08541

ℹ Tourist-Information, Stadtpl. 27, ✆ 208114, @ msr338

🏛 Afrika-Museum, Schweiklberg 1, ✆ 2090 ♿ Ancient African art and ethnology give an insight into the mysterious old African tribal life. @ twg735

🏛 Stadtgalerie im Stadtturm (city gallery in the city tower), Obere Vorstadt 15, ✆ 1334 ♿ In the gallery constantly changing exhibitions of contemporary artists take place. @ ljy753

⛪ St. Barbara, Kapuzinerstr. The late Gothic church houses an interesting rococo altar from 1750.

⛪ Stadtpfarrkirche Johannes der Täufer (city parish church of St. John the Baptist), Kirchpl. 19. The Gothic church, erected in the 13th/14th c., was redone in baroque style in 1803.

⛪ Wallfahrtskirche Maria-Hilf (pilgrimage church), Kapuzinerstr. The domed building in the shape of a Greek cross dates from 1692.

⛪ Benediktinerabtei (Benedictine abbey), Schweiklberg 1, ✆ 208112, ✆ 208114 🕐 The abbey was built in 1905 with a school, boarding school, church, monastery and workshops. Today it works mainly in missions in Africa, South America and Korea. @ pev685

⛪ Stadtturm (city tower), Stadtpl. A landmark of the city built in its present form in 1643-47. @ aec886

✦ BierUnterwelten (BeerUnderworlds), Stadtpl., ✆ 208112 🕐 The rock cellar of the beer brewer family Groll, a 90 m long vault, became an exhibition room and gives a lot of information about beer and the pub culture. @ pkq384

✦ Kunst im öffentlichen Raum (Art in public space) 🕓 Sculptures by Lower Bavarian, Upper Palatinate and Austrian artists can be admired in the middle of the historic old town. @ nhd828

✦ Rathaus & Galerie (Town Hall & Gallery), Stadtpl. 27, ✆ 208107. The four-storey building was built in the 16th c. In the vaulted rooms on the ground floor, local artists exhibit paintings, sculptures and photographs. @ swv157

🏊 Hallen-, Freibad (in- and outdoor pool), Vilsfeldstr. 50, ✆ 8757. With brine bath, steam sauna, adventure showers and much more. @ bco471

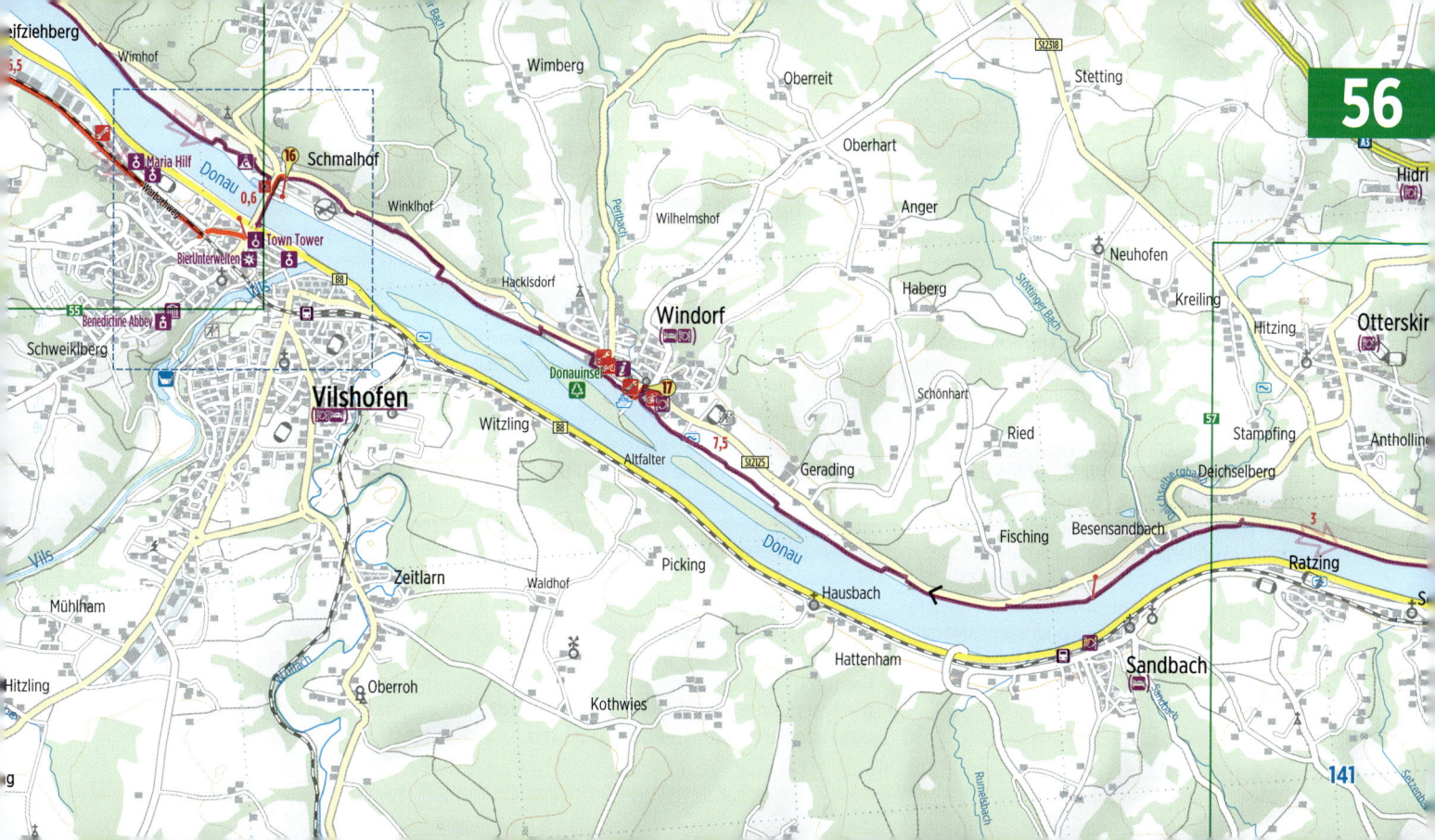

141

Donau

Vils

Vils

Wimhof

Maria Hilf

Wanderhafen

BierUnterwelten

Town Tower

16 Schmalhof

0,6

Winklhof

Wimberg

Oberreit

Stetting

Hidri

Oberhart

Anger

Wilhelmshof

Neuhofen

Kreiling

Hitzing

Otterskir

Haberg

Schönhart

Stampfing

Antholling

Benedictine Abbey

55

Schweiklberg

Hacklsdorf

Windorf

Donauinsel

17

7,5

Altfalter

Gerading

Ried

57

Deichselberg

3

Ratzing

Vilshofen

Witzling

Picking

Fisching

Besensandbach

Mühlham

Zeitlarn

Waldhof

Hausbach

Sandbach

S

Hitzling

Oberroh

Kothwies

Hattenham

g

Schmalhof

Right bank   28,7 km

After taking the ferry from Niederalteich, ride up the road to Thundorf.

Thundorf (Osterhofen)

- **Fußgänger- und Radlerfähre „Altaha" Thundorf-Niederalteich (Pedestrian and bicycle ferry),** ☎ 0170/9252435 🕿, @ vfj152
- **Wallfahrtskirche Maria Himmelfahrt und St. Quirinus (pilgrimage church).** The church offers magnificent Rococo decor. The pilgrimage, serviced by the Benedictine abbey, has been proved since the 11th c.

Keep left by the church in Thundorf ⌁ then immediately turn left after crossing the ditch ⌁ follow the bicycle path along the dike out of Thundorf ⌁ in **Aicha** keep left and follow the path along the top of the dike to **Haardorf** ⌁ take the path to the left along the Danube ⌁ after the small bridge continue along the river bank past the houses of Mühlham ⌁ **A** at the end of the village you reach a small side street.

Mühlham (Osterhofen)

EXCURSION From here you have the option of visiting Osterhofen or taking advantage of the shorter alternative route to Künzing.

Osterhofen

prefix: 09932

- **Tourist-Information,** Stadtpl. 13, ☎ 4030, @ kll212

- **Heimatmuseum (local museum),** Stadtpl. 15, ☎ 4030 🕓 A presentation of the history of the town from the old handicraft to the local glass and children's toys.
- **Hallenbad (outdoor pool),** Lahrstr. 20, ☎ 908956, @ mws174
- **Hallenbad (indoor pool),** Seewiesen 21/2, ☎ 90586, @ pna134

The main route out of Mühlham continues along the dike ⌁ near **Polkasing** be sure to continue straight ahead along the dike ⌁ you reach a large road bridge, which you can use to connect with the route along the left bank, otherwise continue straight ahead under the bridge ⌁ follow the dike all the way to **Schnelldorf, B** where you follow the right bend in the road ⌁ continue past the houses of Schnelldorf to the T-intersection in **Gramling (Endlau)** ⌁ turn left and follow the street out of the village to Langkünzing.

Künzing

prefix: 08549

- **Tourist-Information,** Osterhofener Str. 2, ☎ 973112, @ cmf844
- **Museum Quintana,** Osterhofener Str. 2, ☎ 973112 🕓 Here you can experience 7,000 years of settlement history from the Neolithic Age to the Roman Age and Late Antiquity. @ mty888

Turn left and ride on the bicycle path along the main road to Pleinting ⌁ turn right after the first buildings ⌁ after passing the outdoor pool keep left onto the path past the tennis courts ⌁ continue along **Thanneter Straße** to the intersection.

Pleinting

Turn right and follow the main street **Hauptstraße** through Pleinting ⌁ **C** before the main road, turn right and ride through the railway underpass ⌁ keep left and follow the street parallel to the railway line out of Pleinting ⌁ keep left after passing under the bridge and continue beside the railway line into Vilshofen ⌁ at the end of the street take the pedestrian and bicycle path and turn left under the railway line ⌁ turn right, first exit, at the roundabout and ride to the next intersection by the historic gate tower (Stadtturm). The historic centre of Vilshofen, centred on the **Stadtplatz,** lies straight ahead through the Stadtturm. Turn left to reach the bridge over the Danube and the main route to Passau on the left bank.

Vilshofen an der Donau   see page 140

Vilshofen to Passau   25.4 km

16 Follow the bicycle path to Windorf ⌁ turn right as you reach the houses ⌁ follow the bicycle path along the river bank then left by the creek up to the main street. **17**

Windorf

prefix: 08541

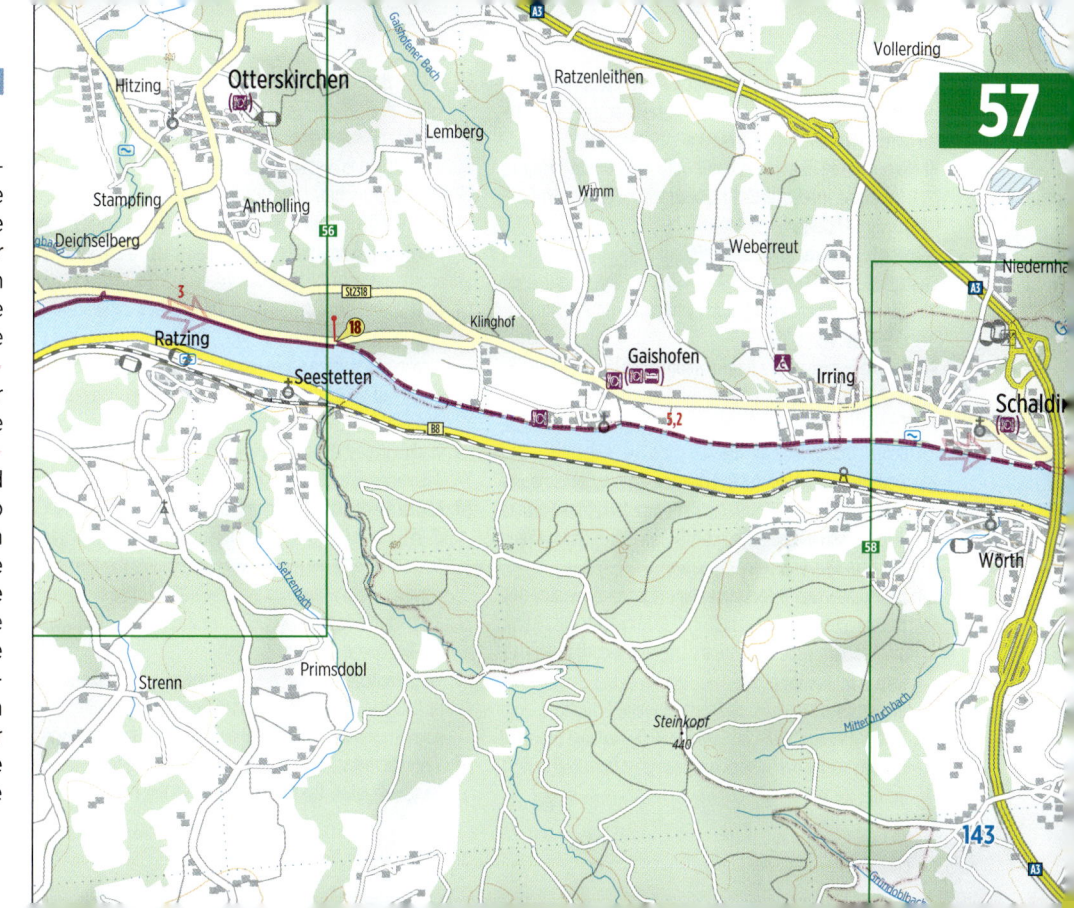

Tourist-Information, Marktpl. 23, ✆ 962640, @ fmp563

17 Turn right across the bridge and immediately right again ～ now simply follow the bicycle path along the river ～ you pass the ferry landing to Sandbach and shortly after the village of **Besensandbach** ～ **18** continue on the unpaved path along the river bank all the way to **Schalding** ～ turn right past the little marina and ride under the freeway bridge ～ after the underpass you cross the bridge over the river Gaißa ～ you now follow the bicycle path along the left side of the main road continue along the street past **Donauhof** and **Wörth**, then back onto the bicycle path into **Maierhof** ～ take the underpass under the main road in Maierhof and continue on the bicycle path along the right side of the road past the transformer station ～ turn right before the railway bridge ～ ride over the bridge by the **Kachlet locks** ～ **19** and continue over the barrage to the right bank of the Danube ～ turn left and follow the bicycle path along the river bank ～ under railway bridge and road bridge ～ at the T-intersection turn right and cross the main road ～ you now follow the bicycle path along the right side of **Regensburger Straße** all the way into the centre of Passau.

EXIT If you would like to get straight to the railway station, turn right into the **Bahnhofstraße** after the multi-storey car park.

Passau

prefix: 0851

ℹ️ **Tourist-Information (Tourist information)**, Rathauspl. 2, ✆ 955980, @ fap284

ℹ️ **Tourist-Information (Tourist information)**, Bahnhofstr. 28, ✆ 955980, @ enr843

ℹ️ **Tourist-Information Passauer Land (Tourist information)**, Dompl. 11, ✆ 397600, @ ruw547

⛵ **Donauschifffahrt Wurm & Noé (Danube shipping society Wurm & Noé)**, Höllg. 26, ✆ 929292 ⓐ Three river tours from March to October, daily scheduled service to Engelhartszell, Schlögen and Linz from April to October. @ duh285

🏛️ **Domschatz- und Diözesanmuseum (Cathedral treasury and diocese museum)**, Residenzpl. 8, ✆ 3930 ⓔ Precious historic artifacts from what was once the largest bishopric in the Holy Roman Empire, @ goo213

🏛️ **Glasmuseum Passau (Passau glass museum)**, Schrottg. 2, Close to town hall square, ✆ 35071 ⓐ The 30,000 exhibits provide a comprehensive overview of European glass from 1650 to 1950. @ ugd368

🏛️ **MMK - Museum Moderner Kunst (Museum of Modern Art)**, Bräug. 17, ✆ 3838790 ⓔ Alternating international exhibitions of 20th and 21st c. art presented in one of the most handsome old buildings in Passau. @ dlq537

🏛️ **OberhausMuseum**, Oberhaus 125, ✆ 396800, ✆ 396812 ⓐ Historical city museum with exhibitions on city history; Böhmerwaldmuseum, firebrigade museum etc., viewing tower. Shuttle bus from the town hall. @ gbu153

⛪ **Dom St. Stephan (St. Stephan's Cathedral)**, ✆ 3930. Its roots go back to the early Middle Ages. The cathedral received its Baroque form when it was rebuilt by Italian builders after the city fire of 1662. The nave is the largest Italian-Baroque, ecclesiastical space north of the Alps. The cathedral houses the world's largest church organ, with 17,974 pipes, 233 stops and 4 Glockenspiele (chimes). @ vrx157

⛪ **Kloster Niedernburg (Niedernburg convent)**, Klosterwinkel 1, ✆ 955980. On the eastern tip of the city, established in 740 and active until 2013, the monastery church houses the late gothic grave of Gisela, who joined the Benedictine Abbey as Queen of Hungary in 1045, dying in 1065. The convent contains 800 year old, Romanesque frescos. @ ghl547

⛪ **Veste Niederhaus**, Ferdinand-Wagner-Str. 1, ✆ 396800. It was probably built in the 14th c. in front of the upper house. In the 17th c. it served as prison, later as workhouse. Today it is privately owned.

⛪ **Veste Oberhaus**, Oberhaus 125. Besides cathedral and pilgrimage church Mariahilf, the fortress is one of the three urbanistic dominants of the city. It is one of the largest preserved castles in Europe and was founded in 1219. Contains the Oberhaus Museum. @ xje244

🎭 **Stadttheater (town theatre)**, Gottfried-Schäffer-Str. 2-4, ✆ 9291913. The former prince-bishop's opera house was built in 1783 and still maintains its early-classical form. @ wcl444

✴️ **Neue Bischöfliche Residenz (New Episcopal Residence)**, Residenzpl. 8, ✆ 3930. Built in 1712-1730 for the prince-bishop in the Viennese, late-Baroque style. The Rococo stucco interior dates from 1768 and the late-Baroque, early-classical facade dates from 1770.

✴️ **Rathaus (town hall chambers)**, Rathauspl. 2, ✆ 955980 ⓐ In the town hall there are two representative chambers in baroque style with colossal paintings from the 19th c. Glockenspiel in the town hall tower: Mo-Su 10:30 am, 2 pm and 3:30 pm.

✴️⛪ **Universitätskirche St. Nikola (St. Nicolai university church)**, Innstr. In the former collegiate church the crypt from the 11th c. has been preserved, and more than 90 frescoes shine in full splendour after years of restoration. @ asq156

✴️ **Dreiflüsseeck (Three rivers confluence)**. The spot where the three rivers Inn, Danube and Ilz Rivers come together.

🏊 **Passauer Erlebnisbad (Passau adventure bath)**, Messestr. 7, ✆ 560260. With outdoor and indoor swimming pools, sauna world and wellness area. @ efu285

Passau, the three-rivers city, occupies a dramatic narrow peninsula formed by the Danube and Inn rivers. The third river, the Ilz, joins the Danube from the north

Niederhart

Gaißbach

A3

57

Schalding

Wörth

St2175

Danube

Heining

Reuth

Reisch

Rittsteig

A3

Eichet

Neustift

Richterbach

Haarschedl

Kohlbruck

Walding

Engbolding

Donauhof

5.5 Wörth

B8

19

Maierhof

Unteröd

Auerbach

Haidenhof

Moos

Partriching

Korona

Eck

Ries

Neureuth

B85

Sturmsölden

Hacklberg

2,6

B8

St. Nikola

University Church St. Nikola

Repensburger Str.

Bahnhofstr.
Passau Hbf.

Oberilzmühle

Ilzleiten

Oberöd im Ilztal

Ilz

Kuchlhof

Anger

Danube

Passau

Veste Oberhaus

1,6

Fritz-Schäfer-Promenade

St. Stephan's

MMK

Three-rivers Confluence

Roman Museum Boiotro

Pilgrimage Church Mariahilf

Inn River Trail

Inn

Kinsing

Kirnberger Bach

Reut

Sieglgut

Sieglberg

Hals

B12

Stromlänge

Untersölden

Ilzstadt

Obersölden

B388

Sandberg

Erdbrustbach

St2319

Grubweg

Linda

Haibach

Rosenau

Lindenthal

Neusaming

Waging

Hamberg

Ingling

Rad

Schwendt

Inn

145

B12

Füssing

Passau

near the city's eastern tip. Passau's history extends back to around 500 years BC. The original Celtic settlement was succeeded by the Romans around the time of Christ. In 460 AD St. Severinus, also known as the Apostle to Noricum, established a monastery here. In the 6th century, the Bavarii took control of what was the last Roman outpost on German soil. Batavis became Bazzava which finally became Passau. In 1161, the emperor withdrew from Passau and presented the Niedernburg Abbey to the high monastery of Passau, which governed the city until 1803. In 1568 Austrian nobles filled the prince-bishop's seat until Napoleon restored the city to Bavarian rule.

Passau's cathedral has gone through numerous incarnations. In the 13th century it was rebuilt as a Gothic church. In 1407, Hans Krumenauer was instructed to build a completely new cathedral. It and large parts of the city were destroyed in a great fire in 1662. Because the city could not afford to build a new church at the time, the Italian architect Carlo Lurago added a baroque long-church to surviving elements of the Gothic choir and transept. Today the church's interior is regarded as the largest baroque church space north of the Alps. The church also has five organs which can be played simultaneously from a single main console. It is considered the largest church organ in the world.

The city lies to the west of the Dreiflüsseeck, the point of the peninsula at which the three rivers join to form the Danube as it enters Austria. To the south lies the Innstadt, with the Mariahilf pilgrimage church. The Ilzstadt to the north is dominated by the lower Veste Niederhaus and the upper Veste Oberhaus fortress that offers excellent views on the panorama. Across from the cathedral one can find the "Passau Tölpel, " or "idiot," jokingly considered the city's mascot. It is actually a fragment from a statue of St. Stephen, which fell from the cathedral's south tower and shattered during the fire of 1662.

CONNECTION In Passau you have the possibility of continuing your tour down the Danube, with detailed maps and information about the route from Passau all the way to the Black Sea available in the *bikeline* guides.

You have now reached the end of this cycling journey. We hope you had an interesting and enjoyable cycling holiday and we are pleased that you chose a *bikeline*-cycling guide to accompany you on your journey.
The *bikeline* team wishes you a safe and enjoyable return trip!

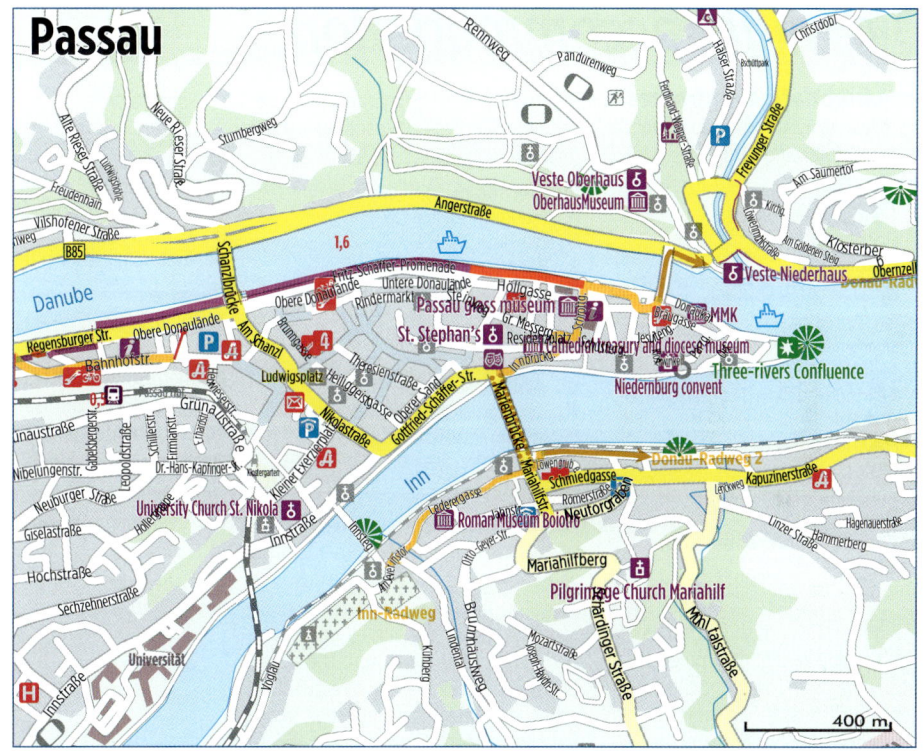

Passau

Overnight accommodation

Accommodation addresses

The following list includes accommodation in the following categories:

Categories

- 🛈 Tourist-Information
- H Hotel, Inn
- Hg Hotel garni
- BB Bed and Breakfast, Boarding House, Farm
- Ho Hostel
- Mo Motel
- AH Aparthotel, Holiday Flat (selection)
- B Bungalow
- Hh Hay hotel
- S Other
- 🛏 Youth hostel
- 🏕 Camp ground
- ⛺ Tent site (nature tent site)

We have not attempted to list every possible place where visitors can spend the night, and listings should not be construed as any kind of recommendation. Because we wish to expand this list and keep it up-to-date, we welcome any comments, additions or corrections you

may have. There is no charge for a single-line entry, for lack of space we cannot guarantee one.

Identification

I	Price Range less than € 25,–
II	Price Range € 25,– to € 35,–
III	Price Range € 35,– to € 50,–
IV	Price Range € 50,– to € 70,–
V	Price Range € 70,– to € 100,–
VI	Price Range over € 100,–
o.F.	no breakfast
HP	with breakfast and dinner
🛁	only room with shared bathroom
☺	Bed+Bike Accommodation
2.5	distance to the route in kilometres

Prices

These categories are based on the price per person in a double room equipped with shower or bath, with breakfast. The indicated price categories correspond to the status of the survey or revision period and may differ from the actual prices. Price fluctuations are possible, especially during trade fairs, due to different room types and not least due to

seasonal factors.

Bike Workshops and Rental

- 🔧 Bike workshop
- 🚲 Bike rental
- 🔌 E-Bike charging station
- 🚲 E-Bike rental
- 🔒 lockable parking facilities

Distance

The blue number (2.5) at every accommodation shows the distance to the route in kilometres. Please note that this number refers to the linear distance, the difference in altitude and the actual distance covered is not included.

Updates

For further corrections concerning the overnight accommodation list see the LiveUpdate at www.esterbauer.com

Donaueschingen

Area Code: 0771

- 🛈 Tourist-Information, Karlstr. 58, ✆ 857221
- BB **Ziegelhof, Dürrheimer Str. 65, ✆ 3373, ✆ 0176/63064463, II**
- H Concorde, Dürrheimer Str. 82, ✆ 83630, III-IV
- H Linde, Karlstr. 18, ✆ 83180, IV-V ☺
- H Zum Hirschen, Herdstr. 5, ✆ 8985580, III ☺
- H Bora, Friedrich-Ebert-Str. 18, ✆ 3376, III
- AH Jägerhaus, Buchberg 37, ✆ 7346, II-III ☺
- 🔧🚲 Rad Center Rothweiler, Max-Egonstr. 11, ✆ 13148

Allmendshofen (Donaueschingen)

Area Code: 0771

- H Flairhotel Grüner Baum, Friedrich-Ebert-Str. 59, ✆ 80910, III-IV ☺

Ⓗ Adler, Bregstr. 3, ☎ 2401, III

Pfohren (Donaueschingen)
Area Code: 0771
Ⓐ Riedsee-Camping, Am Riedsee 11, ☎ 5511, I

Gutmadingen (Geisingen)
Area Code: 07704
Ⓑ Bensel, Alemannenstr. 20, ☎ 6972, II

Geisingen
Area Code: 07704
ⓘ Rathaus, Hauptstr. 36, ☎ 8070
Ⓑ Villa Arena, Nikolausstr. 1, ☎ 9233980, III ☺
Ⓑ arena gästehaus, Mühltorg. 1, ☎ 9233980, II ☺

Kirchen-Hausen (Geisingen)
Area Code: 07704
Ⓗ Sternen, Ringstr. 1-4, ☎ 8039, ☎ 803500, III
Ⓑ Wagenpark zur Donau, Münsterg. 2, ☎ 360, ☎ 0162/4544991, I 🚲

Zimmern (Immendingen)
Area Code: 07462
Ⓑ Bei Trixi, Kirchg. 3, ☎ 2783, ☎ 0176/47207533, III
Ⓑ Café Waldhorn, Hornensteigstr. 1, ☎ 1284, II
ⒶⒽ Fritz, Wacholderweg 15, ☎ 7180

Immendingen
Area Code: 07462
ⓘ Tourist-Information, Schlosspl. 2, ☎ 24228
Ⓗ Ochsen, Hauptstr. 45, Hattingen, ☎ 6219, II
Ⓐ Radlerzeltplatz, Donauversinkung, ☎ 0173/6668243, OB, I

Möhringen (Tuttlingen)
Area Code: 07462

ⓘ Tourist-Info, Hermann-Leiber-Str. 4, ☎ 94820
ⓃⒻ NFH Donauversickerung, Außer Ort 10, ☎ 91323, I-II ☺
ⒶⒽ Gössler, Schönhalde 11, ☎ 7421, III 🚲

Tuttlingen
Area Code: 07461
ⓘ Tourist-Info, Rathausstr. 1, ☎ 99340
Ⓗ Légère Hotel Tuttlingen, Königstr. 25, ☎ 96160, ☎ 9616410, IV-V ☺
Ⓗ Ritter, Königstr. 12, ☎ 966330, II ☺
Ⓗ Rössle, Honbergstr. 8, ☎ 2913, III ☺
Ⓗ Schlack, Bahnhofstr. 59, ☎ 9440, III ☺
Ⓑ Charly's House, Am Seltenbach 2–3, III. Reservierung nur online möglich
Ⓐ Zeltplatz im Donaupark, Umläufle 1, ☎ 99340
🚲 Dangelmaier, Oberamteistr.26, ☎ 3019
🚲 Radler-Welt, Goethestr. 1, ☎ 72001

Wurmlingen
Area Code: 07461
Ⓗ Traube, Untere Hauptstr. 43, ☎ 9380, IV
Ⓗ Zum Löwen, Karlstr. 4, ☎ 93300, III ☺
ⒶⒽ Lindenkurve, Untere Hauptstr. 58, ☎ 164843, ☎ 0170/5810237, III

Nendingen (Tuttlingen)
Area Code: 07461
ⓘ Tourist-Info, Rathausstr. 1, Tuttlingen, ☎ 99340
Ⓑ Da Nino, Industriestr. 22/1, ☎ 7705288, ☎ 0162/1689745, II

Stetten (Mühlheim an der Donau)
Area Code: 07463

Ⓗ Zum Lamm, Rathausstr. 6, ☎ 393, III

Mühlheim an der Donau
Area Code: 07463
Ⓗ **Zur Linde, Bergstr. 16, ☎ 7855, II**
Ⓗ Hirsch, Hauptstr. 6, ☎ 498, II-III
Ⓑ Gästehaus Theresia Garni, Schloß 8, ☎ 5070, ☎ 0172 6845150, II-III ☺
Ⓑ Nachtwächter, Hauptstr. 28, ☎ 7725, I

Mühlheim-Oberstadt (Mühlheim an der Donau)
Area Code: 07463
ⓘ Verkehrsamt, Schloßstr. 1, im Vorderen Schloss, ☎ 8903, ☎ 0174/3264445
Ⓗ Krone, Tuttlinger Str. 1, ☎ 7043, V

Gasthaus zur Linde
Bergstraße 16
78570 Mühlheim a.d.D.
Tel. 07463 7855
info@linde-muehlheim.de
www.linde-muehlheim.de

Fridingen an der Donau
Area Code: 07463
ⓘ Verkehrsamt Donau-Heuberg, Kirchpl. 2, ☎ 8370
Ⓗ Löwen, Mittlere G. 3, ☎ 99420, III
Ⓗ Sonne, Bahnhofstr. 22, ☎ 99440, III ☺
Ⓑ Landhaus Donautal, Bergsteig 1, ☎ 469, III
Ⓑ ⒶⒽ Pension Sattler, Am Wendelstein 5, ☎ 1325, ☎ 0157/79319000, II
Ⓑ Perazic, Litschenberg 1, ☎ 7634, II
Ⓑ ⒶⒽ Reiser, Martin-Kempter-Str. 4, ☎ 7804, II-III

Wildenstein (Leibertingen)
Area Code: 07466
Ⓜ Burg Wildenstein, Wildenstein1, ☎ 411, I-II

Beuron
Area Code: 07466
ⓘ Tourist-Information, Kirchstr. 18, Hausen im Tal (Beuron), ☎ 07579/92100
Ⓗ Haus Maria Trost, Edith-Stein-Weg 1, ☎ 483, ☎ 484, III
Ⓑ Haus Schönwalder, Donaustr. 5, ☎ 1294, OB, II
Ⓑ Haus im Donautal, Wolterstr. 11, ☎ 910098, ☎ 0176/80576737, II-III

Langenbrunn (Beuron)
Area Code: 07579
Ⓑ Zur schönen Aussicht, Ringstr. 7, ☎ 1634, ☎ 0171/8275278, II
ⒶⒽ Der Talhof, Talhof 2, ☎ 933143, III ☺. Gruppenpension (Schlafsack) 🚲

Hausen im Tal (Beuron)
Area Code: 07579

ℹ️ Tourist-Information, Kirchstr. 18, ☎ 92100
🏨 Bahnhof, Bahnhof 2, ☎ 565, ☎ 0171/7049515, III 🌡️
⛺ Benedikta, Tobelstr.2, ☎ 2192, II
🏕️ Camping Wagenburg, Kirchstr. 24, ☎ 559, ☎ 0160/8449137, I
🚲 Valleybike, Buchheimerstr.8, ☎ 933706, ☎ 0172/7483403

Neidingen (Beuron)
Area Code: 07579
🅱️ Zur Mühle, Neidinger Str. 47, ☎ 523, ☎ 0174/3965120, III

Thiergarten (Beuron)
Area Code: 07570
🏨 Neumühle, Neumühle 1, ☎ 9590, III-II
🅱️ Wolf, Hofstr. 6, ☎ 1443, II
🏠 Jack Rattle Tal der Piraten, Zum Hammer 3, ☎ 550, II

Gutenstein (Sigmaringen)
Area Code: 07570
🏨 Backpackers-Hotel, Burgfeldenstr. 37-1, ☎ 07575/1221, ☎ 0171/5527804, II
🏨 Donauperle, Burgfeldenstr. 16, ☎ 951388, III
🏕️ Jugendzeltplatz Aisnau, Burgfeldenstr. 27, ☎ 487

Dietfurt (Inzigkofen)
Area Code: 07571
ℹ️ Gemeindeverwaltung Inzigkofen, Ziegelweg 2, Inzigkofen, ☎ 73070
🏨 Mühle Dietfurt, Burgstr. 9, ☎ 51715, III

Vilsingen (Inzigkofen)
Area Code: 07571

ℹ️ Gemeindeverwaltung Inzigkofen, Ziegelweg 2, Inzigkofen, ☎ 73070
🏨 Landgasthof Zoller, Dorfstr. 33, ☎ 51089, II
🏨 Donau, Dr.-Josef-Vögtle-Str. 7, ☎ 51669, II
🏨 Zum Donautal, Mühlenweg 2, ☎ 9297555, II

Inzigkofen
Area Code: 07571
ℹ️ Gemeindeverwaltung Inzigkofen, Ziegelweg 2, ☎ 73070
🅱️ Kreuz, Rathausstr. 15, ☎ 51812, III
🅱️ Resort am Nickhof, Nickhof 1, ☎ 50532, V
🏨 Ingrid's Fewo, Kirschenweg 13, ☎ 747924, II

Laiz (Sigmaringen)
Area Code: 07571
🚲 Dany's bike shop, Hauptstr. 15, ☎ 63500

Sigmaringen
Area Code: 07571
ℹ️ Tourist-Information, Fürst-Wilhelm-Str. 15, ☎ 106224
ℹ️ Gasthof Traube, Fürst-Wilhelm-Str. 19, ☎ 64510, III 🌡️
🏨 Jägerhof, Wentelstr. 4, ☎ 744990, IV 🌡️
🅱️ Apartment am Schloss, Fürst-Wilhelm-Str. 36, ☎ 51942, ☎ 01712871422, III
🅱️ Gästehaus Pfefferle, Leopoldstr. 22, ☎ 2448, III
🅱️ Schmautz, Im Muckentäle 33, ☎ 51554, III
🏠 Hohenzollern-Jugendherberge Sigmaringen, Hohenzollernstr. 31, ☎ 13277, I-II 🌡️
🏕️ Camping Sigmaringen, Georg-Zimmerer-Str. 6, ☎ 50411, I

Sigmaringendorf
Area Code: 07571
ℹ️ Gemeindeverwaltung, Hauptstr. 9/Wilhelm-Lehmann-Pl., ☎ 73050
🏨 Beim Rinderwirt, Hauptstr. 17, ☎ 74974100, III
🅱️ Donauhirsch, Lauchertbühl 9, ☎ 7465340, III
🅱️ Gästehaus unterm Regenbogen, Oberdorf 8/1, ☎ 683892, II

Scheer
Area Code: 07572
ℹ️ Stadtverwaltung, Hauptstr. 1, ☎ 76160
ℹ️ Johannslaube I-Punkt, Donaustr. 18, ☎ 767499 @ smr627
🏨 Donaublick, Bahnhofstr. 21-28, ☎ 76380, III 🌡️
🏨 Donau-Spatz, An der Rübhalde 5, ☎ 766441, III

Ennetach (Mengen)
Area Code: 07572
🅱️ Dorfstuben, Ablachweg 6, ☎ 712995, II-III 🌡️
🅱️ Herla, Keltenweg 3, ☎ 8824, I

Mengen
Area Code: 07572
ℹ️ Stadtverwaltung Mengen, Hauptstr. 90, ☎ 6070
🏨 Rebstock, Hauptstr. 93, ☎ 76680, III
🏨 Zum Fliegerwirt, Flugpl. 34, ☎ 760340, ☎ 0160/95838631, III
🅱️ Mattiello's Mengen, Hauptstr. 92, ☎ 7698053, II
🅱️ Nörz, Wilhelmstr. 9, ☎ 786221, ☎ 0157/88105716, I
🚲 Sport Dietsche, Reiserstr. 2, ☎ 76370
🚲 Zweiradcenter Bacher GbR, Mittlere Str. 31-33, ☎ 5696

Blochingen (Mengen)
Area Code: 07572
⛺ Gally, Schweibelweg 2, ☎ 8684

Hundersingen (Herbertingen)
Area Code: 07586
ℹ️ Gemeinde Herbertingen, Holzg. 6, Herbertingen, ☎ 92080
⛺ Adler, Ortsstr. 1, ☎ 378, III
⛺ Heun, Müllershalde 14, ☎ 91017, ☎ 0157/54729574, II

Herbertingen
Area Code: 07586
ℹ️ Gemeinde Herbertingen, Holzg. 6, ☎ 92080
🏨 Engel, Bahnhofstr. 1, ☎ 9217720, III-I
⛺ Fewoni, Angergraben 32 🌡️
⛺ Lucia, Hesslinger Str. 2, ☎ 1748, I

Ertingen
Area Code: 07371
ℹ️ Bürgermeisteramt, Dürmentinger Str. 14, ☎ 5080
🅱️ Buck, Paiters Gässle 11a, ☎ 5866, ☎ 0172 7606199, OB, I-II 🚭
⛺ Keller, Schönblickweg 8, ☎ 5300, ☎ 0151/12875217

Altheim
Area Code: 07371
🅱️ Gentner, Sandgrubenweg 1, ☎ 965144, I

Neufra (Riedlingen)
Area Code: 07371
🏨 Kleinstes Schloßhotel, Schloßberg 12, ☎ 5700, III-IV

Riedlingen
Area Code: 07371
ℹ️ Verkehrsamt im Rathaus, Marktpl. 1, ☎ 1830

H Hirsch, Lange Str. 17, 📞 9665454, 📱 01729857844, III
H Rosengarten, Gammertinger Str. 25, 📞 7336, II
🚲 Radlerrast Weiss, Vöhringerhof 1, 📞 12574, I
🚲🔧 Radsport Günzel, Unterriedstr. 15, 📞 927298

Grüningen (Riedlingen)
Area Code: 07371
H Adler, Adlerberg 1, 📞 93410, 📱 0175/2769926, III 🙂

Unlingen
Area Code: 07371
H Gasthof Eck, Kirchg. 12, 📞 8242, II 🙂 🚲
H Sonne, Hauptstr. 37, 📞 8574, II

Daugendorf (Riedlingen)
ℹ Verkehrsamt im Rathaus, Marktpl. 1, Riedlingen,
📞 07371/1830

Zell (Riedlingen)
Area Code: 07371
H Adler, Januarius-Zick-Str. 6, 📞 2891, OB, I 🚲
B Ferienhaus Fisel, Janarius-Zick-Str. 10, 📞 768, I

Zwiefaltendorf (Riedlingen)
Area Code: 07373
H Zum Rössle, Von-Speth-Str. 19, 📞 643, II
B&B Bauer am Bach, Zum Bahnhof 5, 📞 9216544
B Gästehaus Helga, Zur Donaubrücke 4, 📞 07391/1759,
📞 0174/3274529, II

Baach (Zwiefalten)
Area Code: 07373
B&B Radlerherberge Auchter, Talweg 12, 📞 1422, II–III 🙂
🚲 Autohaus Engst, Riedlinger Str. 50, 📞 92050,
📞 0170/3177725

Zwiefalten
Area Code: 07373
ℹ Tourist-Information, Marktpl. 3, im Rathaus,
📞 20520
B&B AH Forellental, Mühlweg 1, Gossenzugen, 📞 92190,
II–III
⛺ Jugendzeltplatz, Beim Höhenfreibad, 📞 20520, I

Obermarchtal
Area Code: 07375
ℹ Bürgermeisteramt, Hauptstr. 21, 📞 205
H Berghofstüble, Reutlingendorferstr. 5, 📞 266, III 🙂
B&B Bildungshaus Kloster Obermarchtal, Klosteran-
lage 2/1, 📞 95050, III
AH Petrushof, Maierstorweg 12, 📞 9225233, II

Rechtenstein
Area Code: 07375
ℹ Bürgermeisteramt, Braunselweg 2, 📞 244
H Bahnhofsgaststätte, Bahnhofstr. 1, 📞 315

Untermarchtal
Area Code: 07393
ℹ Infozentrum, Bahnhofstr. 4, 📞 917383
B&B Bildungsforum Kloster Untermarchtal, Margarita-
Linder-Str. 8, 📞 30250, III

Munderkingen
Area Code: 07393
ℹ Tourist-Information, Alter Schulhof 2, 📞 9534581
Hg Café Knebel, Donaustr. 21, 📞 1314, III 🙂
H Rose, Donaustr. 2, 📞 1726, II 🙂
B&B Adler Brasserie, Martinstr. 17, 📞 91424, II 🙂
B Nöbel-Tress, Gerhard-Hauptmann-Weg 12,

📞 919283, 📱 0162/6803947, I
⛺ Zeltplatz Bodenösch am Alten Wasserwerk, Kugel-
wert, 📱 0160/8709619, I

Rottenacker
Area Code: 07393
ℹ Bürgermeisteramt, Bühlstr. 7, 📞 95040
H Rosi's Dorfwirtschaft, Bogenstr. 19, 📞 5988203, III–IV
⛺ Zeltplatz Badesee „Heppenäcker", 📱 0171/6825016,
I

Dettingen (Ehingen (Donau))
Area Code: 07391
H Donau Stüble, Höllweg 5, 📞 7741875,
📱 0171/9293307, III
H Knupfer, Rottenackerstr. 15, 📞 2488, II 🙂

Berg (Ehingen (Donau))
Area Code: 07391
H Landgasthof und Landgut-Hotel Zur Rose, Graf-
Konrad-Str. 5, 📞 70830, III–IV 🙂

Ehingen (Donau)
Area Code: 07391
ℹ Tourist-Info, Marktpl. 1, 📞 503216
H Adler, Hauptstr. 116, 📞 500460, III–IV
H Best Western Plus Bierkulturhotel Schwanen,
Schwaneng. 18/20, 📞 770850, III–IV 🙂
H Ehinger Hof, Lindenstr. 72, 📞 77070, III
H Ehinger Rose, Hauptstr. 10, 📞 2737, III 🙂
H Zum Ochsen, Schulg. 3, 📞 770530, III–IV 🙂
H Sonne, Sonneng. 5, 📞 6885, II
🚲🔧 Fahrradmobilitätszentrum Rad und Sport Ersing,
Hauptstr. 195, 📞 7819642

🚲 s´ Fahrradlädle, In den Rübteilen 8, Mundingen,
📞 07395/961481

Allmendingen
Area Code: 07391
ℹ Gemeindeverwaltung, Hauptstr. 16, 📞 70150
H Dietz, Hauptstr. 23, 📞 770760, II
B Schlossmühle, Schwenkstr. 6, 📞 2008
B Sportgaststätte, Sportplatzweg 1, 📞 71270

Schmiechen (Schelklingen)
Area Code: 07394
H Hirsch, Hauptstr. 40, 📞 2364, II
H Zur Sonne, Hauptstr. 50, 📞 916100, II
B Felsenhäusle, Hauptstr. 4, 📞 1566, 📱 0174/7463011, I

Schelklingen
Area Code: 07394
H HGS³, Heinrich-Günter-Str. 3, 📞 931490, III
H Sonne, Marktstr. 9, 📞 933375, II
H Zur Traube, Stadtschreibereistr. 8, 📞 931985, II

Weiler (Blaubeuren)
Area Code: 07344
H Forellenfischer, Aachtalstr. 5, 📞 5024, III
AH Ebert, Siedlungsstr. 17, II

Blaubeuren
Area Code: 07344
ℹ Tourist-Information, Kirchpl. 10, 📞 966990
H Löwen, Marktstr. 1, 📞 928050, II
H Ochsen, Marktstr. 4, 📞 969890, III–IV
H Blautopf, Blautopfstr. 4, 📞 952466, OB, II 🚲
AH Bacher, Ritterg. 5, 📞 5922, II
🏠 Jugendherberge, Auf dem Rucken 69, 📞 6444, I–II

🚴 🛠 Bike-Station, Karlstr. 66, ✆ 922707

🚴 🛠 Rund ums Rad - Käppeler, Karlstr. 52, ✆ 6398

🚴 Velo Blaubeuren, Karlstr. 18, ✆ 1779903,
✆ 0152/52721982

Gerhausen (Blaubeuren)
Area Code: 07344

🏨 Blautal, Eisvogelweg 10/12, ✆ 917169,
✆ 0174/5798942, I-II

Arnegg (Blaustein)
Area Code: 07304

🅱 Kreuz, Erminger Str. 2, ✆ 43198, ✆ 0151/54270117,
II-III

Herrlingen (Blaustein)
Area Code: 07304

🅷 Lindenmeir, Bahnhofstr. 9, ✆ 921328, OB, II

Blaustein
Area Code: 07304

ℹ️ Tourist-Information, Boschstr. 12, ✆ 802162

ℹ️ Stadtverwaltung, Marktpl. 2, ✆ 8020

🅷 Blue-River-Side, Kurt-Mühlen-Str. 5,
✆ 07311/4394480, III

🅷 Wirtshaus Brauerei Klingenstein, Ulmer Str. 30,
✆ 436990, III-V 😊

🚴 Radsport Pfister, Max-Hilsenbeck-Str. 7, ✆ 42192

Klingenstein (Blaustein)
Area Code: 07304

🅱 Blaustein-Mitte, Josefweg 11, ✆ 2028,
✆ 0179/2009262, OB, I

Ehrenstein (Blaustein)
Area Code: 07304

🅷 Zur Ente, Martinstr. 22, ✆ 3474, I-II

Griesingen
Area Code: 07391

ℹ️ Gemeindeverwaltung, Alte Landstr. 51, ✆ 8748

🅷 Pizzeria Adler, Alte Landstr. 12, ✆ 8373, III

🏨 Radlerquartier, Alte Landstr. 26, ✆ 757670,
✆ 0176/51071666, II

Öpfingen
Area Code: 07391

ℹ️ Gemeindeverwaltung, Schlosshofstr. 10, ✆ 70840

🅷 Ochsen, Darreng. 42, ✆ 6129, ✆ 53150

Ersingen (Erbach)
Area Code: 07305

ℹ️ Ortsverwaltung, Mittelstr. 11/1, ✆ 9262880

🅷 ⛺ Gasthaus Hirsch, Rißtisser Str. 4, ✆ 4160, I-II

⛺ Radwanderzeltplatz, Am Badesee, Auskunft DLRG,
✆ 3539, ✆ 6345, ✆ 0157/34615815, I

Oberdischingen
Area Code: 07305

ℹ️ Gemeinde, Schlosspl. 9, ✆ 931130

🅷 Bräuhausschenke, Bräuhausg. 5, ✆ 0170/1606923,
III

Donaurieden (Erbach)
Area Code: 07305

🅷 Da Vinci, Erbacher Str. 1, ✆ 6309, III

🅱 Steinle, Kirchenberg 12, ✆ 5216, II 😊

Dellmensingen (Erbach)
Area Code: 07305

🅷 Adler, Adlerg. 2, ✆ 931190

🅷 Hirsch, Alte Landstr. 1, ✆ 956680, III

Erbach
Area Code: 07305

ℹ️ Stadtverwaltung, Erlenbachstr. 50, ✆ 96760

🅷 Kögel, Ehingerstr. 44, ✆ 8021, III

🅷 Zur Linde, Bahnhofstr. 8, ✆ 931100, III-IV 😊

🅷 Schwabenpfanne, Donaustetter Str. 21/1, ✆ 24444,
II-III 😊

🚴 Radsport Scheck, Am Wall 8, ✆ 4872

🚴 e-motions e-Bike Welt Ulm, Heinrich-Hemmer-
Str. 14, ✆ 9347150

Donaustetten (Ulm)
Area Code: 07305

🆖 Kreuz, Alb-Donau-Str. 17, ✆ 7160, ✆ 0170/8339639,
II 😊

🅱 „Bed & Breakfast", Eichbühlstr. 68, ✆ 4610, I

Gögglingen (Ulm)
Area Code: 07305

🆖 Am Zehntstadl, Bertholdstr. 17, ✆ 96130, III-IV

🅷 Zum Ritter, Bertholdstr. 8, ✆ 956540, II

Wiblingen (Ulm)
Area Code: 0731

🅷 Löwen, Hauptstr. 6, ✆ 8803120, IV

🚴 Andys Bike, Fischerhauser Weg 84,
✆ 0151/23028848

Grimmelfingen (Ulm)
Area Code: 0731

🅷 Adler, Kirchstr. 12, ✆ 938080, III-IV

🅷 Hirsch, Schultheißenstr. 9, ✆ 937930, III-IV

🅾 O Sole Mio, Eisenbahnstr. 47, ✆ 382575, III

Ulm
Area Code: 0731

ℹ️ Tourist-Information, Münsterpl. 50, ✆ 1612830

🅷 Anker, Rabeng. 2, ✆ 63297, II-III 😊

🅷 Centro Hotel Stern, Sterng. 17, ✆ 15520, III-IV

🅷 Economy-Hotel, Blaubeurer Str. 63, ✆ 8804940, III

🅷 Hotel am Rathaus, Kroneng. 8-10, ✆ 968490, III-IV

🅷 LeoMar-Hotel, Blaubeurer Str. 35, ✆ 93490, III-IV

🅷 Maritim Hotel Ulm, Basteistr. 40, ✆ 9230, IV-VI

🆖 B&B Hotel Ulm, Ehinger Str. 11, ✆ 176330, III

🆖 Ibis Ulm City, Neutorstr. 12, ✆ 96470, III-IV

🆖 Lehrertal, Lehrer-Tal-Weg 3, ✆ 954000, III 😊

🆖 Schiefes Haus, Schwörhausg. 6, ✆ 967930, V

🆖 Ulmer Münster Hotel, Münsterpl. 14, ✆ 55218674, III-
IV 😊

🚴 „Das Schmale Haus", Fischerg. 27, ✆ 60272595,
✆ 0176/47377380, V

🚴 Andy's Sportbikes, Wengeng. 16, ✆ 65222

🚴 Klapprad, Frauenstr. 28, ✆ 55212721

🚴 Radlbauer Ulm, Blaubeurer Str. 16, ✆ 176800

🚴 🛠 Reich's Radl Shop, Platzg. 29, ✆ 21179

Neu-Ulm
Area Code: 0731

ℹ️ Tourist-Information, Münsterpl. 50, Ulm, ✆ 1612830

🅷 Golden Tulip Parkhotel, Silcherstr. 40, ✆ 80110, IV-V

🆖 City-Hotel, Ludwigstr. 27, ✆ 974520, III-IV

🆖 Donauhotel, Augsburger Str. 34, ✆ 97690, III

🅱 Brickstone Hostel, Schützenstr. 42, ✆ 7082559, OB, I
🏴 😊

🅱 B&B Hotel Neu-Ulm, Memminger Str. 31,
✆ 7053936-0, III

🚲 Radweg, Industriestr. 12, 📞 9723890

Pfuhl-Offenhausen (Neu-Ulm)
Area Code: 0731

H Sonnenkeller, Leipheimer Str. 97, 📞 71770, III

Hg Kreuzäcker, Augsburger Str. 196, 📞 9742325, III

Hg Schmid, Hauptstr. 67, 📞 9799014, III

🚲 Tretbar, Spielbergstr. 12, 📞 3782898

Böfingen (Ulm)
Area Code: 0731

H Best Western Plus Atrium, Eberhard-Finckh-Str. 17, 📞 92710, IV

Thalfingen (Elchingen)
Area Code: 0731

H Austüble, Austr. 26, 📞 263135, 📞 0171/7876331, III-IV

Oberelchingen (Elchingen)
Area Code: 07308

H Krone, Klostersteige 38, 📞 2586, III

Elchingen
Area Code: 07308

🚲 Gemeindeverwaltung, Pfarrgässle 2, 📞 0731/20660

Unterelchingen (Elchingen)
Area Code: 0731

H Landgasthof Zahn, Hauptstr. 35, 📞 3007, III-V

B Pia Schneider, Hauptstr. 34, 📞 07308/6521

AH Hartmann, Klosterstr. 15, 📞 07308/922641, 📞 07308/92264-2, 📞 0175/3592235, II

AH Huber, Klosterstr. 21a u. Hauptstr. 25a, 📞 07308/922641, 📞 0175/3592235, II-IV

Riedheim (Leipheim)
Area Code: 08221

Hh 🏕 Schwarzfelder Hof, Schwarzfelder Weg 3, 📞 72628, I ☺

Leipheim
Area Code: 08221

ℹ Tourist-Information, Schloßpl. 1, Günzburg, 📞 200444

ℹ Stadtverwaltung, Marktstr. 5, 📞 7070

H Zur Post, Bahnhofstr. 6, 📞 2770, III-IV ☺

H Brauereigasthof Hirschbräu, Ulmer Str. 1, 📞 71411, II-III ☺

H Bären, Günzburger Str. 15, 📞 0152/36107983, II

🚲 Zweirad - Schlosserei Biedenbach, Güssenstr. 25, 📞 7555

Bubesheim
Area Code: 08221

BuB Gästehaus Kirchenbauerhof, Leipheimerstr. 7, 📞 6388, 📞 0162/3043368, III ☺

Günzburg
Area Code: 08221

ℹ Tourist-Information, Schloßpl. 1, 📞 200444

H EuroHotel, Spielplatzstr. 6, 📞 206660, IV

H Goldener Löwe, Ichenhauser Str. 62, 📞 36680, III

H Hirsch, Marktpl. 18, 📞 5610, III

H Rose, Augsburger Str. 23, 📞 2068221, III ☺

H Zettler, Ichenhauser Str. 26a, 📞 36480, IV

Hg Römer, Ulmer Str. 26, 📞 367380, III ☺

B Astrid, Roseng. 14, 📞 33716, I

B Geduld, Auf der Bleiche 5, 📞 33673

🏕 Camping Gutshof Donauried, Heidenheimer Str. 115, 📞 2076946 ☺

🚲 Saiko's Velo, Schlachthausstr. 37, 📞 2049800, 📞 2049801

Denzingen (Günzburg)
Area Code: 08221

B Zum 8 Mädchenhaus, Ichenhauserstr. 53, 📞 1719, II 🚭

Offingen
Area Code: 08224

ℹ Verwaltungsgemeinschaft, Marktstr. 19, 📞 96970

H Krone, Hauptstr. 34, 📞 1739, III

BuB Fleißiger Michel, Bahnhofstr. 42, 📞 967848

Peterswörth (Gundelfingen an der Donau)
Area Code: 09073

BuB Gaststätte Wünsch, Offinger Str. 2, 📞 508, II

Gundelfingen an der Donau
Area Code: 09073

ℹ Kulturamt im Rathaus, Prof.-Bamann-Str. 22, 📞 999118

H Landgasthof Sonne, Hauptstr. 56, 📞 7334, II-III ☺

H Stadion Gaststätte am Badesee, Stadionstr. 1, 📞 2406, II

BuB Zur Alten Kanzlei, Am Wehrgang 9, 📞 969159, 📞 0176/21032286, III ☺

🚲 Hausmann, Schulstr. 5-7, 📞 7257

🚲 Intersport Seeßle, Bahnhofstr. 3, 📞 95800

Echenbrunn (Gundelfingen an der Donau)
Area Code: 09073

H Sonne, Lauinger Str. 52, 📞 958640, III

Faimingen (Lauingen (Donau))
Area Code: 09072

AH Appartement Lauingen, Sudetenstr. 69, 📞 9695813, II

Lauingen (Donau)
Area Code: 09072

ℹ Stadtverwaltung, Herzog-Georg-Str. 17, 📞 9980

H Hotel und Restaurant Kastanienhof Lauingen, Bahnhofstr. 4, 📞 96030, III

H Drei Mohren, Imhofstr. 6, 📞 95890, III

H Genießerhotel Lodner, Imhofstr. 7, 📞 95890, III ☺

H Kannenkeller, Dillinger Str. 26, 📞 7070, IV

🚲 Bike & Tec, Riedhauserstr. 3, 📞 921250

🚲 Radhaus Lauingen, Pfarrfeldstr. 1, 📞 991808

Hausen (Dillingen a.d.Donau)
Area Code: 09071

H Zur Sonne, Wittislinger Str. 9, 📞 2201, 📞 2027, III

AH Dillinger Schwabennest, Wittislinger Str. 7, ✆ 5839376, ✆ 0152/28863344, III

Dillingen a.d.Donau

Area Code: 09071

i Tourist-Information, Königstr. 37/38, ✆ 540

H Dillinger Hof, Rudolf-Diesel-Str. 8, ✆ 58740, III ☺

H SleepySleepy, Kapuzinerstr. 35, ✆ 7749690, IV

Hg Zur Donau, Donaustr. 7, ✆ 5838170, III ☺

H ▲ Eichwaldstuben-Donaucamping, Georg-Schmid-Ring 45, ✆ 728445, ✆ 0162/7655099, II. (jugenherbergsähnlich)

H Osteria zur goldenen Traube, Königstr. 46, ✆ 726060, III

Steinheim (Dillingen a.d.Donau)

Area Code: 09074

B&B Miller, Dillinger Str. 3, ✆ 5252, ✆ 0172 7079624, II

AH Müller, Dillinger Str. 18a, ✆ 5229, ✆ 0176/96908106, I-II

Höchstädt a. d. Donau

Area Code: 09074

i Bürgerservicebüro, Herzog-Philipp-Ludwig-Str. 10, ✆ 440

H Berg, Dillinger Str. 17, ✆ 958990, ✆ 0171/5226629, III

H Zur Glocke, Friedrich-von-Teck-Str. 12, ✆ 957885, III

B&B Maier, An der Bleiche 23a, ✆ 6691, ✆ 0162/7632612, II ☺

B&B Thomas, An der Bleiche 26, ✆ 0172/6057531, OB, I

B Geirhos, Bachg. 26, ✆ 2191, ✆ 0160/95591735, I-II

Sonderheim (Höchstädt a. d. Donau)

Area Code: 09074

H Heigl, Paulstr. 1, ✆ 1066, II

H Zur alten Donau, Hauptstr. 7a, ✆ 3220, III

Blindheim

Area Code: 09074

B&B Breisachmühle, Nebelbachstr. 15, ✆ 6166, II

B&B Konle, Schloßstr. 2, ✆ 91027

Schwenningen (Donau)

Area Code: 09070

H Schloss Kalteneck, Kirchstr. 26b, ✆ 9602840, ✆ 0175/3308280, III

H Zum Lamm, Bundesstr. 7, ✆ 258, I

Erlingshofen (Tapfheim)

Area Code: 09070

H Kartäuser Klause, Donauwörther Str. 7, ✆ 302, ✆ 0157/81053326, III

Zusum (Donauwörth)

Area Code: 0906

B&B Gerstmeier, St.-Sebastian-Str. 5, ✆ 4513, I-II

Donauwörth

Area Code: 0906

i Städt. Tourist-Information, Rathausg. 1, ✆ 789151

H Donau, Augsburger Str. 6, ✆ 7006042, III-IV ☺

H Im Ried, Hindenburgstr. 30, ✆ 9998480, IV

H Zur Promenade, Spindeltal 3, ✆ 70593440, III-IV

Hg Goldener Greifen, Pflegstr. 15, ✆ 7058260, III-IV

B&B Graf, Zirgesheimer Str. 5, ✆ 5117, II

B&B Jünger, Schützenring 8, ✆ 7057871, ✆ 0151/61323017, II

AH Danubio - Tagen-Feiern-Schlafen, Schützenring 10, ✆ 01777/167683 ☺

▲ Zeltmöglichkeit beim Kanu-Club, An der Westspange, ✆ 22605, ✆ 0170/1866165, I

⚡ Top Bike Brachem, Kapellstr. 25, ✆ 8077

⚡ Zwei-Rad Uhl, Dillinger Str. 57, ✆ 9816060

Riedlingen (Donauwörth)

Area Code: 0906

B&B Sonnenhof, Sandacker 14, ✆ 1240, ✆ 5669, II

B Degginger, Posthof 2a, ✆ 28418, II

Berg (Donauwörth)

Area Code: 0906

🏠 Jugendherberge Donauwörth, Goethestr. 10, ✆ 5158, II ☺

Parkstadt (Donauwörth)

Area Code: 0906

H Parkhotel, Sternschanzenstr. 1, ✆ 706510, IV

H Zum Deutschmeister, Hochbruckerstr. 2, ✆ 8095, III

Hg M&s, Andreas-Mayr-Str. 11, ✆ 4039, III

Nordheim (Donauwörth)

Area Code: 0906

B&B Dietenhauser, Rainer Str. 50, ✆ 9800677, II

Zirgesheim (Donauwörth)

Area Code: 0906

Hg Mayer, Schenkensteiner Str. 9, ✆ 706690, III

B Leberle, Schießerhof 1, ✆ 1323, II

B Mebes, Lederstätterstr. 6, ✆ 22035, II

Altisheim (Kaisheim)

Area Code: 09099

H Grünenwald, Hopfenweg 4, ✆ 09097/266

B&B Steidle, Donaustr. 34, ✆ 09097/1212

Leitheim (Kaisheim)

Area Code: 09097

H Schloss Leitheim, Schlossstr. 1, ✆ 485980, V

Graisbach (Marxheim)

Area Code: 09097

AH Graf-Reisach, Graf-Reisach-Str. 13, ✆ 251, II-III

Marxheim

Area Code: 09097

H Bruckwirtschaft, Flößerstr. 8, ✆ 920435, ✆ 0176/49505965, II

H Land-Steakhaus Bürger, Bayernstr. 16, ✆ 239, ✆ 0171/7576785, III-II

B Schütz, Pfalzstr. 10, ✆ 1047

Schweinspoint (Marxheim)

Area Code: 09097

B Weigl, Am Hang 5, ✆ 288

Bertoldsheim (Rennertshofen)

Area Code: 08434

i Markt Rennertshofen, Marktstr. 18, Rennertshofen ✆ 94070

B Gästehaus Manuela Seefried, Finkenstr. 14, ✆ 1806, II ☺

B Roßkopf, Lerchenstr. 7, ✆ 650, II

Rennertshofen

Area Code: 08434

i Markt Rennertshofen, Marktstr. 18, ✆ 94070

Hatzenhofen (Rennertshofen)

Area Code: 08434

B Hager, Graspointstr. 19, ✆ 1302, I

154

Stepperg (Rennertshofen)
Area Code: 08434
- **B** Gästehaus Kimmerling, Poststr. 5, ☎ 9163, II
- **AH** Krallert, Hatzenhofener Str. 50, ☎ 1602, I

Bittenbrunn (Neuburg an der Donau)
Area Code: 08431
- **H** Kirchbaur Hof, Monheimer Str. 119, ☎ 619980, IV

Laisacker (Neuburg an der Donau)
Area Code: 08431
- **BB** Dollinger, Gietlhausener Str. 42, ☎ 7234, II
- **BB** Jagdschlößl, Gietlhausener Str. 43, ☎ 2700, II
- **BB** Memmelhof, Brunnenstr. 13, ☎ 2529, II

Neuburg an der Donau
Area Code: 08431
- **i** Tourist-Information, Ottheinrichpl. A 118, ☎ 55240, ☎ 55241
- **H** Am Fluss, Ingolstädter Str. 2, ☎ 67680, IV
- **H** Das Acker Hotel, Am Maschinenring 2, ☎ 907660, IV-V
- **H** Hotel & Brauerei-Gasthof Neuwirt, Färberstr. 88, ☎ 2078, III
- **Hg** Im Schrannenhaus, Schrannenpl. C153 1/2, ☎ 67210, II-III
- **H** Blaue Traube, Amalienstr. A49, ☎ 8392
- **JH** JUST Jugendübernachtung, Adolf-Kolping-Str. 298 1/2, ☎ 57285
- **A** Campingplatz des Donau-Ruder-Clubs Neuburg, Oskar-Wittmann-Str. 5, ☎ 6449643. (300 m unterhalb der Donaubrücke rechts)
- **A** Jugendzeltplatz Schwaighölzl, Grünauer Str.,

☎ 57285
- **B&B** Behr Eduard, Münchener Str. 162-164, ☎ 44889
- **B&B** Bike-Markt, Münchener Str. 169, ☎ 42573
- **B&B** Fahrrad Appel, Ingolstädter Str. 20, ☎ 9076819
- **B&B** Fahrradladen Kneißl, Weinbergstr. 38 1/2, ☎ 42428, ☎ 0176/83149439

Rohrenfeld (Neuburg an der Donau)
Area Code: 08431
- **H** Golfclub Hotel, Rohrenfeld 102, ☎ 9085950, IV

Weichering
Area Code: 08454
- **H** Vogelsang, Bahnhofstr. 24, ☎ 91260, III
- **B&B** B&M Gästehaus Weichering, Bahnhofstr. 26, ☎ 8503

Ingolstadt
Area Code: 0841
- **i** Tourist Information im Ingolstadt Outlet Shopping

Village, Otto-Hahn-Str. 1, ☎ 8863100
- **i** Tourist-Information am Hauptbahnhof, Elisabethstr. 3, ☎ 3053005
- **i** Tourist-Information am Rathausplatz, Moritzstr. 19, ☎ 3053030
- **H** **enso, Bei der Arena 1, ☎ 885590, IV-V** ☺
- **H** ARA, Schollstr. 10a, ☎ 95430, III-IV
- **H** Adler, Theresienstr. 22, ☎ 35107, ☎ 17099, III-IV
- **H** Block, H.-P.-Müller Str. 15, ☎ 953450, V-VI
- **H** Donauhotel, Münchener Str. 10, ☎ 965150, III-IV
- **H** Hecht, Regensburger Str. 77, ☎ 58507, III
- **H** Schumann Stuben, Schumannstr. 21, ☎ 81435, ☎ 481395, II
- **Hg** Bauer, Hölzlstr. 2, ☎ 67086, ☎ 66099, III-IV
- **Hg** Bayerischer Hof, Münzbergstr. 12-14, ☎ 934060, III-IV
- **JH** Jugendherberge Ingolstadt, Friedhofstr. 4 1/2,

☎ 3051280, I-II ☺
- **A** Azur Waldcamping Auwaldsee, Am Auwaldsee 1, ☎ 9611616
- **B&B** Fahrrad Brenner, Unterlettenweg 5, ☎ 62891

Friedrichshofen (Ingolstadt)
- **H** Kleines Brauhaus, Levelingstr. 86, ☎ 0841/81077, ☎ 0841/3053088, III

Großmehring
Area Code: 08407
- **i** Gemeinde Großmehring, Marienpl. 7, ☎ 92940
- **H** Am Interpark, Gutsweg 2, ☎ 9649093, III
- **H** Schäringer, Prinz-Karl-Str. 10, ☎ 287, ☎ 0176/53144794, II
- **B&B** Delagera, Nibelungenstr. 51, ☎ 373, II
- **B&B** Meininghaus, Uferstr. 12, ☎ 0157/56216587
- **B&B** Hallermaier, Marienpl. 3, ☎ 9153, ☎ 0171/22470482

Irsching (Vohburg an der Donau)
Area Code: 08457
- **B** Kuhn, Germanenstr. 11, ☎ 1096, II

Menning (Vohburg an der Donau)
Area Code: 08457
- **H** **A** Unterer Wirt, Ingolstädter Str. 17, ☎ 929412, II

Vohburg an der Donau
Area Code: 08457
- **i** Tourismusbüro, Agnes-Bernauer-Str. 1, ☎ 9369700
- **i** Stadtverwaltung, Ulrich-Steinberger-Pl. 12, ☎ 92920
- **H** Boutique Hotel zur Post, Donaustr. 31, ☎ 9368000, III-IV
- **H** Stöttner-Bräu, Donaustr. 9, ☎ 1219, III

🅱 Zimmervermietung Vohburg, Buchenstr. 3, ✆ 431035, OB, II 🏠

Dünzing (Vohburg an der Donau)
Area Code: 08457

🅱 Wolfsteiner, Am Ölberg 1, ✆ 1751
AH Amberger, Dorfstr. 34a, ✆ 2951

Wackerstein (Pförring)
Area Code: 08403

🛈 Verkehrsamt, Marktpl. 1, Pförring, ✆ 92920
🅱 Gästehaus Schulte, Vohburger Str. 82, ✆ 0157/80323440 od. 0151/16803580, I–II
🅱 Nachreiner, Vohburger Str. 10, ✆ 741
🅱 Pfaller, Schloßberg 2, ✆ 1202

Pförring
Area Code: 08403

🛈 Verkehrsamt, Marktpl. 1, ✆ 92920
🅷 Jägerwirt, Marktpl. 8a, ✆ 1380, I–II

Neustadt an der Donau
Area Code: 09445

🛈🅲 Tourist-Information Bad Gögging, Heiligenstädter Str. 5, Bad Gögging (Neustadt an der Donau), ✆ 95750, ✆ 0800/46344464
🅷 Amtmann, Herzog-Ludwig-Str. 9, ✆ 2872
🅷 Gigl, Herzog-Ludwig-Str. 6, ✆ 9670, III–IV ☺
🅰 Campingplatz Felbermühle, Felbermühle 1, ✆ 516, I

Bad Gögging (Neustadt an der Donau)
Area Code: 09445

🛈🅲 Tourist-Information Bad Gögging, Heiligenstädter Str. 5, ✆ 95750, ✆ 0800/46344464
🅷 Apparthotel Minerva-Diana, Zur Limestherme 3,

✆ 880, ✆ 88195, III–IV ☺
🅷 Centurio, Am Brunnenforum 6, ✆ 97220, ✆ 972212, IV ☺ 🔲
🅷 Eisvogel, An der Abens 20, ✆ 9690, IV–VI 🔲🔲
🅷 Kaiser Trajan Kurhotel, Römerstr. 8, ✆ 9660, ✆ 966100, IV ☺
🅷 Marc Aurel, Heiligenstädter Str. 34-36, ✆ 9580, ✆ 958-0, IV
🅷 The Monarch Hotel, Kaiser-Augustus-Str. 36, ✆ 980, IV–VI 🔲
🅷 Zur Sonne, Trajanstr. 3-5, ✆ 95470, III 🔲
B&B Eichschmid, Römerstr. 4, ✆ 7525613, II
B&B Schwaiger, Schulstr. 7, ✆ 95670, II

Eining (Neustadt an der Donau)
Area Code: 09445

🅷 Abusina Stubn, Abusinastr. 38, ✆ 8359, I–II
🅷 Treitinger, Abusinastr. 29, ✆ 7880, II

Weltenburg (Kelheim)
Area Code: 09441

🅷 Gästehaus St. Georg, Asamstr. 32, ✆ 6757500, III
🅷 Klostergasthof Schweiger, Alte Dorfstr. 3, ✆ 1370, II
B&B Köglmaier, Am Keltenwall 4, ✆ 7103, ✆ 0170/3539606 od. 0171/3813289, II
B&B Probst, Auf der Weiß 10, ✆ 9546, II

Kelheim
Area Code: 09441

🛈 Tourist-Information, Ludwigspl. 1, ✆ 701-234
🅷 Frischeisen, Regensburger Str. 69, ✆ 50490, II
B&B Anita's Alstadtpension, Benefiziateng. 2, ✆ 7038790, III–IV

B&B Carlbauer, Schloßbuckel 4, ✆ 50380, III
B&B Zum Schwan, Fischerg. 30, ✆ 29298, III
🚲 ZRad Jessen, Schäfflerstr. 12, ✆ 504850, ✆ 504848
🚲 Bike Station, Kelheimwinzerstr. 101, ✆ 179880
🚲 Radsport 2000, Schäfflerstr. 14, ✆ 4732

Affecking (Kelheim)
Area Code: 09441

Hg Sperger, Regensburger Str. 190, ✆ 3420, III
🚲 Ebike plus, Saueracker 19, ✆ 3024

Lengfeld (Bad Abbach)
Area Code: 09441

🅷 Gut Deutenhof, Deutenhof 2, ✆ 953230, III
🅷 Schreiner, Teugner Str. 11, ✆ 1717, II

Kelheimwinzer (Kelheim)
Area Code: 09441

🅷 Winzer, Dorfring 23, ✆ 5899, ✆ 0171/7475686, I–II
🅱 Glaser, Pfarrer-Plass Weg 7, ✆ 9158, II
AH Weinzierl, Dorfring 17, ✆ 4947, II–III

Herrnsaal (Kelheim)
Area Code: 09441

🅰 Camping auf dem Bauernhof, Herrnsaaler Ring 26, ✆ 9607, I

Kapfelberg (Kelheim)
Area Code: 09405

🅰 Campingplatz Kapfelberg, Bootsweg 3, ✆ 5335, I

Poikam (Bad Abbach)
Area Code: 09405

🅷🅰 Donaulände, Kanalstr. 22, ✆ 4431, II

Bad Abbach
Area Code: 09405

🛈 Kurverwaltung / Tourist-Information, Kaiser-Karl-V.-Allee 5, ✆ 95990
🅷 Elisabeth, Ratsdienerweg 4-8, ✆ 95090, III
🅷 Parkresidenz Bad Abbach, Kochstr. 18-20, ✆ 95000, IV ☺
B&B Café Rathaus, Kaiser-Karl-V.-Allee 6, ✆ 5009060, III ☺
B&B Stark, Tannenstr. 5, ✆ 3621, ✆ 0160/93491988, II
🅱 Claudia, Frauenbrünnlstr. 24, ✆ 1031, III
AH Gästehaus Turmblick, Kurallee 1, ✆ 956950, III ☺
🅰 Freizeitinsel, Inselstr. 1a, ✆ 9570401, ✆ 0176/96631729
🚲 OMV Tankstelle, Kaiser-Karl-V.-Allee 60, ✆ 1398. Fahrradersatzteile

Oberndorf (Bad Abbach)
Area Code: 09405

B&B Gästehaus Lodermeier, Donaustr. 68a, ✆ 941583, III
B&B Lodermeier, Donaustr. 68a, ✆ 941583, III
B&B Schröppel, Donaustr. 56, ✆ 957808, II

Matting (Pentling)
Area Code: 09405

🅷 Fänderl, Wirtsweg 2, ✆ 2105
🅷 Zur Walba, Unterirading 1, ✆ 2102, III ☺
AH Gebhard, Hanselbergweg 4, ✆ 3118, ✆ 0157/56100462, III

Pentling
Area Code: 0941

🅷 Homey, Hohengebrachinger Str. 29, ✆ 9465610, V

Mariaort (Pettendorf)
Area Code: 0941

H Krieger, Heerbergstr. 3, ☏ 81080, II-III

Dechbetten (Regensburg)
Area Code: 0941

H Best Western Premier, Ziegelsdorfer Str. 111, ☏ 463930, IV

H Dechbettener Hof, Dechbetten 11, ☏ 35283, III

Regensburg
Area Code: 0941

ℹ Tourismusbüro Landkreis Regensburg, Altmühl-lstr. 3, ☏ 4009495

ℹ Tourist-Information Altes Rathaus, Rathauspl. 4, ☏ 507-4410, ☏ 507-4411

ℹ Zentrale Zimmervermittlung, Rathauspl. 4, ☏ 5074410

🔧 Bikeambulanz, Bahnhofstr. 18, ☏ 5998808, ☏ 0177/4608460

H Am Peterstor, Fröhliche-Türken-Str. 12, ☏ 54545, III-V

H Atrium im Park, Im Gewerbepark D90, ☏ 40280, OB, III-IV

H B&B Hotel Regensburg, Landshuter Str. 111, ☏ 784910, II

H Bischofshof Braustuben, Dechbettener Str. 50, ☏ 2082170, V

H Castle Hotel, St. Petersweg 3, ☏ 20919283, III-IV

H Hansa Apart, Friedenstr. 7, ☏ 99290, IV

H Hottentotten Inn, Auweg 1a, ☏ 69099999, III

H Kaiserhof am Dom, Kramg. 10-12, ☏ 585350, III-IV

H Lux, Stadtamhof 24, ☏ 85724, III

H Mercure Hotel Regensburg, Grunewaldstr. 16, ☏ 78820, IV

H Orphée Andreasstadel, Andreasstr. 26, ☏ 596020, IV-V

Hg Münchner Hof und Dependence „Blauer Turm", Tändlerg. 9 und 14, ☏ 58440, IV ☺

H Kolpinghaus Regensburg, Adolph-Kolping-Str. 1, ☏ 595000, III ☺

B&B Holzgarten, Holzgartenstr. 77, ☏ 78036550, ☏ 0151/54091325, II

🛏 Brook Lane Hostel, Obere Bachg. 21, ☏ 6965521, I-II

🛏 Jugendherberge Regensburg, Wöhrdstr. 60, ☏ 4662830, III ☺

⛺ Azur Camping, Weinweg 40, ☏ 270025, I

🔧 Bikehaus, Landshuter Str. 19, ☏ 46520781

🔧 Fahrrad Rosenhammer, Lappersdorfer Str. 2, ☏ 84223

🔧 Zweirad Scheffthaler, Großprüfening 3, ☏ 31626

🔧 Zweirad-Center Stadler, Kirchmeierstr. 22, ☏ 37880

Tegernheim
Area Code: 09403

H Dream Inn, Von-Heyden-Str. 12, ☏ 9529379, II-III

H von Heyden, Von-Heyden-Str. 26, ☏ 954499400, III-IV

H Götzfried, Donaustr. 13, ☏ 961665, III

Donaustauf
Area Code: 09403

ℹ Tourist-Information, Maxstr. 24, ☏ 9552929

H Forsters Posthotel, Maxstr. 43, ☏ 9100, V-VI

H Kupferpfanne, Lessingstr. 46-48, ☏ 95040, III

B Kastenmeier, Ludwigstr. 30, ☏ 1014, I

🔧 Fahrradservice Zdenko Francuski, Prüllstraße 2, ☏ 0941/962330

Hammermühle (Donaustauf)
Area Code: 09403

H Hammermühle, Thiergartenstr. 1, ☏ 96840, III

Demling (Bach an der Donau)
Area Code: 09403

B Elfriede Wagner, Alleestr. 14, ☏ 2250, ☏ 0151/28741691, OB, I

B Vitus Kaiser, Rosenstr. 6, ☏ 8506, ☏ 0170/7285659, I

Bach an der Donau
Area Code: 09403

B&B Held, Hauptstr. 44, ☏ 1881, II

B&B Weinstube Heitzer, Obere Bachg. 9, ☏ 954832, ☏ 0160/90190328, II

B Gästehaus Gmeinwieser, Obere Bachg. 7, ☏ 2529, ☏ 0171/9281293, I

Wörth an der Donau
Area Code: 09482

ℹ Tourist-Information, Rathauspl. 1, ☏ 94030

H Butz, Kirchpl. 3, ☏ 9510, II-III

H Geier, Josef-Feller-Str. 1, ☏ 2250, II ☺

B&B Bayerisches Gästehaus, Osserstr. 5, ☏ 2805, I

B AH Fuchs, Hungersdorfer Str. 2, ☏ 2856, ☏ 0151/12597672, II

AH Monte Castello, Schlossberg 14, ☏ 938048, I-II

Wiesent
Area Code: 09482

B&B Rösch, Regensburger Str. 10, ☏ 3706, II

AH Stadler, Ettersdorfer Str. 9, ☏ 3536, I

Hofdorf (Wörth an der Donau)
Area Code: 09482

H Pflamminger, Dorfpl. 3, ☏ 1770, III

Pillnach (Kirchroth)
Area Code: 09428

🔧 Fee Wheels, Pfalzstr. 35, ☏ 948990, ☏ 0179/4880696

Oberzeitldorn (Kirchroth)
Area Code: 09428

B&B Radl-Pension, Hauptstr. 10, ☏ 8116, II

Kirchroth
Area Code: 09428

H Zur Lacke, Dekan-Seitz-Str. 8, ☏ 324, II

B&B Golfpension Bauer, Bachhof 5, ☏ 7368, I

B&B Weiss-Hof, Regensburger Str. 40, ☏ 542, II

Kößnach (Kirchroth)
Area Code: 09428

B&B Groß, Straubinger Str. 23, ☏ 1574, ☏ 7102, II

Sossau (Straubing)
Area Code: 09421

H Reisinger, Sossauer Pl. 1, ☏ 1897500, III

Straubing
Area Code: 09421

ℹ Tourist-Information, Fraunhoferstr. 27, ☏ 94460199

H Asam, Wittelsbacherhöhe 1, ☏ 788680, V-VI ☺

H Franziska, Regensburger Str. 42, ☏ 180480, IV

H Gäubodenhof, Theresienpl. 32, ☏ 12275, III ☺

H Theresientor, Theresienpl. 51, ☏ 8490, IV-V ☺

H Villa, Bahnhofpl. 5b, ☏ 963670, IV

H Wenisch, Innere Passauer Str. 59, ☏ 99310, IV-V

⛺ Campingplatz Straubing, Wundermühlweg 9, ☏ 89794, I

🔧 Radhaus Lang, Chamer Str. 36, ☏ 88353

🚲 Zweiradcenter Stadler, Chamer Str. 47, ✆ 99200

Reibersdorf (Parkstetten)
Area Code: 09421
Ⓗ Winklmeier Hof, Richprechtstr. 15, ✆ 12295, II–III
Ⓑ Schaller, Richprechtstr. 19, ✆ 10157, I

Bogen
Area Code: 09422
ⓘ Stadt Bogen, Stadtpl. 56, ✆ 5050
Ⓗ Wurm, Bärndorf 7, ✆ 2137, III
Ⓗ Zur schönen Aussicht, Bogenberg 6, ✆ 1539, II
ⒷⒷ Schreiber, Stadtpl. 23, ✆ 806993, II
ⒶⒽ Mosandl, Straubinger Str. 2, ✆ 2201, II
🚲 E-Bike-Verleih, Straubinger Str. 4, ✆ 8593285, ✆ 0151/40176320

Breitenweinzier (Bogen)
Area Code: 09422
ⒷⒷ Eberth, Breitenweinzier 1, ✆ 805373, II

Pfelling (Bogen)
Area Code: 09422
Ⓗ Zum Donauufer, Pfelling 23, ✆ 2306, III ☺

Waltendorf (Niederwinkling)
Area Code: 09906
Ⓗ Plank-Hof, Waltendorf 19, ✆ 492, ✆ 0171/3866335, II

Loham (Mariaposching)
Area Code: 09906
Ⓗ Stöberl, Riedstr. 6, ✆ 201, II

Mariaposching
Area Code: 09906
ⒷⒷ Killinger, Stadtfeldstr. 10a, ✆ 783, ✆ 0160/7217532, II

Kleinschwarzach (Offenberg)
Area Code: 09906
ⒶⒽ Schreiber, Kleinschwarzach 1, ✆ 879, ✆ 0991/21376

Metten
Area Code: 0991
Ⓗ Markt Metten, Krankenhausstr. 22, ✆ 998050
Ⓗ Café am Kloster, Marktpl. 1, ✆ 9989380, II ☺
ⒷⒷ Christa, Egger Str. 1, ✆ 9959877
ⒷⒷ Grabmeier-Keller, Deggendorfer Str. 27, ✆ 9355, ✆ 0160/96653460, II
Ⓗ s´ Platzl, Marktpl. 9a, ✆ 98159429, ✆ 0160/94722176

Deggendorf
Area Code: 0991
ⓘ Tourist-Information, Oberer Stadtpl. 1, im Alten Rathaus, ✆ 2960535
Ⓗ Donauhof, Hafenstr. 1, ✆ 38990, III
Ⓗ Hotel-Gasthof Höttl, Luitpoldpl. 122, ✆ 3719960, III
Ⓗ Pielmeier, Hafenstr. 18, ✆ 5423, ✆ 0160/99113484, II
Ⓑ ⒶⒽ Haus Gawlik, Regerstr. 5, ✆ 8791, I
Ⓐ Camping Donaustrandhaus, Eginger Str. 42, ✆ 4324
🚲 Biller Bikes, Pferdemarkt 18, ✆ 30440
🚲 Fahrradshop Deggendorf, Untere Vorstadt 10, ✆ 0176/26250190

Fischerdorf (Deggendorf)
Area Code: 0991
Ⓗ Georgenhof, Altholzstr. 9, ✆ 4716, III

Natternberg (Deggendorf)
Area Code: 0991
Ⓗ Burgwirt, Deggendorfer Str. 7, ✆ 30045, III

Seebach (Deggendorf)
Area Code: 0991
Ⓗ Landgasthof Zwickl, Schwarzacher Str. 3, ✆ 09901/6306, II

Niederalteich
Area Code: 09901
ⓘ Verkehrsamt, Guntherweg 3, ✆ 93530
Ⓗ Gästehaus St. Pirmin, Mauritiushof 1, ✆ 2080, FB, IV
Ⓗ Habereder, Uferstr. 13, ✆ 5657, II
ⒷⒷ Zum Glück, Donaustr. 14a, ✆ 9589992, ✆ 0151/43246307, II–III

Osterhofen
Area Code: 09932
ⓘ Tourist-Information, Stadtpl. 13, ✆ 4030
Ⓗ Bayerischer Löwe, Vorstadt 10, ✆ 1497, III–IV
Ⓗ Pirkl, Altstadt 1, ✆ 1276, II–III
ⒷⒷ ⒶⒽ Fohlenhof, Raindlinger Weg 17, ✆ 908351, ✆ 0171/8572284

Rossfelden (Osterhofen)
Area Code: 09932
Ⓐ Camping Meierhof, Rossfelden 1, ✆ 2276

Künzing
Area Code: 08549
ⓘ Tourist-Information, Osterhofener Str. 2, ✆ 973112
Ⓑ Duschl, Girchinger Str. 4, ✆ 1227, I
ⒶⒽ Brumm, Schaibinger Boindl 12, ✆ 1719, I

Pleinting (Vilshofen)
Area Code: 08549
Ⓗ Baumgartner, Hauptstr. 32, ✆ 910060, II

Winzer
Area Code: 09901
ⓘ Markt Winzer, Schwanenkirchener Str. 2, ✆ 93570
Ⓗ Zur Burgschänke, Passauer Str. 11, ✆ 7348, ✆ 9497494, I
ⒷⒷ Falter, Böhmerwaldstr. 9a, ✆ 949256, II–III ☺
ⒶⒽ Steinke, Bergstr. 6, ✆ 7270, II
🚲 Fahrrad-Studio, Geißkopfstr. 11, ✆ 0170/7273603

Neßlbach (Winzer)
Area Code: 08545
Ⓗ Augenstein, Deggendorfer Str. 7, ✆ 341, II
ⒶⒽ Kralitschek, Nelkenstr. 3, ✆ 8307, ✆ 0160/2834363, II
Ⓐ Camping Donautal, Schillerstr., ✆ 1233, ✆ 1021, I

Hofkirchen
Area Code: 08545
ⓘ Tourist-Information, Rathausstr. 1, ✆ 97180
Ⓗ Buchner, Kaiserstr. 14, ✆ 911033, III
Ⓗ Eichelberger, Anger 74, ✆ 0170/5269738

Vilshofen
Area Code: 08541
ⓘ Tourist-Information, Stadtpl. 27, ✆ 208114
Ⓗ Bairischer Hof, Vilsvorstadt 29, ✆ 5065, II
Ⓗ Schlemmerhof Schmalzl, Hundsöd 30, ✆ 5103, III
Ⓗ Wittelsbacher Zollhaus, Donaug. 10-12, ✆ 969600, III
Ⓗ Wolferstetter Bräu, Stadtpl. 14, ✆ 967935, ✆ 0160/4065689, II
ⒷⒷ Gäste- und Tagungshaus St. Benedikt, Schweiklberg 1, ✆ 209270, III
Ⓑ Sagerer, Alte Fischerg. 4, ✆ 7779, ✆ 075/1987127, I–II

Campingplatz, Beim Bootssportverein, ☎ 0171/4534140

🚲 Gierster, Vilsvorstadt 15, ☎ 202554

🚲 Zweirad Würdinger, Kapuziner Str. 107, ☎ 910710

Windorf
Area Code: 08541

ℹ️ Tourist-Information, Marktpl. 23, ☎ 962640

Ⓗ Zum Goldenen Anker, Marktpl. 42, ☎ 96650, III-IV

Ⓗ Moser, Marktpl. 40, ☎ 8275, III ☺

Ⓑ Donaublick, Nömerberg 20a, ☎ 967593, ☎ 0170/4332728, I-II

🚲 Fahrradladen Passau, Zweigstelle Windorf, Marktpl. 56, ☎ 0151/12547962

Gaishofen (Windorf)
Area Code: 08546

Ⓗ Endl, Nibelungenstr. 15, ☎ 322, I

Ⓗ Heller´s Fischerstüberl, Fischerstr. 21, ☎ 624, III

Irring (Tiefenbach)
Area Code: 08546

🔺 Dreiflüsse-Camping, Am Sonnenhang 8, ☎ 633, I

Maierhof (Passau)
Area Code: 0851

Ⓗ Halli-Galli, Kachletstr. 16, ☎ 0171/7208490 od. 0171/4579741, III

Passau
Area Code: 0851

ℹ️ Tourist-Information, Rathauspl. 2, ☎ 955980

ℹ️ Tourist-Information, Bahnhofstr. 28, ☎ 955980

ℹ️ Tourist-Information Passauer Land, Dompl. 11,

☎ 397600

🔺 **Zeltplatz Ilzstadt, Halserstr. 34, ☎ 41457, ☎ 0160/2856778**

Ⓗ Cultellus, Kleine Messerg. 12, ☎ 49095204, ☎ 0160/94641829, III-IV ☺

Ⓗ Dreiflüssehof, Danziger Str. 42/44, ☎ 72040, III-IV

Ⓗ Geizkragen, Regensburger Str. 21, ☎ 75682363, ☎ 0170/3575285, III

Ⓗ Morgentau, Bräug. 19, ☎ 49095599, III-V

Ⓗ Rotel Inn, Haisseng. 10, Hauptbahnhof/Donauufer, ☎ 95160, II 🍴

Ⓗ Herdegen, Bahnhofstr. 5, ☎ 955160, III-IV ☺

Ⓗ König, Untere Donaulände 1, ☎ 3850, IV

Ⓗ Residenz, Fritz-Schäffer-Promenade 6, ☎ 989020, IV-VI

Ⓗ Spitzberg, Neuburger Str. 29, ☎ 955480, III-V

Ⓗ Goldenes Schiff, Unterer Sand 8, ☎ 34407, II-III

Ⓑ Panorama, Angerstr. 59, ☎ 88199078, OB, II 🍴

🏠 Jugendherberge Passau, Oberhaus 125, ☎ 493780, I ☺

🚲 Bikehaus Bikeambulanz, Bahnhofstr. 29, ☎ 9662570, ☎ 0151/12834224

🚲 Denk bike + outdoor, Ludwigstr. 22, ☎ 31450

🚲 Fahrrad-Klinik, Bräug. 10, ☎ 33411. und Radwerkstätte

🚲 Fahrradladen Passau, Wittg. 9, ☎ 72226

🚲 Zweirad Seidel, Spitalhofstr. 83, ☎ 57813

🚲 Zweirad Würdinger, Regensburger Str. 22, ☎ 6346

🚲 Zweirad-Center Zeller, Graneckerstr. 4, ☎ 56302

Innstadt (Passau)
Area Code: 0851

Ⓗ Dormero, Kapuzinerstr. 32, ☎ 386401, III-V

Ⓑ Vicus, Johann-Bergler-Str. 2, ☎ 931050, III

Ⓑ Vilsmeier, Lindental 28a, ☎ 36313, II

Geographical Index

Page numbers from page 148 refer to the list of accommodations